MASTERS OF THE BAIZE

Masters of the Baize

Cue Legends, Bad Boys and Forgotten Men
in Search of Snooker's Ultimate Prize

Luke Williams and Paul Gadsby

MAINSTREAM
PUBLISHING

EDINBURGH AND LONDON

First published in Great Britain in 2005 by
MAINSTREAM PUBLISHING COMPANY (EDINBURGH) LTD
7 Albany Street
Edinburgh EH1 3UG

ISBN 1 84018 872 3

A catalogue record for this book is available
from the British Library

Typeset in Ellington and Century Gothic

Printed in Great Britain by
Antony Rowe Ltd, Chippenham, Wiltshire

Acknowledgements

The authors would like to thank:

Everyone at Mainstream Publishing, especially Bill Campbell, Graeme Blaikie, our editor Deborah Warner and, for the cover design, Emily Bland;

For sharing their memories and thoughts with us, Steve Davis, Ken Doherty, Terry Griffiths, Stephen Hendry, John Parrott and Joy Lindrum Gillan. We also greatly appreciated the assistance, guidance and expertise of Andrew Ricketts in Australia, Domenic Aquilina in Malta, Stewart Weir at sports management agency 110sport and Bill Borrows;

For valued help and support, the staff of the British Newspaper Library in Colindale, David Flegg at the State Library of Victoria in Melbourne and Jenny Bentall, Saul Brookfield, Greg Demetriou, Matt Dimmock, John Exon, Jill Fenner, Ben Gallop, Ivan Hirschowitz, Andy Jacques, Nick Johnson, Roger Lee, Mike Morris, Joe Pepler, Luke Riches, Rowland Stone, Chris Straw, Eric Whitehead, Gerry and Zoe Williams.

Above all, we wish to thank Roana and Emma, without whose support and patience none of this would have been possible.

We would also like to thank the following for their kind permission to quote extracts from copyrighted material:

David & Charles Ltd for *Ray Reardon* by Ray Reardon with Peter Buxton (1982); Virgin Books for *The Breaks Came My Way* by Joe

Davis (W.H. Allen, 1976); Gillon Aitken Associates Ltd for *Pocket Money* by Gordon Burn (Heinemann, 1986) © Gordon Burn, 1986; Matchroom Ltd for *Frame by Frame* by Dennis Taylor (Futura Publications, Macdonald and Co., 1986) and *Steve Davis: Snooker Champion* by Steve Davis, as told to Brian Radford (Arthur Barker Ltd, 1981); Orion Publishing Group for *Ronnie: The Autobiography of Ronnie O'Sullivan* by Ronnie O'Sullivan with Simon Hattenstone (2003); Penguin Books Ltd for *Griff: The Autobiography of Terry Griffiths* by Terry Griffiths with Julian Worthington (Pelham Books/Stephen Greene Press, 1989) © Matchroom Ltd; The Random House Group Limited for *Behind the White Ball* by Jimmy White with Rosemary Kingsland (Hutchinson, 1998), *Playing for Keeps* by Cliff Thorburn (Partridge Press, 1987) and *On Snooker* by Mordecai Richler (Yellow Jersey Press, 2002); Robson Books for *Right on Cue* by John Parrott (1991); Clive Everton for extracts from *Snooker Scene* and *World Snooker* magazines, 'Joe Davis: The Master of the Green Baize' and *The Embassy Book of World Snooker* (Bloomsbury Publishing, 1993); BBC Sport Online for 'Snooker's forgotten man' by Peter Sanderson, 'Griffiths: Williams to rule the roost' and 'Welsh Open is just the start' by Steve Davis; *The Guardian* for 'Nursery Cannons' and 'Davis returns to snooker's top table' by Simon Hattenstone; *The Independent* for 'I'd rather be in the bingo hall than in the players' lounge' by Nick Townsend; Jonathan Rendall for 'A breed apart' which appeared in *The Observer* and 'Join the cue' which appeared in the *Independent on Sunday*; *Sydney Morning Herald* for 'Crowe ties the knot' by Richard Jinman; *The Times* for 'Snooker Pool: World's Professional Championship' and 'The world could soon be in his pocket' by Sydney Friskin, 'A champion at all costs' by Peter Batt and 'Mr Interesting sticks to work ethic in quest for greatest feat' by Andrew Longmore; Jim White for 'The Peter Ebdon Interview' and 'The Stephen Hendry Interview' which appeared in *The Guardian*; *The Observer* for 'Why gentlemen prefer Jimmy' by Will Buckley; World Promotions for 'The Greatest Player' (embassysnooker.com) and *World Snooker* for 'Marvellous Mark going for the treble' (Embassy World Snooker Championship programme, 2004).

CONTENTS

FROM JUBBULPORE WITH LOVE

As this book goes to print, it is 130 years since snooker came into being. Such an anniversary provides an opportune time for reflection on the forces and personalities that shaped its development from an afternoon diversion in an outpost of the British Empire to a major televised spectacle and multimillion-pound industry.

Unlike golf or tennis, where there are four major tournaments every year, snooker essentially revolves around just one event: the World Championship, played every spring at the Crucible Theatre in Sheffield. There are other tournaments that make up the snooker calendar, but the players, as well as the fans, are under no illusions – the World Championship, inaugurated in 1927 through the vision of Joe Davis, has always been the sport's most hallowed prize. It is the piece of silverware all snooker players dream of winning when they first pick up a cue, the trophy they must lift to be considered a true great. This prestige, coupled with the unique pressure-cooker atmosphere of the Crucible, has enabled it to become a firm fixture in the British sporting calendar.

Every player's career incorporates relatively few Crucible appearances and, once they are there, they must handle the extra pressure which comes with it. The consequences of defeat in snooker are no higher than in Sheffield. Winning and losing there is what defines every professional and crossing the winning line in the final, having never done so before, is the severest test of nerves in this most psychologically gruelling of sports. Once a player is beaten, his season is over and it is that performance which he is left reflecting on throughout the summer. The 17-day event is a marathon of the mind as well as the body. It is for this reason that this book focuses solely on those players (with one notable exception) who have lifted the World Snooker Championship.

The origins of billiards (which gave rise to snooker) stretch back centuries and have been the subject of much debate. Some historians argue that primitive forms of the game can be traced to the Roman Empire under Caligula or even ancient Egypt, while others believe it was brought to Europe after the First Crusade by the Knights Templar. However, the most widely accepted interpretation is that it developed from various outdoor lawn games played in France in the late fourteenth or early fifteenth centuries in which sticks or maces were used to hit balls towards targets. This certainly accounts for the derivation of the term 'billiards', which echoes the French word *bille* meaning 'tree trunk' or 'stick'.

The earliest reference yet found to an indoor cue sport played on a table is in an inventory of the accounts of King Louis XI of France (r. 1461–83), whose enthusiasm for the sport ensured it became an accepted court tradition. During the sixteenth century, billiards spread across Europe assisted by Henri III of France (r. 1574–89), who referred to it as 'the noble game'. Tables soon sprang up in taverns across the country to cater for the lower classes, while aristocrats constructed ever more elaborate tables with which to impress billiard-playing guests.

The game also acquired a significant foothold in Britain. Mary Queen of Scots (r. 1542–67) played billiards to help while away her many days of incarceration. This privilege was withdrawn as her execution approached and she wrote a letter to the Archbishop of Glasgow to protest. After she was beheaded, her body was wrapped in the green baize from her billiards table prior to burial.

The growing popularity of billiards was also demonstrated by its appearance in the literature of the time: in 1591, Edmund Spenser described it as a 'thriftless game'; William Shakespeare gave Cleopatra the line, 'Let's to billiards' in *Antony and Cleopatra*; and Ben Jonson referred to the smoothness of billiard balls in his 1616 play *The Devil is an Ass*.

Throughout the seventeenth, eighteenth and nineteenth centuries, billiards acquired many celebrated fans, from Louis XVI and Marie Antoinette to Napoleon, Mozart, Pope Pius IX and Mark Twain. Along the way, different countries and regions developed their own specific rules, customs and idiosyncrasies. In Britain by the mid-nineteenth century, billiards was the country's leading indoor sport. Queen Victoria had a table installed in Windsor Castle in 1838 and Britain's greatest players attracted popular attention and acclaim. One, the great John Roberts junior, was appointed 'Court Billiards Player for Life' by the Maharajah of Jaipur while it is estimated that, annually, 12,000 elephants were slaughtered to provide ivory balls to satisfy the British lust for the game.[1]

As skilled players became accustomed to building lengthy breaks, more sociable forms of billiards were devised, such as pyramids, life pool and black pool, which involved more than two players and were centred around betting between participants. So it was, by common consent, that snooker took shape one long, rainy day in 1875 in the officers' mess of the Devonshire Regiment in Jubbulpore, India. Colonel Sir Neville Chamberlain, then a subaltern, was bored with the games of black pool to which officers were devoting so much time and suggested adding yellow-, green- and pink-coloured balls (blue and brown were introduced later) to the existing 15 reds and single black used in black pool.[2] Chamberlain suggested that every time a player potted a red, a colour should then follow, which would be re-placed on the table if potted. Once all the reds were potted, the colours would then be attacked in sequence. The word 'snooker' itself was a slang term used to denote first-year cadets at the Royal Military Academy in Woolwich, London. Chamberlain adopted it as the sport's name, arguing that he and his fellow players were all inexperienced 'snookers' at this new game.

Snooker caught on in Britain's gentlemen's clubs as retiring officers introduced the game to friends and fellow members, but its rules were not formalised until the establishment of the Billiards Association and Control Club (BA&CC) in 1919.[3] Snooker still laboured in billiards' forbidding shadow, though. Its transformation into a major sport was gradual and hard-earned, incorporating many peaks and troughs from the 1930s onwards until steady growth in the 1970s gave way to a dramatic explosion in popularity during the 1980s.

One of the major factors that enabled snooker to become part of the British sporting establishment was the decision, from 1977 onwards, to base the World Championship at one venue, the Crucible.[4] The X-factor of that arena increased the tournament's status greatly. Don't take our word for it – listen to the players, who recognise that the mystique surrounding the Crucible makes the World Championship the only tournament that really matters. Terry Griffiths, the 1979 world champion and now a respected coach, told the authors, 'It's a very special place. I've been there and played my best snooker ever, and I've also been there and collapsed in a nervous heap. Every time I go there, I get so excited, and I'm not even playing any more. There's so much history there – so much has gone on there. Something happens there every year. When you're in the Crucible . . . you're just there . . . and it's the whole world at that moment in time.'

There are, of course, other factors why snooker has succeeded in capturing the hearts and minds of the British public over the past quarter of a century. It was perfect for colour television and benefited from that innovation enormously. Furthermore, in the 1980s, with football struggling in the shadow of the Heysel disaster and the Valley Parade fire at Bradford, and live attendances for most sports dwindling, snooker was able to balloon from a curiosity into a national obsession in living-rooms up and down the country.

Aside from social and cultural factors, snooker's top exponents also played their part by constructing a series of striking narratives. In the 1980s, the sport's colourful cast of characters – '*Coronation Street* with balls' to borrow promoter Barry Hearn's famous sobriquet – was as frequently on the front pages of newspapers as in the sports sections, and the sponsors and broadcasters lapped it up. Alex Higgins's tearful 1982 World Championship win captivated 14 million viewers, while Dennis Taylor's fairy-tale 1985 black-ball victory against Steve Davis persuaded a record 18.5 million people to watch BBC2 past midnight – a staggering achievement that, in these days of digital and cable television, is unlikely to be surpassed. Such moments have imprinted themselves on the nation's consciousness, as confirmed by the way snooker continues to thrive in the lists of 'great sporting moments' that frequently appear on television programmes and in newspapers.[5]

Today, outwardly at least, little has changed from snooker's peak in the 1980s – the World Championship retains its pre-eminent status and the final, in particular, still commands outstanding viewing figures. Indeed, the peak audience of 7.1 million which tuned in for the Mark Williams–Ken Doherty final in 2003 exceeded those attracted by the FA Cup final the same year.

For all its strengths, though, snooker is at a crossroads. Organisational shortcomings, political infighting and lawsuits have blighted the sport for several years, while it has been increasingly relegated to the 'sport in brief' sections of newspapers from which it laboured for so many years to escape. Due to the British government's ban on tobacco advertising, prize money and sponsorship are falling. Embassy's long-running and valued sponsorship of the World Championship, which began in 1976, ends this year, while the professional circuit has been slashed from 128 players to 96, with a further reduction to 64 planned for the 2005–06 season.

By cruel irony, the pool of talent in the game has never been deeper – seeds in ranking tournaments are no longer guaranteed sedate opening matches and the competition for top-16 places grows fiercer every season. In 2004, Glaswegian Stephen Maguire, ranked 41 in the world at the beginning of the season, won the European Open – the idea of such a lowly ranked player lifting a major title would have been unthinkable in the 1980s. Further proof of snooker's strength in depth came at the UK Championship that November, when none of the top 8 reached the quarter-finals in a tournament that, played over longer-distance matches, has traditionally favoured the higher-ranked players.

A consequence of the improved level of professionalism is the frequent criticism that snooker lacks the 'characters' of yesteryear. However, such assertions are based more on the British capacity to idealise the past than on hard facts. No sport in which three of the leading competitors are Ronnie O'Sullivan, Jimmy White and Paul Hunter could be said to be low on personality. Yet in a world where media mantras invariably stick in people's minds, this unfounded criticism has damaged the public perception of the game.

A regrettable offshoot of this trend is that the literary world has served the sport poorly in recent years. In the 1970s and '80s every top player seemed to have a finger in a literary pie, while snooker encyclopedias and yearbooks also filled the bookshelves; in fact, such was the game's popularity that there were even a couple of snooker-themed films made in the mid-1980s.[6] However, the majority of these books have now fallen out of print and snooker has been one of the few sports to miss out on the recent boom in sports-related publishing. The shelves of Sportspages bookshop on Charing Cross Road, London, buckle under the weight of football, cricket, rugby and boxing literature, while the snooker section is relegated to a side annexe where its small selection of tomes compete with water polo and mountain climbing for space. Save for a handful of player biographies, technical guides and the invaluable *Snooker Scene* magazine, there is little literature catering for aficionados of the game – somewhat surprising when you consider snooker enjoys fans in high literary places such as Martin Amis, A.S. Byatt and Julian Barnes.

This book, which offers a comprehensive guide to the lives and careers of the men who have won the sport's most coveted prize, was conceived for the benefit of loyal fans of the game whom we believe have been somewhat starved of snooker literature in recent years, as well as for more casual followers of the sport. Rather like the way the pre-Premiership football era has been airbrushed out of history by Sky TV, snooker fans are often deprived of any sense of what the game was like before the transfer of the World Championship to the Crucible, which is why we have devoted as much attention to forgotten stars such as Horace Lindrum and Walter Donaldson as the more well-known modern professionals.

The 21 men profiled in this book are the greatest in snooker history and while we seek to assess and compare their abilities and historical impacts in the pages that follow, any criticisms we make are relative. Similarly, it should be noted that while purists may decry two of our inclusions – Lindrum and White, for different reasons – we felt the story of the World Snooker Championship was not complete without their presence.

It is to the players featured in these pages, many of whom shared memories of their careers with us, that this book is truly dedicated and in a spirit of love for snooker that it was written. During our two years of research, we have become ever more confident in the game's ability to thrive well into the future. Its history is rich and, in terms of subtle psychological drama, it remains a sport without peers. Its future may appear outwardly uncertain, but if its past has taught us one thing, it is that snooker possesses the capacity to survive through uncertain times and emerge stronger.

Ultimately, any sport stands or falls on the virtues of its players and in the case of snooker the production line of young talent shows no sign of abating. In 2004, Bristol's Judd Trump became the youngest player, aged 14, to compile a maximum 147 break, while the recent emergence of Chinese youngster Ding Jun Hui offers the tantalising prospect that the game, which has traditionally been restricted to the Commonwealth, might still achieve its oft-stated ambitions of global influence.

However, in order to approach and attack the future with confidence, it is always wise to take heed of the lessons of the past, starting with the man who, even more than Sir Neville Chamberlain, shaped the development of modern snooker . . .

ONE

JOE DAVIS

It Began with a Legend

If it hadn't been for Joe Davis, there probably wouldn't even be a World Snooker Championship as we know it today. We might be living in a surreal world where there's no Crucible fortnight to look forward to every year, no television cameras and no sponsors handing out big pay cheques to the winners.

Davis was not only a player of monumental talent; his desire to establish an organised tournament to decide who could call themselves the world's best gave the sport the lift-off it needed. Once an undisputed champion could be named on a regular basis, snooker was transformed into a sport people queued up to watch in their thousands, rather than being merely a relaxing pastime.

Davis was never beaten in a World Championship match: he won the tournament a staggering 15 times and looked untouchable throughout his career. His classic cue action is still used as a starting point for most of today's players and he also developed the tactic of splitting the reds and break-building around the black to chalk up as many points as quickly as possible.

His command of the table reached such levels that he even won frames without his opponent taking a single stroke. This involved breaking off with a strong two-cushion shot that banged into the pack off the top cushion, sending a red arrowing into a corner pocket. From there, he'd go on to clear the table.

His pure ability drew in the crowds, not just for his world-title matches, but also for his exhibitions. Sometimes a long mirror, placed at a certain angle on a trestle and supported by chains, was set up by the side of the table so the whole crowd could see the reflection and watch in detail a master at work. Davis once overheard a man saying to his friend after watching one session, 'Joe can make those balls do everything but talk.'[1]

Born in the Derbyshire coal village of Whitwell on 15 April 1901, Davis had to wait until he was 11 years old for his first taste of the green baize. Before that, his life had followed a rather unsettled path. When he was just two, his father, Fred, decided to give up being a miner and move into the pub trade, taking over the Travellers' Rest in Whittington Moor, near Chesterfield, along with his wife, Elizabeth. The couple, who later had another boy called Fred and a daughter, Gladys, were an ambitious pair who spent the next nine years saving up so the family could move into a bigger place, the Queens Hotel, just 200 yards away. The new pub was in a different league. As well as being much larger, it had a licence to serve spirits, a crown bowling green and, crucially, a full-size billiards table.

There's no doubt that anyone who rises to the very top of their profession needs luck somewhere along the way. Davis certainly had this on his side in having a table in his own home, but the way the table was set up was another handy piece of fortune that played a major role in hastening the youngster's progress. The previous tenant of the Queens Hotel had been concerned about the spectators' view when building his billiards room and, to give them as good a vantage point as possible, he had lowered the table several inches. This forced most players to bend over more than usual to take a shot, but for Davis it meant he could reach the table and play without having to rely on the rest too often.

Davis practically lived in that room. Every weekday morning before leaving for school he'd knock the ivory balls around the table, working out his angles and perfecting his technique, and do the same again after rushing home during his lunch break. The evenings were a problem, though, as the customers would want to use the table, with Davis acting as the scorer. However, this again had its advantages – the devious youngster would often add a few points to the score of the leader behind the players' backs, thus speeding up the game and increasing his chances of bagging the table for himself.

His father, noticing the consummate ease with which his son was playing the game (and probably twigging that his customers were getting a little irked at their lack of table-time), thought Joe could do with some proper guidance and looked around for a suitable coach. Ernest Rudge, one of the best players ever seen in the local area, had just opened a billiards hall in Chesterfield, having moved from Normanton in Yorkshire, and it wasn't long before he took Joe under his wing. 'It was the finest introduction I ever had,' Davis recalled years later. 'He became a sort of second father.'[2]

Rudge had built a private billiards room at the bottom of his garden where Davis popped along for regular lessons and his constant, meticulous practice soon paid off. He was the local amateur billiards champion by the time he was thirteen, just two years after first picking up a cue, and turned professional five years later. He was so proficient that, when he was playing for money, many of his wary opponents would only oblige if Davis played left-handed. So the foxy youngster soon perfected this skill as well, which meant he seldom had to use the rest. It wasn't long before he was holding his own against the best players the country had to offer at the plush venues in London.

Davis would soon switch his attentions to snooker, however, since billiards was beginning to crumble as a public entertainment. The top players of the 1920s – Walter Lindrum, Tom Newman, Davis himself and Clark McConachy – were making so many breaks of 1,000-plus it looked too easy and spectators were getting bored. Instead, they were flocking in to watch – and bet on – 'the tomato game', as some called it. If a billiards session happened to finish early, many pros would throw in a cheeky frame of snooker afterwards so the crowd would feel they got their full money's worth. This 'filler' arrangement was soon extended to two frames as it was becoming so popular. In fact, the punters, now feeling blasé about watching huge billiard breaks, wanted all that out of the way as soon as possible so the snooker could begin.

This view was not shared by many high-profile cuemen, who looked down on snooker as a coarse knockabout that appealed to those not talented or patient enough to test themselves at billiards. Davis, it appears, also felt this way during snooker's early years. Although he has historically been regarded as a major figure in championing snooker's cause, his decision to switch from billiards wasn't as smooth as many have been led to believe. Even as late as 1934, whilst on tour in Australia, he wrote an article in the *Sporting Globe* newspaper promoting the case for billiards: 'I regard snooker as a slap-dash, agricultural game as compared with billiards, in which artistry and scientific methods are essential to the development of skill. It is deplorable that snooker has become far more popular than billiards.'[3]

Despite this disappointment at the demise of his favoured discipline, Davis, from about the mid-1920s, had always been realistic enough to realise that snooker was the way forward if he was going to make a living out of cue sports, and no one can deny he worked tirelessly to promote and develop the 22-ball game. His enthusiasm wasn't matched by some of his peers, though. When Davis told Willie Smith, another billiards great, about his vision of the future, Smith simply replied, 'They'll fall for a lot of things, but they'll never fall for this.'[4]

However, Davis didn't give up. After years of trying, he eventually persuaded the BA&CC to stage a major tournament and so helped organise – and draft the conditions for – the inaugural World Snooker Championship at Camkin's Hall in Birmingham in 1927. There were ten entrants, the BA&CC spent half of the players' entry fees on a trophy (the same one that is still fought for at the Crucible today) and battle commenced. Not only did he have a hand in setting the thing up, Davis went on to win it, beating Tom Dennis 20–11 in the final to claim his winning prize of £6 10s. And to think Mark Williams spent his first title winnings on a Ferrari.

Davis was now busy fashioning a reputation for himself as the greatest player of the times and went on a winning run that saw him clinch every World Championship until 1940, a stunning 14 in a row, before the war years interrupted his progress. His domination wasn't over, however, and he went on to beat Australian Horace Lindrum in the first post-war final in 1946 for his 15th and final title. 'He was so overpowering that he put everybody else in the shade,' John Pulman, a future world champion, would later remark.[5] The nearest Davis came to defeat during this unstoppable run was in the 1940 final when his younger brother, Fred, pushed him all the way before going down bravely 37–36.

Davis was, without doubt, a legend. *Daily Mail* cartoonist Tom Webster christened him 'The Emperor of Pot' (this was in more innocent times, don't forget) and, playing on his links with Chesterfield, Webster once depicted Davis standing beside the town's famous church with a tongue-in-cheek caption stating he must have a good eye because he was quick to notice the spire wasn't straight.

His eyesight, strangely enough, was far from perfect. Unable to focus with his right eye, Davis used his left one instead to line up each shot, which meant resting the cue to the left side of his chin. This one-eyed stance seemed so natural to him that it was only towards the end of his career that he went to see a specialist about his lazy right eye. He was told it could only have responded to treatment at an earlier age and that it was too late to cure at that stage. It wasn't all bad news, though. The specialist told Davis the condition may have even been advantageous for him anyway, as focusing with two eyes was rarely accurate because most people have one eye which is stronger than the other.

Davis, having perched comfortably on top of the snooker tree for so long, developed many great rivalries during his prime years. One of them was with the aforementioned Horace Lindrum, Walter's nephew. Walter shared hostilities with Davis over the billiards table, but it was in snooker that Horace thrived.

In 1934 Davis travelled to Australia in what was initially an attempt to reclaim his world billiards crown (Walter had won it the previous year and adopted a 'come and get it' stance – if anyone wanted it back, they had no choice but to head Down Under). Davis was beaten by just 875 points and, after failing to make any money on the tour, was preparing to head back to Blighty to drown his sorrows when another door opened. Horace's mum, Clara, commonly known as Vi, threw down the mother of all challenges – an unofficial World Championship snooker contest against her son. Vi, Walter's sister, became Horace's manager and she took her job very seriously. Davis himself claimed, 'She dominated Horace . . . she doted on him and smothered him.'[6]

According to Davis, the 'fiery red-headed' Vi never spoke to Walter after he once claimed Horace would never match him, but she held an even bigger vendetta against Davis. In a number of newspaper articles, she demanded to know why he walked around calling himself the world champion when Horace had made a 139 break, 25 points higher than Davis's best effort. Davis replied, via the same newspapers, that Horace's break was not registered and he had beaten it unofficially himself. 'Rubbish,' replied Vi. 'Davis is a phoney.'[7]

Davis realised there was only one way to settle this unexpected but certainly riveting public feud, so, in an interview with the *Sydney Sun*, he announced he would meet Horace if the price was right. The next morning he arrived at the newspaper's office to gauge the reaction to this challenge and was not entirely surprised to see Vi storming in. 'Calls himself world champion,' she screamed, waving her handbag in

Davis's direction. 'I could beat him myself. You know, I pot a thousand balls a day for practice. I've got secret strokes that would paralyse the Pommy bastard.'[8] She challenged him to play Horace, and Davis, who had had enough, eventually wilted. Slapping £300 on the table, he said he'd play if she matched it. She did and the battle, the unofficial World Championship, in effect, was now on.

The match was played at the Tivoli Billiards Hall in Melbourne, but, in the end, Horace didn't have the trousers to match his mother's mouth. Not used to playing in such a pressure-cooker atmosphere, he struggled to keep up with Davis, who raced to a 42–22 win. It was a double victory for Davis – not only was his reputation as the world's best restored, the extra gate receipts picked up thanks to Vi's publicity techniques meant he could afford his ticket home with a little something to spare.

The pair met again, this time back in England for the 1936 World Championship final. Lindrum had picked up a number of impressive wins since sailing over to Britain and was firmly established as the main contender to Davis's crown. The Australian even led 27–24 on the final day, but Davis rolled up his sleeves and knocked off the remaining frames without reply to triumph 34–27.

Lindrum was beaten by Davis again a year later, but it may not have turned out like that – well, not if one man had anything to do with it. During the build-up to the final, Davis, winner of the previous ten world tournaments, was so heavily fancied to make it eleven in a row that no bookmaker would take a bet on him. A man who appeared to be a very keen snooker enthusiast started showing up at virtually every afternoon and evening session in which Davis played. The pair soon got chatting and lunched together on several occasions, during which the conversation always got round to one thing – gambling and, more specifically, Davis's chances of winning the title.

When asked how much he would make by winning the championship, Davis replied, 'Oh, not very much. As a matter of fact, very little. If it wasn't for the prestige value, it would hardly be worthwhile.'

'Why? Don't you play for a side stake?'

'No, we don't, and even if we wanted to, I wouldn't be able to find anyone to back Horace.'[9]

No need to worry about that, thought the man, who told Davis he'd ask around his contacts and friends to see if anyone would take up the bet and back the Australian. After a few days without a word, the punter finally rang Davis while he was practising at Thurston's snooker club to say he wanted to see him in private. They met in a flat Davis had in Notting Hill Gate where the man revealed he and a few friends were willing to bet substantial cash on Horace to win – providing he was certain to do so. In other words, if Davis lost, the man and his friends could make a fortune.

'There's £1,000,' he said, opening a small attaché case full of notes and promising Davis even more if he agreed to lose. Davis promptly told him to get lost, but the stubborn man wouldn't take no for an answer and even had the audacity to show up at the opening session of the final, sending Davis a note saying the offer still stood if he wanted to change his mind. To prove that he didn't, Davis went out and duly sealed another victory and world title 32–29, with poor Lindrum wondering where Joe's extra motivation had come from.

Lindrum had his chance to exact revenge when the pair met yet again in that first post-war final of 1946. The Aussie had already knocked Fred Davis out in the semi-finals and 1,200 fans per session packed into the Royal Horticultural Hall in Westminster, twice a day for two weeks, to watch a marathon of a final to be played over 145 frames. It was broadcast live on the radio, both in the UK and Australia, with commentary from Willie Smith and women's professional Joyce Gardner. Microphones were even set up over the table to magnify the sound of the balls clicking. It was tight and tense, not to mention tiring, but Davis, of course, came out on top, 78–67, knocking in a very impressive six centuries on the way. Box-office receipts for the match passed the £12,000 mark and 8,000 programmes were sold, a far cry from the 1931 final which Davis won playing in the back room of a Nottingham pub owned by his opponent, the aforementioned Dennis. In 1946, both players came out of the competition with around £1,500 for two weeks' work. It was the only time Davis made any real money from his World Championship career.

There are few, if any, sports stars who could ever claim to have been the best there was for 20 years, but that's exactly what Davis could say when he announced his retirement from World Championship snooker after that 1946 final. He was presented with a replica of the trophy he had helped establish and had successfully defended so many times, and no one was left in any doubt about his greatness.

Certainly the best player of the first half of the twentieth century, many experts believed Davis was the greatest of all time until Stephen Hendry walked off with his seventh world crown in 1999. But legendary commentator Ted Lowe has always hailed Davis as the all-time best, even after the Scot's achievement:

Joe was the complete artist. I'm sure he would have been able to deal with the fantastic potters that we have in the game today. He had the perfect all-round game and made every shot look so easy, even though they played with much heavier snooker balls in those days.[10]

Comparing him with today's stars is such a tricky business because of that reason and also the fact that the cloths were different and the old equipment made modern power-shots impossible. Davis, as Lowe points out, had everything. He set new record breaks 12 times and, in 1955, achieved the first officially registered 147 maximum against Willie Smith – ironically, the man who said snooker wouldn't catch on – at Leicester Square Hall in London.

However, a look at the hard facts suggests that, admittedly with the benefit of hindsight, Davis's World Championship record – although 100 per cent – does not compare as favourably against Hendry's as you may imagine. Four of Davis's fifteen world titles were won by beating just one player, and on only one occasion did he have to win more than three matches. Although none of this was his fault, as he couldn't control the standard of competition at the time, modern-day players are clearly tested much more vigorously in the game's biggest event. It mustn't be forgotten, though, that Davis could only beat what was put in front of him and was never found wanting. With his undeniable quality and determination, it's hard to imagine him struggling to meet the demands of any era.

The television commentator and editor of *Snooker Scene*, Clive Everton, agrees with Lowe about Davis's capacity to succeed anytime, anywhere:

In the quality of his close control, and even more through the force of his personality, he would have been a top player in any era . . . Even uprooting him unchanged from his peak in the 1940s and '50s, he would have enjoyed considerable success in the modern game.[11]

So why did Davis make the switch to snooker so easily, while many other great billiards players struggled to adapt? The first answer lies in the fundamentals. Davis used a short and heavy cue (one that he bought second-hand for seven shillings and sixpence in 1923 and used for his entire career) which matched his short and crisp style. Whereas billiards predominantly requires an exceptional knowledge of angles, snooker demands the ability to strike the ball with 100 per cent accuracy, along with a command of screw and stun. A simple cannon in billiards involves aiming at a larger target, while in snooker there's no margin for error when the cue ball strikes the object ball – if you want to keep position. Davis's action was always dead level, and his no-nonsense short-back movement of the cue helped him control his stroke from start to finish and kept his shots right on line.

Davis also took full advantage of the introduction in 1929 of Crystalate balls, which replaced the ivory ones he had grown up with. The new balls were a lot more receptive to stun and screw shots, techniques in which Davis was already supremely skilled, but he could now take it to another level. The cue ball was rarely at the mercy of the nap of the cloth and Davis could put it to within an inch of where he wanted it on a more consistent basis. These new balls were still nothing like as receptive as the modern ones pros use today, but they were hailed as the new big thing back then and no one exploited the advance in technology more than Davis.

Another attribute that made him stand out from the rest was his character. Davis was an intimidating player at the table, and this wasn't just because of his exceptional skill or the amount of time he made his opponent sit in his chair throughout a match. His will to win and desire to roll over anyone who came across his path was too much for all the rest.

Davis's proud record didn't pass without some controversy, however. Throughout his entire career only one player beat him on level terms – his younger brother Fred. This was mainly due to Joe's habit of rarely playing anyone without giving them a head start in points (although not in championship play) to ensure his 'level terms' record stayed intact. 'He wanted to have it both ways,' said Everton. 'He did not want to risk defeat, but he wanted to be regarded as the best player.'[12] Whether this ploy was a selfish act or not, Davis still had to win those World Championship matches and no one but a legend could have achieved that.

Some pundits also questioned his commitment to the game after he walked away from the championship in 1946 and limited his appearances to other, less prestigious tournaments and exhibitions, but Davis himself was in no doubt that the sport was better off for it. He said it wasn't profitable for the event to be dominated by one man and that it was time for the emerging players to battle it out for the game's biggest prize amongst themselves.

There were also other reasons why it wasn't all plain sailing for

Davis. The Depression of the 1920s and '30s forced him into even more exhibitions as he travelled the country trying to make ends meet. He was sometimes fitting five of them into one day and on a tour of South Africa in 1937 squeezed in 85 exhibition games over 105 days.

Endless rows with other competitors, mostly over money or handicap points awarded for certain tournaments, added to the stress (he had a long-running feud with Walter Lindrum) and Davis admitted that he found the pressure of living up to the crowds' expectations difficult to handle. He recalled once being followed by an enthusiastic fan during a week of exhibition matches in Sheffield. On the opening night, he made a 97 break and the punter said to him afterwards that it was a failure because he'd missed out on a century; the next night Davis duly obliged with a ton, but missed the final black – a mistake which the fan leapt on, claiming Davis should have cleared the table. 'It must be blood you want,' replied Davis, who got the century and sank the final black the following evening only for the customer to retort, 'Wasn't it a shame there were no more balls on the table? – then you could have broken your record.'

'It was ever thus,' reflected a clearly frustrated Davis.[13]

Davis also learnt another valuable lesson while performing in exhibitions – know exactly who and what you're working with. Most of the time, he finished a session with his famous machine-gun shot. This involved lining eight reds up along the baulk line, then playing the cue ball softly from the side cushion with enough pace to eventually roll into the corner pocket before rattling the other eight balls into the same pocket before the white got there. This always required the help of an assistant who had to be pretty quick with his hands to pick out the first few balls so there was enough room for all nine to fall into the pocket. In 1947 at Drill Hall in Truro, Davis let Albert James, who had been refereeing him all afternoon, do the honours.

Davis instructed his man to stand close and pick the first few balls out quickly to make room for the rest. Unfortunately, James didn't expect them to come at him so quickly and the pocket was soon full. As he bent down to try and clear things up, Davis fired the last ball which struck the previous one which was still stuck in the pocket. It flew up and gave James no time to react, hitting him plump on the forehead, and knocking him backwards and straight to the ground. He was unconscious for a good ten minutes 'with a lump the size of an egg between his eyes', remembered Davis.[14] The poor referee recovered later and went on to carry out his duties that evening, although he understandably gave the trick shots a wide berth.

Despite not playing in the World Championship, Davis still remained a hugely influential figure in the sport. As chairman of the Professional Billiard Players' Association and co-leaseholder of Leicester Square Hall, the game's prime venue at the time, it was he who called the shots. If a player wanted to move from amateur to professional level, he needed Davis's approval, and it was Davis who conducted early negotiations with the BBC for snooker on TV in the 1950s. But without his presence, the World Championship suffered. In 1957 it was down to four entrants and from 1958 until 1963 it wasn't held at all. Many fans blamed Davis, saying he had put his own interests above all else, but few could deny that without him it would have been a lot worse. 'He became a dictator, but the alternative, without any effective governing body, was anarchy,' wrote Everton.[15]

He eventually retired from the game altogether in 1964, a year after being awarded the OBE (in the days before gaining such an honour seemed almost automatic for sportspeople). After such a long career, retirement came as something of a relief. He later admitted:

> The burden of knowing every day that I had to travel somewhere to give yet another display, and that every display would be watched with that hyper-critical eye which audiences the world over reserve for those who are regarded as prime exponents of any sport . . . had been taken from my shoulders.[16]

Davis had knocked in an incredible 687 centuries and 83 billiard breaks of over 1,000 by the time he called it a day.

He was still invited to many tournaments, as well as onto television's flagship snooker programme, *Pot Black*, as an honoured guest to hand out prizes. His love for snooker didn't stop at promoting the sport through the broadcast media, either. Davis wrote, and got much satisfaction out of, a number of self-help books. First off was *How I Play Snooker*, then along with Walter Lindrum he published *Advanced Snooker*, before both volumes were incorporated into *Complete Snooker for the Amateur*. These books weren't there just to gather dust, either. Steve Davis read them religiously when first taking up the game and another future world champion, John Parrott, once said, 'Dad swore by the Joe Davis method when he coached me as a youngster,'[17] adding, 'He had thoroughly absorbed the lessons embodied in Joe Davis's books.'[18]

He had dedicated his life to cue sports from the moment he set eyes on that lowered table in his parents' pub and it was snooker that eventually played its part at the very end. Davis was feeling unwell and was suffering from back pain after watching Fred play in an emotional roller-coaster of a match in the 1978 world semi-finals in Sheffield. After being driven back to his London home the next day, Joe collapsed and was taken to hospital. Despite a successful six-and-a-half-hour operation, he died a few weeks later from a chest infection at the age of 77.

'Nothing I have seen in recent years will change my mind about Joe Davis,' adds Lowe. 'Snooker would not have become one of the most popular sports in the world if it wasn't for him. He was, without doubt, the greatest.'[19]

Colour television and a batch of larger-than-life characters – not to mention some hell-raising ones – from the 1970s and '80s all played their part in establishing snooker as a worldwide spectacle, but the sport needed something to snowball from, someone to kick-start the whole thing. If Davis – even if it was initially against his own wishes – hadn't switched from billiards to take up snooker before most people even respected the game, then there's no guessing where snooker would be now.

Today's pros possess a vast array of skills that, due to the times he played in, Davis wouldn't even have dreamt about. However, all you can do is be the best of your era and not only did Davis obliterate every player he faced, his enthusiasm for the sport and his desire to develop the game and bring it to the masses earned him the title of the father of modern snooker.

TWO

WALTER DONALDSON

The Great Imperturbable

Decades before the likes of Stephen Hendry and John Higgins established Scotland as a snooker superpower, Walter Donaldson flew the flag of St Andrew. At first glance, his career is one of considerable achievement – he was only the second man to get his name engraved on the World Championship trophy and, by the time he quit the professional ranks, he had contested eight World Championship finals (all of them against his great rival Fred Davis) and won two of them. Yet today his name is virtually unknown by the public at large and his reputation kindles little legend.

How is it that a two-time world champion could become so forgotten? The answer is partly due to the formidable Joe Davis, and the way that snooker simultaneously owed its popular existence to him, but also suffered from his dominance. It is never easy to follow in the footsteps of a legend and by retiring from the World Championship in 1946 before suffering the ignominy of defeat, Davis solidified his own reputation, but also devalued the efforts of those who immediately followed him. To make matters worse, while Davis did not enter the World Championship, he did still participate in other tournaments and exhibitions – to the public at large he *was* snooker and those who succeeded to his throne were merely pretenders.

Perhaps a highly charismatic champion might have succeeded in filling the void left by Davis, but Donaldson was a softly spoken man with little sense of humour and a reputation for being a somewhat graceless loser. He was certainly not equal to the task of lightening the mood of a nation which had just emerged from the rigours of the Second World War ravenous for sport, leisure and entertainment. As Clive Everton notes:

> His dour approach and thrust-out, determined Scottish chin symbolised his approach to the game and indeed to life. He was a literal kind of man and he played a literal point-by-point type of game, making few concessions to the public.[1]

Yet a closer inspection of Donaldson's career reveals it to be a fascinating and complex one, and proves he merits his place in snooker folklore. His gritty character and no-nonsense approach to life can be traced to his birth in Coatbridge, a Scottish town nine miles east of Glasgow and three miles west of Airdrie, on 2 February 1907. Then the eighth-largest town in Scotland, Coatbridge was an important industrial centre known as the 'Iron Burgh'. With more blast furnaces than any other town in the country, it was consequently bedevilled by pollution and not a place for the faint-hearted.

Donaldson's father was the proprietor of a billiards hall, although he initially forbade his son from playing the game despite his obsessive interest in the sport from an early age. Eventually, the five-year-old Walter's pleas broke his father's will and he was handed a short cue and told, 'All right, my boy, play – and see you make a champion!'[2]

The portents for success were not good. Although Scotland possessed a nascent professional billiards scene, it was hardly a hotbed for cue sports and had never produced a top-class player. Donaldson was something of a prodigy, though, and at the age of just 15 he travelled to London to take part in the first Under-16 United Kingdom Billiards Championship. Organised by journalist Harry Young and involving 37 participants, the event took place at Burroughes & Watts snooker hall, Soho Square, between 5 and 16 June 1922. The young Donaldson battled his way through five matches to reach the final against one H. Renaut of Leyton. With the famous English billiards player Melbourne Inman an interested spectator, Donaldson won by over 300 points and earned perhaps his first newspaper write-up in the *Manchester Guardian*, which reported, 'The small, exquisitely self-possessed Scottish boy . . . could probably have given all elderly person[s] present, with one exception, 50 behind in 100 and disgraced him.' The exception referred to, of course, was the great Inman, whose demeanour the writer compared to 'an Eastern Buddha at a ping-pong tournament'.[3]

The reward for Donaldson's endeavours was a 50-guinea silver cup, a 'gold' medal, a cue and case, and a new suit donated by one of the Strand's tailor shops. Encouraged by this success, Donaldson turned professional the following year.

Realising that to make a decent living he would have to relocate south of the border, he moved to Rotherham and then Chesterfield, where he combined managing billiards halls for the Davis family, one of which he later bought, with long practice sessions. In the mean time, he also added the Scottish billiards and snooker titles to his mantelpiece in 1928.

In common with many others, Donaldson had sensed that the great era of billiards was coming to an end and moved increasingly towards snooker. Nevertheless, he elected not to enter the World Championship until its seventh staging in 1933. By then, his style of play had evolved into that of a 'grinder' – a man who played each shot on its merits, took the minimum of risk and had little time for trickery such as side or screw. His stance was narrow and compact while his cue action was as straight as a gun barrel. His main asset was his flair for incredibly accurate long potting, although his unwillingness to risk missing a pot by playing for position for his next shot meant he made fewer big breaks than many other top players.

One of only five entrants in the 1933 championship, Donaldson overcame W. Leigh 13–11 to progress to a semi-final meeting with reigning champion Davis. The match was a disaster, though, Donaldson being thrashed 13–1. He was so demoralised by the experience that he went away to work on his game for another six years. On his return to World Championship play in 1939, Donaldson reached the quarter-finals where he faced Sidney Smith, the young Doncaster prodigy. A losing finalist to Davis the previous year, Smith edged Donaldson out in a decider 16–15 en route to another defeat to Davis in the final. In 1940, Donaldson faced Davis again, this time in the last four, and lost 22–9 without putting up much of an argument.

The relative trivialities of sport were soon overshadowed by the spectre of global conflict. While Davis remained in Britain and embarked on a morale-boosting series of exhibitions that generated £125,000 for the war effort, Donaldson served as a Royal Signals sergeant with the Fourth Indian Division of the Eighth Army. Often in the front line of the action, he was stationed across North Africa, and in Greece and Italy. When he was demobbed in 1946, he had barely picked up a cue in six years, but he soon threw himself into intense practice to bring his game back up to scratch. Although he won the Albany Club Professionals' Snooker Tournament within months of his return to Britain, when it came to the first post-war World Championship he was no match for Davis, losing 21–10 in the first round. Thereafter, Davis won his 15th world title, defeating Horace Lindrum in the final.

The fates then conspired to make Donaldson an offer he could not refuse. With Davis announcing his retirement from championship play, a vacancy at the top suddenly appeared and the 1947 World Championship was wide open. Joe's brother, Fred, a beaten finalist in 1940, and Lindrum, who had fallen three times at the final hurdle, were the favourites, but no one had taken into account Donaldson's determination. After tucking himself away in a neighbour's attic in Belvedere, Kent, for yet more unrelenting practice, he pulled off a major shock by defeating Lindrum 39–32 in the semi-finals to set up a final against Fred.

The Davises were confident of success. 'I fancied Fred to keep the "Davis Cup" in the family,' Joe observed[4] and with tradition, reputation and the bookmakers all pointing towards a victory for his younger brother, the finalists convened at Leicester Square Hall in October for the two-week final. Donaldson, relishing being in the limelight after labouring in relative obscurity for so many years, sensed this was his moment and revelled in the role of underdog. In front of large crowds, he played the game of his life, securing a winning lead of 73–49 en route to victory 82–63. Donaldson's father, by then 70, was on hand to witness his son's triumph and join in the post-match celebrations at the Albany Club in Savile Row.

The Scot's tactics had consisted of making small breaks of between 30 and 50, and then retreating to baulk as soon as he ran out of position. This made Davis impatient and he took on, and missed, several tricky half-chances while seemingly every attempt to snooker Donaldson ended with him engineering a miraculous escape. Davis made the only three centuries of 145 long frames, but sportingly said of his conqueror that he had played 'the best snooker I have ever seen'.[5] In later years, he tempered this praise somewhat by claiming he had gone into the game overconfident and unprepared for the improvements Donaldson had made.

Although *The Billiard Player* hailed Donaldson as 'The Great

Imperturbable', the risk-free manner of his victory led to little other acclaim. His triumph did earn him the dubious right to challenge Joe on level terms, though. Victory would have solidified his claim as champion, but he succumbed 49–42 after failing to capitalise on an excellent start. A second match between the two in February 1948, on Donaldson's home territory at the Kelvin Hall in Glasgow, was a great box-office hit, attracting 10,000 spectators over the course of a week, but it too ended in defeat for the Scot. For snooker fans, that settled the issue: Donaldson might have been 'world champion', but it was a paper crown he wore – Davis was still the greatest player around.

Such lack of recognition must have grated on Donaldson. To add to his woes, his reign as world champion ended after only six months due to the scheduling of the 1948 championship and his 84–61 defeat against Fred Davis in the final. It was a dour encounter. Fred had learnt his lesson from the previous year and his play was unrelentingly safe, forcing Donaldson to take some risks. It was not pretty, with several six-frame sessions lasting four hours or more, but, in the end, Davis succeeded in beating the Scot at his own game.

With Joe still refusing to compete in the championship, Fred and Donaldson proceeded to dominate the tournament for the next three years, contesting the final on every occasion. Fred retained his title in 1949 before Donaldson won his second, and last, title in 1950. The 51–46 scoreline in favour of the Scot was considered a major shock. Typically, he received little credit, with many observers putting Fred's defeat down to a lack of recent match practice – and, besides, brother Joe was still the undisputed king of snooker. As if to prove the point, Donaldson took part in a televised snooker match on the BBC on 8 September 1950 – his opponent, inevitably, was Joe, who received top billing despite the fact that he was no longer champion.

Fred beat Donaldson again in the 1951 final and in 1952, after a split between the professionals and the BA&CC, two World Championship events were held. This incident will be examined in full in Chapter 4, but, for the time being, suffice it to say that while Horace Lindrum and Clark McConachy contested the 'official' title, over the next few years, Donaldson, Davis and the rest took part in the World Professional Matchplay Championship. Davis won the first three by beating Donaldson in the final each time. Retrospectively, this event has been granted World Championship status by snooker historians.

By this stage, snooker was in serious trouble, with public interest low, and the governing body and players still racked in conflict. In 1954, Donaldson announced his retirement from championship play, telling *The Billiard Player* that he found the effort of getting in top shape to compete too much of a strain and that he wanted to spend more time on his smallholding in Buckinghamshire. Donaldson continued to compete in the *News of the World* tournament until it came to an end in 1959, but, in a potent symbol of his disillusionment with the sport, he eventually converted his snooker room in Bucks into a cow shed and dismantled his table, using the slate underneath the baize as makeshift paving stones for a new path.

Ironically, Donaldson's death in 1973 at the age of 66 came as snooker was rapidly expanding in popularity. While contemporaries such as Fred Davis and John Pulman benefited from the sport's growth with a burst of late fame, Donaldson's name and reputation continued to fade. By way of a final insult, when Hendry lifted the World Championship trophy for the first time in 1990, he was wrongly lauded in some quarters as the first Scot to win the title.

On a measured analysis of the facts, it seems fair to conclude that in achievement, if not personality, Donaldson was one of the most underrated champions, as well as a giant of the pre-Crucible snooker era. For one, he redefined the standards of long potting and, if his safety-first style of play engendered little excitement (he was never in much demand for exhibitions), then the fact that he ended the Davis family's monopoly of the championship was a considerable feat.

Most impressive of all is that, through utterly single-minded determination, Donaldson twice won snooker's ultimate prize. It is somewhat tragic, then, that today the only faint reminder of his career in his home town of Coatbridge is a Riley's snooker centre. Donaldson deserves better, but then, as his story demonstrates, sometimes single-mindedness is not enough.

THREE

FRED DAVIS

The Ambassador Supreme

The likes of Fred Davis will surely never be seen on the snooker circuit again. Some of his career statistics simply defy sense, and would cause younger fans of the sport to look again and still shake their heads in disbelief. A World Championship semi-finalist at the age of 64, he was still in the world's top 16 at 67 and a pro 11 years later, making him the oldest active professional sportsman in the world at the time.

It's hard to imagine many of today's win-at-all-costs players being predominantly remembered in years to come for their charm, so focused are they on winning and gaining ranking positions. For, despite holding claim to a more than commendable eight World Championship titles, Davis is generally referred to as a great ambassador for the game and one of the most enchanting players the sport has ever produced.

However, his popularity must not be allowed to conceal his on-table skill and tenacity. Davis was the only player to beat the mighty Joe Davis – his older brother – on level terms. He managed this an incredible four times and was the only man to seriously threaten, albeit sporadically, Joe's dominance of the baize.

Born on 13 August 1913 in Whittington Moor near Chesterfield, Fred was 12 years Joe's junior. Although Joe was clearly an inspiration, young Fred never received any on-table help or coaching from his older brother. Like Joe, Fred's first love was billiards and he played regularly at the old Lyceum Cinema which his father had bought after the First World War and converted into a billiards hall. At 15, he won the National Under-16 Championship in London, but, as a young boy lacking confidence at this time, was so terrified by the prospect of making his winner's speech he asked a friend to do the honours for him.

Although confident in his own abilities, Davis had yet to acquire a hardness for match competition and in these early years was not the most dedicated of players on the practice table. He was a shy, quiet young man in stark contrast to Joe, who was concerned by his younger brother's laid-back attitude to the sport and didn't want the Davis family name being disparaged in any way. Fred was clearly very self-conscious and when he noticed in his 20s that his eyesight was deteriorating, he initially refused to do anything about it. However, this decision was to haunt him in his first World Championship match in 1937 against Welshman Bill Withers at the popular Thurston's venue. There was plenty of expectancy heaped on Fred going into the game, but his poor vision had now got to the stage that he could hardly see the balls properly, and he fell to a shock 17–14 defeat. By his own admission, Fred should have won easily and he was forced to incur Joe's wrath afterwards.

His reputation was in tatters and he was devastated, but the Withers defeat drove him to do something about his eyesight. He went to an optician who confirmed he was suffering from short-sightedness and had him fitted with a pair of special swivel-lens glasses. These had an extra hinge which allowed him to swivel the frame against the eyebrows and therefore look through the lenses, rather than over the top of the frame, when bending down to play a shot. No leading professional had ever worn glasses before, so Fred was slightly apprehensive about the whole thing, but they did the trick and his assault on the 1938 World Championship was a lot more spirited. After beating Herbert Holt and Alec Brown, he lost to the highly accomplished Sidney Smith in the semi-finals.

Davis reached the last four again twelve months later, but Joe beat him 17–14, although he went one better in 1940, going all the way to the final before losing a very tight contest 37–36, again to his older brother. Some cynics suggested Joe, the game's indisputable master, had taken it easy on his kid brother, but Fred was always quick to denounce such claims, both during his career and for years afterwards.

In 1946, following the Second World War, throughout which Davis was in the army and hardly played at all, the championship reconvened and he lost another semi-final. After that, the event had a completely new look – Joe retired from the tournament with his proud undefeated record going back to 1927 still intact and limited his appearances mainly to handicap-based events and exhibitions. There's no doubt that this decision devalued what should have been the one competition that confirmed who was No. 1 and who wasn't. Many players, Fred included, were frustrated to see the official championship miss out on the outstanding form which Joe went on to produce in exhibitions and other tournaments until the 1960s.

However, with Joe out of the way, Fred reached the final in 1947 and was the clear favourite against Scotsman Walter Donaldson. But Donaldson, with his relentless powers of concentration and perseverance, made full use of his excellent long-potting skills and no-risk approach to win 82–63. A year later, though, Davis got his revenge, beating the gritty Donaldson by taking no chances in a slow-paced final – it was the only way to win the prize his brother had done so much to establish.

Despite being the official world champion, Davis found it difficult persuading the game's followers that he was the true king of the sport rather than just Joe's younger brother. It was a frustrating time for him, now in his prime and in a position to challenge anyone, anywhere, anytime – including fans' favourite Joe. In a pro-handicap tournament during the 1948–49 season, he achieved his first level-terms win over Joe and repeated the feat a few months later. But still Joe was referred to as the best, many people putting that second defeat down to exhaustion after a recent trip to Bermuda.

In the early 1950s, Fred collected a further two wins over his illustrious elder, making four in total. Considering no one else ever managed this, to do it four times was a staggering achievement that was never taken as seriously as it should have been. Around this time, Fred was playing some superb snooker, those self-conscious days of refusing to make a public speech well behind him. But Joe's reputation, and, some claim, his commanding influence with the media and therefore the public, ensured the elder Davis was always seen as the true No. 1.

Fred had to make do with dominating the World Championship, which he did with consummate professionalism. He successfully defended his crown in 1949, lost it again to Donaldson a year later, but wins from 1951–54, all against the durable Scot, made him the man to beat. Donaldson then surprisingly retired from the championship and a new pretender to the throne emerged in the shape of John Pulman, a player who had been creeping up the professional ladder during the previous decade. Davis was too strong for him in the 1955 final and beat him again 38–35 the following year, claiming his eighth and last world title.

One of Davis's great strengths during this period of domination was his ability to size up his opponent from a psychological angle and adjust his game accordingly. Just as he did with Donaldson in 1948, Davis applied various tactics in order to frustrate his opponent or expose his weaknesses. Many players, for instance, often put too much emphasis on bad luck during a match, while Davis always took a step back to look at the whole picture, maintaining a balanced and objective view.

Davis's chances of fighting for a ninth world crown were diminished, however, as the game suffered a serious decline in the late 1950s, the result of which was that no promoter was prepared to stage the tournament. The advent of television meant more people had entertainment in their own homes and many sports, including snooker, were hit by falling attendance figures. The fact that the same faces were appearing in nearly every snooker final gave the sport a predictable look and, as a result, Davis, disillusioned with how the game had dropped off the public radar, pulled out of the 1957 tournament. The event was eventually held in Jersey with only four participants and Pulman went on to win the title.

These were dark days and Davis himself had serious concerns about whether the game would recover – one winter he didn't play at all. He occasionally got to play Joe in one-off games on BBC television, but these were mostly used as fillers if bad weather had affected the favoured outdoor sports and television schedulers were looking for something to use up airtime.

In 1964, however, fellow professional Rex Williams helped reorganise the event on a challenge basis. Styled on the system used in boxing, an existing title-holder would defend his crown against the top challenger in one-off matches. With Davis still seen as the main threat to champion Pulman, he was given first rights to try and win his title back. He made a good start and was leading 13–11 when a poor mistake cost him dearly. Davis was awarded a free ball, but, despite it being obvious which colour he was aiming for, he failed to nominate it audibly (at the time, all free balls had to be nominated whether they were obvious or not), and the referee called a foul. This proved the turning point and Pulman went on to win 19–16.

Throughout the match, it was clear that both players had lost their sharpness; however a year later Davis had another chance to reclaim the crown, but lost to the same player 37–36 despite having led 36–35. He had another attempt in 1966, but lost again to Pulman, before a sponsorship deal with tobacco company John Player & Sons in 1969 ensured the tournament would revert back to a knockout system.

New players like Ray Reardon and John Spencer had just turned professional and fans were relishing the prospect of these fresh challengers taking on proud stalwarts like Pulman and Davis. The first strike for the newcomers came early on when Spencer sent Pulman, theoretically the holder of the title since 1957, tumbling out in the first round.

Davis, looking to prove he was still a major force in the game, found himself in trouble against Reardon, but a late rally saw him edge the Welshman out 25–24 in a match played in Stoke. The table they were playing on was very damp and made it very difficult to control the cue ball so Davis, as ever adjusting to the conditions, slowed up the game by concentrating on making sure of his pots and otherwise leaving the cue ball safe on the baulk cushion. Playing in his first knockout World Championship for 13 years, Davis was still short of match practice, though, and was easily beaten by another up-and-coming professional, Gary Owen, in the semi-finals.

The following season, Davis lost to Reardon in the opening round and then, in May 1970, he suffered his first heart attack, putting him out of the next World Championship. In 1972, it looked as though Davis had recovered well. He'd lost some weight and was in good shape going into the tournament, but didn't have the reserves of energy he thought he had and ran out of steam at the quarter-final stage against Spencer.

In 1973, Crystalate balls were changed in favour of new lighter Super Crystalate versions, which were less predictable, but would respond better to spin, stun and screw shots. This meant more adapting for the likes of Davis, who also had to get used to the new format of the World Championship that year, held at the City Exhibition Halls in Manchester. Rather than having the tournament spread over several months with matches that lasted a week or perhaps a fortnight, the whole event was compressed into two weeks, with multiple tables, big crowds and a bustling atmosphere the order of the day. Players had to concentrate on their game while the crowds were moving around from match to match. For well-established players like Davis, who had spent years working to the old system, it was like asking a long-distance runner to take up sprinting. Davis was up against the then world champion Alex Higgins in the quarter-finals, a match which included a bizarre rain delay (this was Manchester after all) caused by a leaking roof, and covers had to be brought on. When play eventually resumed, Davis, trailing 15–14 and needing only a pink and black to square it up, missed the pink, gifting Higgins the match 16–14.

Although he suffered a second coronary that winter, Davis got his revenge on the Northern Irishman a year later, winning the last three frames to send Higgins packing 15–14. The veteran ran into problems in the semi-final against Reardon, though. The table they were playing on was slightly higher than normal, causing Davis – by no means the tallest of players – to rub the skin on the knuckles of his right hand against the side of the table throughout the match, which he lost 15–3. When Davis mentioned the height of the table to an official after the match, ironically he was told it wasn't a case of the table being too high but the floor being too low.

Despite that mishap, things were hotting up for a revitalised Davis. He had fully recovered from his two heart attacks and was hitting the ball better than he had in years, but luck was deserting him at the World Championship. A narrow 15–13 defeat to Eddie Charlton in the quarter-finals in 1976 was followed by an even closer 13–12 reverse at the hands of a back-in-form Pulman in the opening round in 1977, the first year the event had been moved to the Crucible.

This defeat meant Davis, now wearing contact lenses after discarding the glasses, had to go through qualifying to reach the two-week showpiece the following spring. He was drawn to play John Virgo in Stockport and, despite trailing 7–3, staged a fine comeback to sneak through 9–8 and book his place in Sheffield.

It was at the Crucible that a relaxed-looking Davis, by then aged 64, rolled back the years, producing some highly skilled snooker which enthralled the capacity crowds and lit up the tournament. After wins over Dennis Taylor and Patsy Fagan, he was into the semi-finals where he was up against South African Perrie Mans.

Davis won the first session 5–2 but some poor organisation cost him. His routine during that tournament had been to play a morning session followed by one in the evening, but on that particular day the match started in the afternoon and resumed in the evening. As the first session dragged on, there wasn't much time in the interval for Davis to dash back to his hotel and change into evening dress. He managed it just in time, but regretted not keeping everything he needed at the venue, which would have saved him rushing about. By the time the second session had finished, Davis was 8–6 down. The next day, he fought hard to pull it back to 16–14, but missed a pink off its spot in the next frame, gifting it to Mans, who went on to seal an 18–16 victory.

Thereafter, Fred was never able to match that run to the last four at the Crucible, going out to Eddie Charlton the following year after beating Kirk Stevens 13–8 in the first round. The championship, by then an annual colour-television spectacle, had come on leaps and bounds since Davis first dreamt of lifting the trophy. It was fitting that a player of his stature, who suffered in the wilderness years of the late 1950s and early '60s, was able to enjoy the immense fuss surrounding the whole tournament and be a central figure in it.

There's no doubt that a semi-final appearance on the game's biggest stage at the age of 64, especially in an era when several excellent young professionals were coming up through the ranks, was a magnificent achievement. But how did he remain so competitive for so long? Having experience is one thing, but using it to your advantage and exploiting it on a regular basis is another, and few were better at this than Davis. His ability to adapt to certain situations at short notice often saw him claw back a deficit to win. During a tour of Canada in 1958, for example, Davis discovered the locals were using Vitalite balls, which were much lighter than the Crystalate ones he was used to. His opponents were playing a string of deep screw shots which were much easier with the lighter balls, while a deep follow-through action, adopted by Davis on numerous occasions when playing with harder balls, was more or less impossible since the cue ball would often jump. In a match against the highly respected Canadian George Chenier in Vancouver, Davis found himself eight frames down and decided to change his tactics. Even though the deep screw shot was one he would rarely risk playing back home, he applied it more often than ever before in an attempt to get the Vitalite balls to work in his favour and abandoned his follow-through technique. Not only did Davis come back to win the match, he went on to make nineteen century breaks in his six-week tour, an exceptional performance in conditions that were initially alien to him.

As he got older, Davis also took the art of playing within his powers to a new level. He never played too many frames in practice without taking a rest and was always very conscious of relaxing during matches when his opponent was at the table (Cliff Thorburn was once stunned to see Davis fast asleep in his chair in the players' room during a mid-session interval in a match between the pair). Davis was always realistic about his own abilities and this meant his shot selection was nearly always spot on. He would quickly judge the pace of a table and the conditions of a match before acting accordingly, which could mean slowing up play to take the momentum away from his opponent or upping the tempo instead; playing a series of safety shots or going for the jugular if he felt the time was right. He had a knack for finding the correct balance of when to attack and when to defend.

Davis was also a cunning old fox when it came to psychologically analysing his opponent, picking up on any signs of frustration or arrogance to see whether their spirits were up or down. He always seemed to know which kind of shot to play at what time against a certain type of opponent. Pulman once said that, although he regarded Joe as the greatest player in terms of skill, he saw Fred as the greatest matchplayer ever.

In later years, Davis also never shirked from putting himself and his reputation on the line against spirited young players desperate to take his scalp and make a name for themselves. The aforementioned win over Stevens at the Crucible in 1979 was a perfect example, many fans seeing that result as a fascinating triumph for wily craft over youthful exuberance. Davis was always prepared to take on all-comers. When turning up at the Spectrum Arena, Warrington, for a Mercantile Credit Classic qualifying match in the 1984–85 season, he found that a chimpanzee from a local circus had sneaked into the arena. He asked the tournament organisers if this was his next opponent and after being told it wasn't, Davis replied, 'Well, there are so many new professionals these days, I don't know half of them.'

His friendly demeanour and attitude, especially to newcomers, made him popular with many players. Dennis Taylor remembered when he was first starting out:

> Fred always had a genial twinkle, which made him a popular figure . . . I remember meeting him for the first time, we chatted away for about ten minutes before he went to his dressing-room, making me feel very welcome. It was a kind thing for a man like Fred Davis to do for a new professional and I've always remembered it.[1]

40

Another strength that contributed to Davis's longevity was his excellent attitude and temperament around the table. Whether accepting a piece of bad luck or building on a stroke of good fortune, he rarely let the run of the balls dictate his mood. Self-discipline was a major part of his game: his refusal to blame bad conditions or luck for defeats and his determination to look back at what went wrong and work on it (a trait he had demonstrated ever since his decision to see an optician after his infamous 1937 defeat to Withers) always stood him in good stead.

Davis was awarded an OBE in 1977 for his services to billiards and snooker, and following that golden run of '78 he continued playing professionally. In 1979, he captained England in the World Team Cup, where they finished runners-up, and a year later won the world billiards title, which he retained in 1981. In snooker, he was still in the world's top 16 at the age of 67 and even attempted to qualify for world-ranking events until 1992 when he eventually retired from the game aged 78 after arthritis limited his mobility. He died of natural causes in April 1998 at the age of 84.

A man who contributed to so many eras, Fred Davis saw it all. From the early pressures of emulating his illustrious older brother to playing his part in snooker's revival in the late 1960s, then knocking on the door of a world final a decade later, few players have given so much to the sport and few will be so fondly remembered. He may have felt hard done by in the days when he suffered in comparison with Joe, but by the time he packed away his cue Fred Davis had gained more respect and admiration than most.

FOUR

HORACE LINDRUM

Prophet without Honour

Horace Lindrum was a flamboyant and thrilling talent. Fast and fluent with a winning personality, it was little wonder that connoisseurs adored his style. 'When I watch Horace Lindrum sometimes doing smooth, quiet positional shots with a beautiful cue rhythm, I think of velvet,' declared writer C.D. Dimsdale.[1] If Lindrum's panache won him many fans, then it was his grace and humour that marked him out as a true sportsman. In 1952, having become the first player from outside the British Isles to lift the World Snooker Championship, you might have thought legendary status would have beckoned – yet this triumph was, and still is, the subject of heated debate.

Lindrum hailed from a famous cue dynasty. His great-grandfather Friedrich von Wilhelm Lindrum arrived in Australia from Prussia in 1849 and was good enough at billiards to beat John Roberts senior. Friedrich's son, Frederick William II, inherited his father's talent, winning the Australian Native-Born Billiards title in 1887, however it was Horace's Uncle Walter, Frederick's son, who really put the family on the map.

Born in 1898, Walter travelled to Britain in 1929 and established himself as the best billiards player around, entering and winning the World Billiards Championship for the first time in 1933, beating Joe

Davis in the final.[2] At his peak, Walter was almost as fêted as compatriot and cricket legend Sir Donald Bradman, an occasional spectator at his exhibitions. 'Lindrum is to billiards what Shakespeare is to literature,' said John Bissett in 1933, then chairman of the BA&CC.

Walter never embraced snooker, though, and after defending his title against Davis in Australia in 1934, he did not return to Britain again to play competitively. Ironically, he was also one of the reasons for the decline of billiards – with a record of 711 breaks of 1,000-plus, including his 1932 world record of 4,137, the sheer excellence of Lindrum and his contemporaries in sustaining breaks that lasted hours saw many spectators grow bored and drift away.

By the time Walter vacated his title in 1950, there was already a new Lindrum on the block. Horace, born in Paddington, New South Wales, in 1912, was the son of Walter's sister, Vi. Christened Horace Morell, he later adopted the surname Lindrum, which carried a significant cachet, but also inspired high expectations. From an early age, Horace was a regular in his grandfather's billiards room, although his game was never significantly modelled on Walter's. A greater influence was his Uncle Fred, Walter's elder brother and no mean player himself, while he borrowed a few technical flourishes from Willie Smith.

The teenage Horace was an accomplished billiards player, but a snooker enthusiast. 'My grandfather ruled in favour of billiard practice. My adventure into snooker was very much an undercover affair,' he said. 'I was utilising my billiard knowledge toward progressive snooker.'[3] At 16, he knocked in his first snooker century, an astonishing feat given his youth and the standards of his contemporaries.

In the early 1930s, news spread fast about the young prodigy, who for a while played exhibitions on the road with a circus. Travelling with professional entertainers taught Lindrum the value of keeping the customer satisfied, and encouraged him to play with more flair and develop his audience banter. In 1931, he beat Frank Smith junior to win the Australian Professional Snooker Championship, knocking in a series of quick-fire breaks – including a 97 in five-and-a-half minutes and all the colours in just thirty-two seconds. Many of his feats were not ratified as records, though, including a 139 against Smith junior that was far in excess of Joe Davis's official world record at the time. 'This should have been claimed,' Lindrum reflected. 'Due to my own lack of knowledge about record-break procedure, it wasn't.'[4]

By this stage, Lindrum was managed by his mother, a trained pianist who had formed the first Dixieland jazz band in Australia. Whether Vi's influence was to her son's benefit has long been questioned. Fred Davis claimed her attitude made Horace oversensitive to losing, while Joe's autobiography painted an unflattering picture of her. The fairness of such portraits is debatable, however. The Lindrums and Davises were the two biggest families in cue sports and there was a fair degree of rivalry between them. One can also imagine that Joe didn't take too kindly to an Australian, and a woman at that, standing up to him.

Besides, even Joe was forced to admit Vi was a great publicist. In 1934, her pursuit of Davis secured a chance for Horace to test his abilities against the world champion in a lucrative challenge match. Lindrum had just ended Uncle Fred's 27-year reign as Australian billiards champion, but he was beaten 42–22 by the vastly more experienced Davis. Joe was fond of Horace, though. 'An impish, likeable and good-looking snooker player . . . who was to have a profound effect on the game,' he assessed, adding that his 'style, popularity and attitude . . . reinforced my conviction that [snooker] was the game we should be promoting, the game the crowds wanted'.[5]

Snooker's eclipse of billiards was edging closer and Lindrum was one of the major forces that made it happen. Although Davis had persuaded the BA&CC to inaugurate the World Snooker Championship in 1927, public interest in the tournament had always been low, while Davis's own feelings towards snooker in those early days were, as we have seen, more ambivalent than has often been argued. The Melbourne challenge was a landmark event in more ways than one, for it not only further awoke Davis to snooker's commercial power, but also hardened Lindrum's conviction that to reach the peak of his profession he would have to leave Australia and launch himself on the London scene.

Walter Lindrum was already extremely famous in Britain, so the arrival of another Lindrum on the cue-sports scene, and a snooker specialist at that, was huge news. With Walter having departed from Britain and confusion reigning over whether he would defend his billiards world title again, the way was clear for snooker to move out of the shadows. On 14 October 1935, two days after arriving in the UK, Horace made his London debut in an exhibition at Thurston's against Tom Newman. 'The publicity surrounding my claim of being in world class had preceded my arrival and the atmosphere in the hall was expectant,' he remembered.[6]

With the help of Melbourne Inman, Lindrum embarked on a highly successful British tour. When he played Davis at snooker in Birmingham in February 1936, the 2,600 seats in the Woodcock Street Baths sold out before a ball was struck. The following month, Lindrum took his place amongst the record entry of 13 players for the eagerly awaited World Snooker Championship. He won his tournament debut 20–11 on 26 March against B. Terry, before moving up a few gears in the next round against Canadian Clare O'Donnell, triumphing 19–6.[7] In the semi-finals, his impressive form continued as he thrashed Stanley Newman 29–2 to take his place in the final against Davis.

Lindrum was seen as a real threat to the champion and the *Times* correspondent could barely contain his excitement:

> Lindrum's ability to pot a ball probably is quite the equal of Davis's skill. It is just a question of whether Davis's greater experience will enable him to win more games . . . It will be a remarkable achievement if the young Australian is able to win.[8]

After taking the opening frame on the final day of the first-to-thirty-one-frames encounter, Lindrum was 27–24 ahead and looked capable of ending Davis's nine-year reign. However, in a climax eerily similar to Stephen Hendry's rally against Jimmy White in 1992, Davis won seven consecutive frames, and the three dead frames, to triumph 34–27. 'Of all the championships I have contested this was the event I should have won,' the Australian later reflected.[9]

Despite losing, Lindrum was the talk of snooker enthusiasts across the land. His skills were even being showcased in local cinemas. 'The only possible way to play safe on Lindrum would be to take the table away,' declared the commentary of one film clip.[10] Lindrum's appeal was his open, attractive play, while his personality also endeared him to spectators.

In an interview with the authors, Joy Lindrum Gillan, who married Lindrum in 1949, recalled, 'His enjoyment of the game shone through. He would make a witty remark and the audience would be with him. When he bent over the cue, he often looked at someone in the audience – usually a lady! – just before playing his shot. People would feel he was playing for them.' Lindrum would often have to break away from playing a shot because he was laughing, particularly after a fluke. 'He never "pretends" with his audience,' noted C.D. Dimsdale. 'One reason among several why, to the discerning members of the public, he is such an attraction.'[11]

Lindrum's stock rose further when he equalled Joe Davis's world-record break of 114, a landmark he soon extended to 131, only for Sidney Smith to snatch it from his possession the same evening with a 133. In 1937, Lindrum thought he had regained the record with a 141, however, although several newspapers backed his claim, he was denied recognition because the table had not been examined prior to the match by local snooker officials. Such is life, as Australians say, or, more accurately, such was snooker politics. 'I didn't bargain for the fine technical points which would be raised almost every time I scored in world record-breaking class,' Lindrum later reflected.[12]

In 1937, snooker's rapid rise was demonstrated by the transfer of the Gold Cup from a billiards to a snooker event, while, en route to another World Championship final against Davis, Lindrum beat childhood influence Willie Smith in the semi-finals. Once again, he came close to winning the title, only for Davis to deny him 32–29.

Soon after, Lindrum toured Europe by road, taking his own set of balls with him – the first of many trips he would make spreading the snooker gospel. He was back in England for the 1939 World Championship, falling in round two. His career was then interrupted by the Second World War. He returned to Australia to serve in the wilds of the Northern Territory, and after the cessation of hostilities he was back on the baize in time for the 1946 World Championship, showing he had lost none of his ability by beating Fred Davis 16–12 to reach his third final.

Once again, Joe was his opponent in the most hyped final thus far. For two weeks, crowds of 1,200 filled each session at the Royal Horticultural Hall. 'We turned them away from the hall in their hundreds, it was a great occasion,' recalled Joy Lindrum Gillan, who worked for the BA&CC and helped organise that year's championship. In the match itself, Lindrum once again extended, but could not beat Davis, losing 78–67.

Storm clouds were brewing by this stage. Joe Davis's retirement from the championship seemed to devalue the sport and it entered a slump. Lindrum was among the favourites to win the 1947 event, but fell in the semi-finals to Walter Donaldson, whose grinding determination was the antithesis of his own flair. As he adjusted to wearing contact lenses, Lindrum's form suffered and he expressed weariness with the growing predominance of safety in snooker, arguing that it was being used 'without regard for audience appreciation'.[13]

In 1950, Lindrum withdrew from the *Sporting Record* tournament in protest at receiving a 23-point start, bringing him into conflict with Joe. A year later, he reached the World Championship semi-finals, but by now snooker was ready to implode. Lindrum and New Zealander Clark McConachy submitted their World Championship entry forms ahead of the 1951–52 season but were then summoned to a meeting of the Professional Billiard Players' Association, led by Davis, in August 1951. The Association's relationship with the BA&CC had broken down, with players complaining that the governing body was siphoning too much income from the World Championship. Lindrum claimed that when he and McConachy attended the meeting, they were asked to leave without being given a chance to air their views – expressly because they had supported the official championship by entering it.

As a result, while the rest of the circuit participated in the breakaway World Professional Matchplay Championship in 1952, Lindrum and McConachy faced off for the BA&CC title in Houldsworth Hall, Manchester, over a mammoth 143 frames. McConachy went into the final having registered a 147 in an exhibition, albeit one not officially recognised, however he proved inconsistent in Manchester, snaring many difficult pots while missing easier ones. Lindrum led 44–28 at the end of the first week and, although McConachy changed his cue during the second week, Lindrum crossed the winning line at 76–38 on the second Thursday, ending 94–49 ahead after the completion of the dead frames. He later described it as the toughest match of his career. 'I can honestly say I didn't feel happy until I had secured the winning lead,' he said.[14]

Today, the Lindrum–McConachy match has largely been written out of snooker history, which is a shame, for while it was not a fully fledged World Championship tournament, it remains an important part of the sport's history. Although it has become de rigueur for snooker historians to omit Lindrum's name from lists of world champions, it is worth remembering that Fred Davis's and Donaldson's World Championship wins also occurred in less than ideal circumstances – namely without the participation of Joe, still seen by many at the time as the best player. Furthermore, all but one of John Pulman's titles were earned through one-off matches. Although Lindrum's 1952 triumph was not one of the greatest feats in snooker history, crucially his name is on the trophy for which participants still compete today.

Lindrum viewed the controversy philosophically. 'He was a little disappointed, as it was a different sort of championship,' Joy Lindrum

Gillan explained to us. 'He was elated, but he would have rather beaten Joe Davis.' After Lindrum's victory, the previous two champions, Donaldson and Fred Davis, made noises about challenging him in £500 matches, but Lindrum later claimed he did not receive a single written challenge. The issue died down when he left the country on tours of South Africa, India, Sri Lanka, Australia and New Zealand, and for the rest of the 1950s professional snooker was largely stagnant. Lindrum continued to travel and play, though, notching his 500th public century in 1955 in Pretoria in South Africa. Two years later, he announced his competitive retirement.

Thereafter, Lindrum continued to tour, entertaining spectators with his consummate exhibition skills. His repertoire of trick shots was extensive, while he also possessed an astonishing ability to manipulate a ball as accurately with his fingers as with his cue. Lindrum even came back briefly from competitive retirement in 1963, winning the Australian Open, while in 1970 he became the first player to make 1,000 recognised centuries in public with a 133 clearance in Sydney.

Australia today is very different to the country in which Lindrum grew up. Despite his achievements, and those of Eddie Charlton and, more recently, Quinten Hann, snooker is seen by many Australians as a relic of a bygone era. D.H. Lawrence observed that Australians play sport as though their lives depend on it and perhaps that is why Lindrum, with his relaxed style, doesn't fit snugly into the country's idea of what a great sporting hero is. Today, he is one of the forgotten men of Australian sport. He has never been inducted into the Sport Australia Hall of Fame and his name seldom registers on the public radar, although it was heartening to see that one of actor Russell Crowe's wedding presents in 2003 was a cue Lindrum had once wielded.[15]

It is high time that Lindrum was restored to the prominent place in snooker history that his accomplishments deserve, for while the legitimacy of his World Championship win can be questioned, it is undeniable that he electrified 1930s snooker and was the first non-British player to capture the public's imagination. His break-building was among the greatest ever and, alongside Fred Davis, he pushed Joe harder than anyone else. Lindrum has often been dismissed as predominantly an 'exhibition' player who lacked 'competitive steel', but such an analysis does not sit entirely comfortably with fact – his World Championship record, even setting 1952 aside, was outstanding, consisting of three final appearances in six attempts with losses by tight margins that were no disgrace.

Considering that political divisions denied him so much deserved recognition, Lindrum, who died in 1974, also remained laudably philosophical. When he met Joe in the early 1970s, healing the uneasiness that had existed between them for two decades, Davis pointed out that they had arrived in the game too early to cash in on their talents. Lindrum's own view was more sanguine. 'Maybe so,' he wrote of Joe's theory, 'but I am satisfied to have been part of that early pioneering group. We achieved great things in a short period of time and we laid a solid foundation.'[16]

Above all, as well as being one of snooker's great pioneers, Lindrum was also the spiritual father of a lineage of players whose greatest talent was entertaining and enthralling the public. Like Alex Higgins, whose skills he admired, and White and Ronnie O'Sullivan, who he doubtless would have adored, Lindrum's epitaph is not to be found inscribed on trophies or in the record books, but in the fact that, like any true entertainer, he added to the sum of human enjoyment.

FIVE

JOHN PULMAN

For the Love of the Game

John Pulman suffered the unenviable fate of being world champion for the 11-year period between 1957 and 1968 in which professional snooker all but died. During those dark days, he was forced to labour in obscurity for very little financial reward, wearing his crown with as much honour as he could muster. 'His was the name which conjured up a magical world I hadn't even glimpsed,' Alex Higgins once recalled, declaring that Pulman had been his childhood hero, even though he knew very little about him.[1] There was little that was magical about the snooker world during Pulman's reign as champion, though, and if a young, keen player like Higgins knew next to nothing about him, what chance did the rest of the public have?

Yet the tall and distinctive Devonian had no little style. Always immaculately attired, often with diamond and onyx cufflinks, and his swivel-spectacles, he also possessed a sharp crowd-pleasing wit. 'It's wonderful what a good memory will do,' he once quipped after struggling through an exhibition without his glasses. More tellingly, when introduced to an audience with the line, 'He wasn't world champion for 11 years for nothing,' his arch reply of 'Next to nothing' brought the house down.

Although later pigeon-holed as one of the game's old guard, the young Pulman actually had much in common with risk-takers like Higgins and Jimmy White. As likely to miss crucial pots as snaffle them, he also had frequent problems containing his frustration. Woe betide any spectator in Pulman's presence if they rustled a crisp packet while he was lining up a shot. In later years, Pulman curbed these tendencies and also developed a formidable safety game that helped him survive, if not always thrive, in the more competitive snooker environment of the 1970s.

Pulman's long journey to the world title began when he was born in Devon in 1926. His father was an accomplished amateur who opened a billiards hall in Plymouth in 1932. 'You might almost say I was brought up on a billiards table,' Pulman later recalled,[2] although it was not until his father took over a snooker club in Exeter a few years afterwards that the nine year old 'first started to knock the balls around'.[3] In order to reach the table, Pulman had to stand on top of a mineral case, but he was a fast learner and took heed of his father's sound technical advice.

At 12, he made his first billiards century and throughout his teens he honed his snooker skills in local leagues. An excellent athlete, Pulman also represented Exeter at water polo for two seasons and was a schoolboy swimming champion. However, snooker remained his focus and in 1945 he enjoyed a stirring local success by lifting the Exeter Conservative Club Snooker Handicap without losing a frame – despite conceding a jaw-dropping 75 points per frame in the final.

A year later, aged just 20, Pulman exploded onto the national scene by becoming the youngest winner up to that point of the English Amateur Championship, beating Albert Brown 5–3 in the final. Having entered as a virtual unknown, Pulman's triumph was as unexpected as it was spectacular. Years later, he would still maintain, 'I doubt I will ever have a thrill like winning the amateur championship.'[4]

Encouraged by Joe Davis, and widespread acclamation that he was the most promising young player around, Pulman decided to turn professional. He was lucky enough to receive the backing of a Bristol confectioner and baker named Bill Lampard, a friend of Davis's, who let Pulman stay at his house and built a special billiards room for his use.

However, the gap between the professional and amateur game in those days was vast. By way of example, in winning the English amateur, Pulman's highest break in the final had been a mere 25 and it was only after several months as a professional that he achieved his first century – quite a contrast to Ronnie O'Sullivan knocking in a ton at the age of ten.

Pulman's rise through the professional ranks was consequently steady but painstakingly slow, and comprised five years of eight hours' practice a day:

> I studied hard until the time came when, whether I played a shot and got it or missed it, I knew the reason. It is just not good enough to miss a shot and dismiss the fact with a shrug of the shoulders. You must know why. This is the secret of consistency, one of the big differences between the amateur and the professional.[5]

A further complication was that, soon after turning pro, Pulman had to adapt to wearing glasses. In solving this problem, he was indebted to Fred Davis, whose brand of special swivel-lens glasses he adopted. 'I found it a tremendous handicap at first,' he said. 'But knowing how Fred had prevailed I was determined to do likewise.'[6] In this and many other respects, Pulman's ability to analyse in minute detail the finer details of his own game was a major plus.

Another problem he had to surmount was that of his height. The days of standing on that mineral case to reach the table seemed far off by the time he had grown into a strapping lad of 6 ft 2 in. Indeed, he was one of the tallest players yet seen in a sport where shorter men had traditionally dominated – Joe and Fred Davis were both less than average height, while, in the early days of billiards, W.J. Peall, one of the finest potters the game ever saw, stood a mere 4 ft 10 in. It is very easy for taller players to develop an awkward or twisted stance, so Pulman compensated by keeping more of his weight on his back foot and taking care not to plant his legs too far apart, like many taller players do. With this sound stance, he was then able to capitalise on the advantages in reach and power that his height gave him.

In his first season as a pro, Pulman had some early success by winning the qualifying section of the *Sunday Empire News* tournament. This clinched a place in the five-man finals alongside Joe and Fred Davis, Walter Donaldson and Sidney Smith. Aided by a generous handicap, Pulman finished runner-up to Joe and collected a healthy purse of £400, £150 of it for winning the qualifying section. Nevertheless, his debut in the World Championship in 1947 was inauspicious, losing in the qualifying round to old amateur rival Brown. The following year, he negotiated three qualifiers, the last

18–17 against Willie Leigh on the final black to move into the first round, but was beaten 42–29 by Clark McConachy.

A victory against Brown in the first round in 1949 was an improvement and earned Pulman a semi-final spot, but he was thrashed 49–22 by Donaldson. After a first-round exit in 1950, a losing semi-final appearance against Fred Davis followed in 1951. Pulman also twice reached the semi-finals of the World Matchplay Championship, the de facto replacement for the World Championship, but big victories seemed to elude him. More worryingly, snooker itself was in rapid decline. From its high watermark in 1946, when the Davis–Lindrum World Championship final attracted huge crowds, the game was now flirting with disaster.

Joe's withdrawal from championship play had of course been a huge blow, while the growth of television and an attendant stay-at-home culture adversely affected live attendances at snooker matches. To make matters worse, top players such as Donaldson and Lindrum were drifting away from a sport that was plagued with political conflicts. Alarmingly, there was little young blood to replace them – after Pulman and Brown turned pro in 1946 just one further recruit, Rex Williams, joined the circuit over the next 20 years.

Despite the chaos surrounding the sport, Pulman was more concerned with improving his own game. One of his most useful learning experiences came in the lucrative *News of the World* tournament that ran for ten years at Leicester Square Hall. An invitation event, it afforded Pulman the chance to hone his skills against the cream of the snooker circuit in front of decent-sized crowds. In 1954, aided by a generous handicap, he even won the tournament.

By this stage, Pulman had acquired a reputation as a short-tempered player who often let frames slip away by going for a pot too many. This in turn often left him frustrated and could lead to the loss of yet more frames. Interestingly, Pulman himself never felt that this was a significant failing – quite the opposite, in fact:

> I am convinced that [to succeed in snooker] you must have the type of temperament whereby you will get annoyed with yourself when you are not doing as well as you should. The player who gets annoyed with himself . . . will tend to force himself to play better by sheer grit and determination . . . I am sure that only such a person can be a champion.[7]

Whether a failing or not, Pulman's temperament returned to haunt him in 1955 and 1956 when he reached the World Matchplay Championship final at the Tower Circus in Blackpool only to lose on both occasions to Fred Davis, who therefore retained universal recognition as world champion. The second defeat was particularly galling as Pulman established control of the match early on and went into the final day leading 31–29, only to succumb 38–35. It was, Pulman admitted, the bitterest disappointment of his career.

It is testament then to his determination that, from the wreckage of this defeat, Pulman finally won the championship the following year, albeit in far from ideal circumstances. In April 1957, the World Matchplay Championship – still the most effective barometer for assessing the world champion – was staged by the Jersey Billiards Association in the unlikely setting of St Helier in the Channel Islands. With no sponsor in sight, players had to pay for their own travel, with only a share of the gate money to entice them. Unsurprisingly, only four players – Pulman, Rex Williams, Northern Irishman Jackie Rea and former English amateur champion Kingsley Kennerley – elected to contest a tarnished crown, with reigning champion Fred among those to pass.

Rea progressed to the final with a comfortable victory over Kennerley, but Pulman had a far tougher time against Williams. After tight early exchanges, the players were deadlocked at 12–12 going into the final day, with the winning post still seven frames away. Pulman shaded a tense afternoon to go into the evening with a 16–14 lead and held off two late Williams charges to clinch a 19–16 win before also winning the two dead frames.

Promisingly, a new-found steel seemed to have developed in Pulman's game, typified by him clinching several frames on the final black. His ability to identify, and then pot, crucial shots had become formidable. He certainly displayed plenty of grit in the 73-frame final against Rea, which nearly slipped away from him on several occasions. Rea dominated early on, leading 4–2, 8–5 and then 11–8, despite Pulman registering a 101, which turned out to be the only century of the match. From 11–11, Rea pulled away again to establish a 20–15 advantage, but the match then began to swing Pulman's way. Rea came within a missed pink of winning the next and establishing a six-frame lead, but by the end of the third day's play, aided by snatching a frame from 50 behind, Pulman trailed just 20–19.

From then on, he didn't look back. He won Thursday's session 5–2 and also shaded both of Friday's sessions to move into the final

Saturday 32–27 ahead. From this commanding position, he had few difficulties in picking up the five frames he needed for a 37–29 victory (39–34 after the dead frames were played out). To augment the meagre share of the gate money (only around 100 spectators watched the final session), Pulman and Rea were also awarded several pieces of local pottery.

It was a vintage year for Pulman, who also won the *News of the World* tournament for the second time, but any sense of triumph was dissipated by professional snooker's almost total disintegration. Only one newspaper, the *Jersey Evening Post*, had covered the 1957 final in any detail and no one was prepared to risk staging the championship again for another seven long years. Joe continued to play the odd televised exhibition, but with just six professionals on the circuit and young amateur talents simply not given the requisite encouragement or chance to take up the game professionally, snooker looked set for the sporting scrap heap.

In the absence of any major tournaments, Pulman, aided by his sharp wit, threw himself onto the exhibition circuit to earn a crust. Despite struggling to make ends meet, stirringly, his love for snooker and determination to persist with it was unbreakable. 'The essence of any true professional player lies in the fact that he loves the game he plays,' he pointed out. 'At no time did I think of shelving it for something which might have been a little more remunerative.'[8]

In 1964, the same year that Joe Davis brought the curtain down on his career, Pulman finally got the chance to defend his title, thanks to Williams's proposal for reviving the championship based on boxing's 'challenge' system, as explained earlier. Selflessly, Williams, who harboured world-title ambitions himself, recognised that Fred, by virtue of not having lost his 1956 title 'on the table', had the strongest claim to face Pulman.

With the BA&CC sensibly backing the proposal, the contest was on and Pulman duly won a close match 19–16 at Burroughes & Watts in Soho Square to end any doubts about his suitability as champion. The standard of play was not especially high, but a chink of light had appeared at the end of a very dark tunnel – snooker once again had an active World Championship.

Pulman went on to successfully defend his title a further six times throughout the 1960s, repelling challenges from Williams and Eddie Charlton, as well as South Africa's Freddie van Rensberg. However, the closest he came to losing his crown was in a 1965 return with Davis where he won a thriller 37–36. Davis led 36–35 at one point, but

Pulman rallied superbly to snatch victory. These defences showed Pulman's battling qualities at their best; in contrast to his early days as a professional, he was by then an exceptional matchplayer with a rounded attacking and defensive arsenal. By attracting the sponsorship of tobacco company John Player & Sons for an exhibition tour and his defence against Charlton, Pulman also succeeded in helping persuade the company to sponsor a revived tournament-format World Snooker Championship in the 1968–69 season.

By now, though, the passage of time, and a reputation for good living, had caught up with Pulman, who was knocked out in the first round of the 1969 championship by eventual winner John Spencer, one of a trio of new professionals. Although he rallied to reach the final the following year, where he was narrowly beaten by Ray Reardon, Pulman's abilities declined throughout the 1970s almost as steadily as snooker's popularity grew.

Thankfully, his past endeavours and consistent presence on the circuit ensured Pulman enjoyed a great deal of attention as a valued elder statesman of the game. He even enjoyed a renaissance in 1977 when he reached the semi-finals of the first World Championship to be played at the Crucible, before being edged out 18–16 by eventual winner Spencer. His final appearance in the televised stages of the championship came in 1980, when he lost in the first round, and he retired from the game for good in 1982 after he was involved in a bus accident which broke one of his legs. He maintained his contact with the sport and his distinctive Devonian tones became familiar to a whole new generation as a commentator for ITV, most notably on their popular *World of Sport* programme, before he died on Christmas Day 1998 after a fall in his home.

The major question mark that hangs over Pulman's career is undoubtedly that of his temperament. Fred Davis, for one, observed that many people found Pulman more entertaining when things were going badly for him as it meant they were more likely to see fireworks. Such tendencies would have made Pulman a star in snooker's modern era, but it is hard to imagine him, in today's ultra-competitive environment, fighting through several rounds of fierce action at the Crucible to lift the title on anything like as many occasions as he did during his own era. It is worth remembering, after all, that on only one occasion did he have to win more than one match to lift the World Championship.

Conjecture aside, though, Pulman dominated 1960s snooker and it is not his fault that fate dictated his peak was during the sport's weakest era. On reflection, it is probably fair to say that he ranks only behind the Davis brothers among pre-1969 champions. Above all, though, it is for his dedication and love for the game that he should be remembered. Few have toiled so hard for so little reward and for that, as well as for keeping snooker's World Championship flame alive throughout so many difficult years, Pulman deserves the sport's eternal thanks.

SIX

JOHN SPENCER

The Man with the Premier Streak

Being the first to achieve something in sport is always special, a feat that can be logged in the memory bank, safe in the knowledge that in years to come no one else can come along and say, 'I got there first.' By the time John Spencer hung up his cue, he'd had the good fortune to be able to think just that about himself – for on so many occasions during his snooker career, it was he who got there first.

Spencer was the debut winner of the revamped knockout-style World Championship in 1969; the first man to lift the title at the Crucible in 1977; winner of the maiden Benson & Hedges Masters in 1975, as well as the first B&H Irish Masters three years later; and the first player to compile a maximum 147 break in tournament play. During his triumph in 1977, the year many regard as the beginning of snooker's modern era, Spencer also made history by becoming the first player to win the game's major prize using a two-piece cue, an invention that was still very much frowned upon by most professionals at the time.

As well as possessing a knack for winning the inaugural event of so many tournaments, Spencer had many other strings to his bow. He was a fine tactician and his long pots were exceptional, but what also made him stand out from the crowd during his peak in the early 1970s was his immense zest for the sport and his perfection of a stroke few could master – the deep screw shot.

Fans and competitors alike were amazed to see this brash Lancastrian pull off a sublime long-distance pot with the cue ball springing back sometimes as much as eight or nine feet in order to maintain good position. Even in the days before Super Crystalate balls came into use in 1973, Spencer could master these prodigious shots, a revelation at the time, with wonderful accuracy and consistency. During Spencer's prime, even the great Joe Davis was moved to say, 'He plays screw shots bigger and better than anyone I know.'[1]

With such an impressive record of achievement, you'd be forgiven for thinking that Spencer, born in Radcliffe, Lancashire, in 1935, was an early starter. The reality is quite the opposite, as it wasn't until the age of 15 that he took up the sport. He developed a basic stance by playing on a makeshift 4x2-foot table with his brother at home until he stepped up a gear and wandered into his local billiards club. Forcing his brother-in-law to accompany him (minors weren't allowed in unless they were with an adult), Spencer got to work and was soon knocking in half-century breaks on a regular basis, but couldn't fathom out why he kept on breaking down soon after that, unable to complete a century.

He also began playing at the local Church Institute where an elderly member named Jack Westwell gave him a piece of advice he would value for the rest of his career. He suggested Spencer ditch snooker for a while and take up billiards. After an intensive six-week stint at the three-ball game, Spencer was advised to resume snooker and was soon back in the groove, but this time using side and spin much more effectively. The billiards training had helped him develop that aspect of his game and he could thereby maintain his breaks for longer, completing his first century while still only 15.

Spencer was by then taking on opponents for money, and rarely lost, but was once hit in the pocket when, playing for two shillings a frame, his opponent – three frames down and trailing significantly in the fourth – asked Spencer to hold his cue for him while he nipped to the toilet. Half-an-hour later and with no sign of the player, he went looking for him only to find him gone, leaving Spencer with no winnings to show for his efforts and having to foot the bill for the table.

Despite such minor hiccups, he was making a name for himself in the local area and, following a complimentary article about him in the *Bury Times*, was called into his headmaster's office at school one morning. Showing Spencer a copy of the article, the headmaster gave him a strict warning that all this snooker was bad for his education, and advised him to stop playing immediately and concentrate on his school work.

Feeling disheartened, Spencer eventually joined the Royal Air Force when he was 18 to complete his national service, quitting snooker altogether. He spent three years in the forces, during which time he 'never played snooker and completely lost interest in the game'.[2] After leaving the RAF in 1956, he still wasn't tempted to return to the green baize, instead taking up a number of jobs, including a bread-van driver, a labourer in a paper mill and a settler in a betting shop.

Out of the blue, at the age of 28, he received a call from a Radcliffe bookmaker who, thinking Spencer was still playing, wanted him to join a team representing a club in Longsight, who were on the lookout for a player ahead of a big match against a team from a billiard hall in Salford. Spencer accepted and found himself up against Salford's best player, Andy Whiteside, one of the top amateurs in Lancashire at the time. Spencer put in a brave performance and only lost by 17 points, but it was enough for the snooker bug to return.

He set up more matches against highly rated local players over the next few weeks before entering the English Amateur Championship in 1964. Although this was the first serious tournament Spencer had ever played in, all those hours spent playing for a few shillings at a time in his local club meant he knew what it was like to play with something at stake.

Using all this know-how, he went on to win the northern section of the tournament before losing to fellow rising star Ray Reardon 11–8 in the grand final at the Central Hall in Birmingham. Spencer entered the competition again the following year and reached the final once more, but produced a meagre performance, going down 11–3 to Patsy Houlihan at the Tower Circus in Blackpool. Undeterred, he made it through to the final again in 1966, beating Marcus Owen 11–5 in Huddersfield and making the first-ever century break in an amateur final in the process. 'In my first two championships, I had reached the final with a more tactical approach, but in the third final I started to attack more,' he reflected later.[3]

Indeed, Spencer was starting to make serious waves on the national circuit with his elegant, offensive style and enthusiasm for the game. After his success in Huddersfield, he was invited to take part in the World Amateur Championship in Karachi, Pakistan, where he got to the final before losing to Gary Owen – older brother of Marcus – 6–2.

Spencer's snooker career took a dramatic twist on his return to England. Following a row with the sport's governing body over the expenses for the Karachi trip, he withdrew from all amateur tournaments organised for the 1967–68 season and, fed up with the organisation of the game at that level, planned to retire for good unless an opportunity came up for him to turn professional. As it turned out, there was no need to quit the game for a second time – the National Spastics Society offered him some regular exhibitions and Pontin's gave him a contract to tour their summer camps, enabling him to turn pro.

This coincided with the reversion of the World Championship back to a knockout format in 1968–69 and Spencer, after paying a hefty £100 entry fee, made a flying start to his first attempt at snooker's Holy Grail. A 25–18 win over reigning champion John Pulman in the first round was followed by a 37–12 crushing of an out-of-form Rex Williams, putting him in the final against Gary Owen at London's Victoria Hall.

Owen had beaten him in their recent World Amateur Championship clash, but Spencer was learning fast. In this particular tournament, he was focused on going all the way, but at the same time refused to put undue pressure on himself:

> As an amateur I had always thought the top amateurs were out of my class. This was a big help to me as I treated them with the utmost respect when I played them. When I became professional I went in with the same attitude, rating myself as very much the underdog with everything to gain and nothing to lose.[4]

It was around this time that Spencer was also making the most of his dynamic deep screw shots. No one could play them as well as him, keeping sublime control and rhythm throughout. He applied perfect timing and speed when bringing his cue forward to strike the white correctly and avoid the convulsive jerks other players suffered when trying the same shot. Spencer, a supreme technician, never fell into the trap of hitting the ball too hard – he always followed through properly in order to get the maximum reaction possible from the white.

With the final against Owen delicately poised at 8–7 in Spencer's favour, the Lancastrian pulled off one of the most stunning screw shots in his career to take the sixteenth frame. With just three balls left on the table, the cue ball near the pink spot and the blue in baulk,

Spencer smashed the blue into the yellow pocket, screwing the white back a good nine feet – so far back, in fact, that it went beyond the pink, allowing him to pot it into the middle pocket. 'It was just confidence and timing,' he said later. 'A shot like that can really shake your opponent if it comes off.'[5] Now 9–7 up, Spencer had the conviction to go on and clinch a 37–24 victory and the world title at his first attempt, something only Joe Davis had managed up to that point.

Also in Spencer's armoury was a fine judgement of lethal long-range pots, a tactic that, although pleasing on the eye, was considered fairly risky at the time and nothing like as common as it is today. His expert knowledge of how to put the correct amount of side on the cue ball to exploit its bounce off the cushion and aid his positioning was another strength that helped him stand above the rest. His positive approach amongst the balls was also matched by a determination to boss the safety exchanges. Always keen to force his opponent into a mistake, Spencer would more often than not play an attacking safety rather than a containing one. This aggression often forced openings that many players didn't think were there.

Aiming to defend his title the following year, he came up against Reardon in the semi-finals in Bolton. The Welshman had the edge this time, winning through to the final where he would eventually beat Pulman. Still, Spencer took his revenge the following year. The 1971 World Championship was actually played in November 1970 across a number of different venues in Australia and Spencer overpowered Reardon in the last four to set up a four-day final against Australian Warren Simpson. Spencer completely dominated the first two days, at one point knocking in three century breaks (105, 126 and 107) in the space of four frames – a record at the time for the World Championship. Simpson, 18–6 down, staged a recovery on the third day to reduce his arrears to 20–16, but a composed Spencer sealed it on the final day, 37–29.

It was around this time, and particularly during that triple-century burst in the final, that many experts feel Spencer was at the true peak of his powers. World champion for a second time in three years, he was now much more than an exciting prospect with a host of spectacular shots under his belt. He had a proven track record, had won the game's greatest prize in two different continents and looked set to dominate for years to come.

After that success Down Under, he went on a tour of Canada where his confidence levels increased even further with some stunning displays. Making the most of the more receptive Canadian Vitalite balls and slightly bigger pockets, Spencer compiled 29 centuries during his trip, including his first 147 maximum. He also produced 60 breaks of over 80 in 98 frames against Canadian star Cliff Thorburn.

The only drawback of the hugely successful tour was that Spencer picked up a virus and spent a week in bed on his return to England. As expected, he fought through to the final of the 1972 World Championship, but, still a little jaded from his illness, surprisingly went down to buccaneering youngster Alex Higgins 37–32 in the final. 'I tried my best but the spark wasn't there,' reflected Spencer years later.[6]

There was more agony in the 1973 tournament at the City Exhibition Halls in Manchester, the first time the event was squeezed into a fortnight. Leading Reardon 19–12 in the semi-finals, he seemed to lose his concentration, missing a straightforward black to throw away one frame. Reardon, sensing blood, stormed back to claim a 23–22 victory. It was a hard defeat to take and one from which some claim Spencer never really recovered. Although he went on to win further tournaments, *Snooker Scene* editor Clive Everton once remarked it was 'all without quite recapturing the easy confidence and peak form of his greatest years'.[7]

He did win the Norwich Union Open in 1973 and '74, but couldn't seem to produce his best when it mattered most – at the World Championship. Following his devastating loss to Reardon in Manchester, Spencer suffered a first-round exit the following year at the hands of Perrie Mans. Reardon got the better of him again in the quarter-finals in 1975, while Higgins edged him out 15–14 in the last-eight stage the year after.

In 1977, the tournament moved to what turned out to be its modern-age home – the Crucible Theatre in Sheffield – but Spencer was being written off from all angles on the eve of the tournament that spring. He hadn't produced his best in the event for a good six years, while he had just ditched his faithful cue for, heaven forbid, a two-piece model. Up to that point, Spencer had always used the same cue since taking up the sport at the age of fifteen, even after it snapped in four places during a car accident in 1974. A friend had managed to craft it back together, but Spencer could never get the same power out of it again, forcing him to change.

He decided to experiment with a two-piece cue he had been given when he won the Canadian Open in 1976. One-piece cues had, of course, been all the rage since the game's inception and the two-piece invention was regarded as nothing more than a pointless gimmick which was supposed to be used for playing pool. Not only that, all professionals knew a player took years to get fully used to a cue and picking up a new one in the build-up to a major tournament was verging on the absurd.

After a slow start, Spencer (who was awarded the final seeding position of eighth for the tournament) overcame John Virgo 13–9 in the first round, while in the second managed to get one over on his old rival Reardon 13–6 in a match where the Welshman never really got out of first gear. Spencer then bounced back from a poor start against Pulman to win 18–16 and reach his first final since the shock defeat to Higgins five years previously.

Thorburn was his opponent and the Canadian, in his first world final, settled first, opening up a 15–11 lead, but Spencer dragged it back to 18–18 before the final day. Spencer, never an early riser, made a special effort and got out of bed at 7.30 that morning in order to take a long walk in the park so he could focus properly for the 11 a.m. start. He took the first three frames of the day, which set him up for a hard-fought 25–21 win, a lucrative first prize of £6,000 and his third world crown.

'My determination had carried me through,' he later wrote. 'I had proved to myself that I could win with another cue.'[8] As it was, he switched to another two-piece made in Japan a few months later and before long most professionals were dumping their old cues for these new models. Spencer admitted years later that perhaps he had made a mistake in persisting with his original cue for too long following the car crash – his form that year in Sheffield was proof alone that he made the right decision in the nick of time.

Two years before his surprising Crucible success, Spencer had lifted the inaugural Masters Championship, beating Reardon 9–8 on a re-spotted black in the deciding frame of the final at the West Centre Hotel in Fulham. In 1978, it was his turn to win another event making its debut on the circuit, the Irish Masters.

Although the air of invincibility that seemed to follow him during the pinnacle of his career had long gone, Spencer could still beat anyone on his day. His fabulous long potting and screw shots were still putting pressure on his opponents to try risky shots themselves as they knew they couldn't leave him with anything remotely pottable. Spencer would also refuse to get downhearted if he pulled out all the stops on a difficult shot that turned out badly. Applying deep screw sometimes meant he miscued, but if that happened, he didn't allow it to affect his confidence and would still attempt the same shot at the next opportunity.

During that barren six-year spell without a world title, he also avoided the temptation to get bogged down in analysing his technique, as many players do, especially if they go a few years without achieving the results they expect of themselves. 'As soon as a player becomes obsessed with technique, he has written his own death warrant,' he once said, proving that – despite being a keen analyst of the game – he never overdid it.[9]

Spencer, by now approaching his mid-40s, proved yet again that he shouldn't be written off just yet by winning the Holsten Lager International in Slough in 1979. In his quarter-final against Thorburn, he amassed the sport's first 147 maximum break in tournament play. Unfortunately, the feat was not televised because the camera crew covering the event were at lunch and didn't leave the film rolling. To make matters worse, it wasn't recognised as an official break because the middle pockets didn't conform to the official templates. On top of that, the Holsten event was one of the few that didn't pay out a special prize for a maximum. It's fair to say it would have been a tough task for his wife, Margot, to encourage John to look on the bright side that night.

Spencer won the Wilsons Classic in 1980 and was a member of the victorious England World Team Cup side in 1981, but in 1984 he began to suffer from double vision. The problem was so bad that he couldn't practise at all that summer, but, with the help of regular medication, he recovered. He was slipping down the world rankings, but dug deep and surprised many by reaching the quarter-finals of the Dulux British Open in 1987, which helped him regain his place in the top 32. Victories over Tony Meo and Dave Martin set up a last-eight showdown with Jimmy White, but 'The Whirlwind' kept his composure to record a 5–3 win. Spencer still picked up a cool £9,000 for getting that far, the biggest pay day of his lengthy career. He took up television commentary soon afterwards and combined that with playing until finally retiring in 1992. Spencer's love of the game didn't stop there – he served as chairman of the sport's governing body, the World Professional Billiards and Snooker Association (WPBSA), for six years.

Spencer's peak form may not have lasted for as long as he would have wished, or indeed as long as many followers of the game had expected, but his contribution to the sport and the World Championship was immense. Two of his three world titles carried huge significance with them, namely the rebirth of the competition's much-loved knockout system (1969) and the realisation that the event had found its true home (1977). Not bad for a man who didn't pick up a cue between the ages of 18 and 28.

A great snooker thinker and a fine technician, Spencer brought plenty of much-valued panache and elegance to the game with his array of deep screw, spin and stun shots. He was almost untouchable in the early 1970s, while his record, topped with three World Championships, speaks for itself – John Spencer was a class act.

SEVEN

RAY REARDON

The Aura of Greatness

The greatness of Ray Reardon is beyond dispute. A distinctive figure, with his slicked-back dark hair and charming smile, the Welshman dominated 1970s snooker in the way that Steve Davis ruled the 1980s and Stephen Hendry bestrode the 1990s. In his pomp, Reardon always saved his best form for the big occasion – emerging victorious on six of the seven times he reached the World Championship final, including a run of four straight titles from 1973 until 1976. World No. 1 when the rankings were introduced in 1976, he stayed at the summit for six of the next seven years and, like Hendry and Davis, he possessed that indefinable air of authority common to all great champions.

Yet, despite these achievements, Reardon has never been afforded quite the same level of acclaim as some other top players. This is largely due to unfortunate timing. In common with many of his contemporaries, he turned professional relatively late in life and his talents were therefore in decline as snooker approached the zenith of its popularity. As a consequence, just one of his six world titles was won at the Crucible and, aside from his losing appearance against Alex Higgins in the 1982 final, he was never part of a defining snooker moment that fixed him for ever in the public imagination.

Strangely enough, Reardon was also a far from perfect technician. Like many amateurs, he committed the cardinal sin of lifting his head slightly when he played shots, while his cueing elbow jutted out awkwardly. However, he was a master tactician who was adept at coming from behind to win matches and his cold and exacting safety often tied opponents in knots. Ruthless at exploiting mistakes, his potting remained remarkably precise under pressure.

The greatest Welsh cueman of all time was born on 8 October 1932 in Tredegar, Monmouthshire. Reardon's father and his brothers all played amateur cue sports, but it was Uncle Dan who piqued an eight-year-old Ray's interest by setting up makeshift billiard games on the kitchen table. Soon after, Reardon received a small table as a Christmas present and was drawn like a magnet to practise his burgeoning skills at Tredegar Workmen's Institute. By the age of ten, he was visiting the Institute twice a week with his father and, at twelve, was participating in the Welsh Boys' Championship. For the most part, it was billiards that occupied his attention, which helped hone the accuracy of his potting and cue-ball control.

Reardon's father, Ben, was a miner and before the youngster was 15 he followed him into the pits. In order to keep his evenings free for snooker, Reardon worked days on the loading shift. It was a tough life, but mining hardens the hands and sharpens the eyes, as well as adding strength to the arms, shoulders and back, and the long days of toil helped build Reardon's stamina. As he worked, he also took care to keep the tools of his snooker trade, his hands, protected in white gloves. 'I got my leg pulled quite a bit as a result of wearing those gloves,' he admitted.[1]

Reardon was soon playing money matches at the local Lucania snooker club and established an intense but friendly rivalry with one Cliff Wilson. A local steelworker, Wilson was a great talent who possessed an aggressive and fast game and was, along with Londoner Patsy Houlihan, the sort of player who could have reinvigorated snooker in the 1950s and '60s if he had been encouraged to turn professional. Reardon's matches with Wilson drew huge crowds of local fans with much money staked on the results.

This competitive environment helped shape Reardon's temperament, but he showed he had a lot to learn in 1949 when he was thrashed 4–0 by eventual Welsh amateur champion John Ford. The defeat opened Reardon's eyes to the arts of stun and screw, and made him realise that his game was based on potting and little else. Fuelled by a fervent desire to expand the horizons of his game,

Reardon embarked on a month of solid practice of the new techniques he had witnessed. His reward was a maiden century break and the Welsh Amateur Championship in 1950, courtesy of a revenge victory against Ford. It was the first of a remarkable six Welsh titles in a row, with Reardon chalking up several victories against Wilson in the process. Strangely enough, Wilson invariably beat him in the qualifying tournament for the English Amateur Championship.

This stirring rivalry came to an end in 1956 when pit closures forced Reardon's family to uproot to north Staffordshire in search of work. After Reardon's departure, Wilson finally got his hands on the Welsh title, but gradually became disillusioned with snooker, drifting away from the game for 15 years before making a remarkable return in the 1970s.

As for Reardon, his arrival in Staffordshire was marked by a sequence of landmark events. First, he faced the legendary Joe Davis in an exhibition near Stoke-on-Trent organised by Billy Carter, a local businessman. Carter's niece, Sue, who helped sell tickets for the event, was to become Reardon's first wife in 1959. Davis later remarked of Reardon, 'his control and tactics made my old eyes pop'[2] and he invited him to participate in a competition on the BBC television programme *Sportsview*. Each competitor was given five minutes to make a break and Reardon's effort of 21 won him a handmade Davis cue, which virtually became an extra limb.

Not long after, Reardon was given a reminder of his mortality when he was involved in a mining accident at Florence Colliery. A section of the coalface caved in, leaving him trapped for several hours. Struggling against the weight of the rubble, the lower half of Reardon's body went numb before he was finally rescued. It was a sobering but mind-strengthening experience. After a hospital check-up, Reardon was soon back in the pits, but once he married he began to look for employment that offered greater security and more opportunity to practise his snooker.

So it was that in 1960 Reardon joined the Stoke-on-Trent police force as a probationary constable. The training he underwent got him in good physical shape and he performed his duties with distinction, winning a commendation for persuading a man with a loaded gun to give himself up. In the mean time, his snooker was improving all the time and, in 1964, at the age of 31, he finally won the English amateur title, beating John Spencer 11–8 in the final – the first meeting of what would become a splendid rivalry.

The following year, Reardon lost his grip on the title – and the opportunity of another showdown with Spencer – when Houlihan beat him 6–5 from 5–1 down in the semi-finals. Houlihan went on to thrash Spencer in the final, the highlight of a career that never achieved its rich promise. Reardon was determined not to suffer such a fate. Being invited on a six-week tour of South Africa helped convince him he could make a living from the game and he left the police force and officially launched his professional career on 3 December 1967, aged 35.

Although aided by a small retainer paid by snooker equipment manufacturer Riley Burwat, Reardon was taking a mighty risk; professional snooker had been moribund as a major sporting spectacle for at least a decade and, although the recent entry of Gary Owen and Spencer into the ranks had swelled the number of pros, the potential for failure was acute. The early days were tough; he held down part-time work for 12 months to support his family, partly because he took the difficult, but principled, decision not to undersell himself on the exhibition circuit by refusing invitations that did not pay the requisite £20 or £25. 'I wanted the professional snooker player to be worthy of respect and to be properly rewarded,' he said.[3]

This stance paid off when one of the tobacco manufacturers who had begun to explore snooker's sponsorship potential, the Johannesburg Tobacco Company, paid for him to go on another tour of South Africa. As well as giving Reardon's finances a boost, the tour also inspired a rich vein of form, as he knocked in more than 25 centuries. He returned to England for his first tilt at the world title in confident mood.

The 1969 World Championship proved a watershed for snooker. John Player had come forward to sponsor the event and there was a total of £3,500 in prize money on offer for the eight players on the starting grid. Gone was the unsatisfactory challenge system that had seen John Pulman hold the title since 1957, despite playing a meagre nine World Championship games, and back was the traditional, and superior, knockout format.

In many people's eyes, the likes of Owen, Spencer and Reardon started the tournament as underdogs, but this was a misleading assumption, for they had honed their games in the raw competitiveness of the amateur snooker scene, a far more demanding and competitive environment in the 1960s than the professional circuit. Furthermore, although they were not particularly young, the players in their sights were positively ancient by comparison.

The changing of the guard began when Spencer knocked out Pulman in the first round. Meanwhile, Fred Davis needed all his cunning to deny Reardon 25–24 – it was the most constructive snooker lesson the Welshman ever had. 'I absorbed more in that one match with him than I had learned in all the intervening years,' he noted. '[It] taught me new dimensions of the game.'[4] Spencer went on to beat Owen in the final and the high drama of the tournament had confirmed snooker's green shoots of recovery were not a mirage.

Soon after, the game received another major fillip. While BBC producer Phillip Lewis lay in bed one night, pondering ways with which to put the recent introduction of colour television to effective use, he realised that snooker, with its range of coloured balls, was the ideal vehicle for a colour television broadcast. He enlisted snooker impresario Ted Lowe, whose voice was later to become synonymous with snooker commentary, to devise a format that would fill eight weekly half-hour slots on BBC2. Lowe proposed a tournament of one-frame matches and so it was that *Pot Black* was born.

In the past, attempts to televise snooker had been stymied by black-and-white images, but now it was a different story. Colour television graphically conveyed snooker's intimate drama and compulsive rhythm, and viewers were soon seduced. The players themselves might not have liked the one-frame format (finals would later be played over three frames), but from the screening of the first episode on 13 July 1969, the programme was an instant hit and remained a staple of the BBC's schedules until 1986.

By giving players the chance to infiltrate the nation's living-rooms, *Pot Black* was also a significant economic force, enabling professionals to raise their exhibition fees and public profiles. Reardon made the biggest impact possible in snooker's new showcase by winning the inaugural tournament, beating Spencer 88 points to 29 in the final. The BBC weren't keen to let him leave the studio with the gold-plated trophy, but, as an omen of the dominance he would soon exert over the sport, Reardon held his ground and got his own way.

Although his appearances on *Pot Black* made him more recognisable, Reardon craved the World Championship above all else. In 1970, at just the second attempt, he captured it. In a first-round war of attrition in Stoke, he gained revenge over Davis to set up a semi-final showdown against reigning champion Spencer in Bolton. The eagerly awaited match-up, the first meeting of the two players since the 1964 English amateur final, turned out to be a damp squib, mainly due to a table with over-tight pockets. Reardon held his nerve better than his opponent, though, securing a 37–33 win.

Awaiting him in a 73-frame final at the Victoria Hall, London, was Pulman. Reardon dominated from the start and, courtesy of some tremendous long potting, won seven frames in a row to advance from 20–14 to 27–14. At 29–19, he was just eight frames from victory, but he then lost concentration – 'perhaps because it was only the second 73-frame match in which I had played'[5] – and Pulman narrowed the deficit to 34–33. When the former champion also moved ahead on points in the next frame, Reardon began to sense he had blown it. However, Pulman then played a loose safety that left Reardon with a glimmer of a chance. He seized it, squeezing a red into the top pocket and holding position for the green. An artfully constructed break of 38 gave him the frame and, with few alarms, Reardon also won the next two frames to wrap up a 37–33 triumph.

'Nothing will ever surpass the wonder of winning the world crown for the first time,' Reardon later recalled.[6] The winning cheque of £750 was enough to clear his debts and the prestige of becoming world champion meant an instant increase in his earning capacity.

A few months into his reign, while on another tour to South Africa, Reardon had an alarming experience when his beloved Joe Davis cue went missing after an exhibition. As soon as he realised it was gone, Reardon called the police, but extensive searches failed to locate the prized item. Resigned to withdrawing from his forthcoming defence of the title if he did not get the cue back, a devastated Reardon pinned his hopes on an appeal in the *Rand Daily Mail* newspaper. Incredibly, the cue was left outside the newspaper's office the next day along with an anonymous note of apology. The incident made front-page news and ended up being something of a publicity coup for a relieved Reardon.

With the faithful tool of his trade restored to his possession, Reardon set off to Australia to defend his world title a mere six months after winning it. It was far from ideal, but the money on offer persuaded him that the risk of losing his title so soon was worthwhile. In the event, a flawed tournament structure ended up pitting Reardon against Spencer in one semi-final, while Australian representation in the final was assured by the other last-four pairing of Eddie Charlton and Warren Simpson. Unfortunately, Reardon let his irritation at what he saw as a loaded draw affect his play and he lost in tame fashion 34–15.

In the 1972 World Championship, Reardon's exit was again attributable to his inability to put other thoughts out of his mind and get on with the task at hand. His quarter-final against Rex Williams was ill-advisedly played at a succession of venues in Scotland with wildly varying table conditions, but Reardon let it unnerve him more than his phlegmatic opponent and was duly knocked out.

The championship concluded in seismic fashion when a young Belfast maverick named Alexander Gordon Higgins dethroned Spencer 37–32. Although Reardon, Spencer and *Pot Black* had helped snooker win many new fans, Higgins's arrival was the most significant boost the sport had received since the death of billiards – snooker's equivalent of the introduction of the electric guitar into popular music. He might have been unstable and awkward, but he brought new, young fans to the sport and all-important media interest. For his rivals, his effect was more pragmatic; if you played him, your earnings shot up. As Reardon himself put it, 'Someone once said to me, "Would you have any objection to playing Alex?" . . . I said, "He's making me money, how can I have an objection to somebody who's making me money?"'[7]

When Higgins first won the title, many people, not least himself, expected the trophy to remain in his possession for years. The fact it did not was partly due to his mercurial nature (more cautious players were always in with a chance of beating him). However, it is also a measure of Reardon's own greatness that the grip he exerted on 1970s snooker denied Higgins another world title for a full ten years.

From 1973, when Reardon won the title for the second time, until 1976, the Welshman lifted four world titles in a row and chalked up seventeen successive victories in World Championship matches. His swaggering dominance began at the 1973 Park Drive-sponsored World Championship in Manchester, which he entered in a mood of utter determination to regain his crown, having wedded himself to the practice table prior to the tournament. His new-found toughness of body and mind helped him prevail 23–22 from 19–12 behind in a classic semi-final against Spencer.

Drained from this effort, Reardon began the final against Eddie Charlton poorly, trailing 7–0 after the first session. However, without a hint of panic or desperation creeping into his play, he slowly reeled the Australian in, taking a 17–13 lead. At 27–25 in Reardon's favour, the match took a controversial turn. The BBC were recording sections of the final and, ahead of the eighth session, had set up a series of cameras and lights to capture the action. Some of the lights reflected awkwardly on the object ball, which Reardon found particularly distracting.

Rather than put up with it and get on with the game, as Charlton did, Reardon threatened to walk out unless the situation was resolved to his satisfaction. When the organisers refused to back down, Reardon went straight to the sponsors. It was an astonishing display of self-assurance, and it showed that his mindset was now assuredly that of a champion. 'When the television people saw that I was adamant, it suddenly became quite easy to manage without the lights,' he later recalled.[8]

With the offending spotlights duly removed, Reardon kept his nose ahead 31–29 going into the last day before rounding off a 38–32 win. 'Losing it had taught me just how much it meant,' he said of the euphoria of regaining the title.[9] A cheque for £1,500 represented a two-fold improvement on his winnings three years previously, and Reardon had few problems retaining his title in 1974. While Spencer and Higgins succumbed early on, Reardon thrashed Davis in the semi-finals before repelling an intimidated Graham Miles 22–12 in the final.

His assessment of the match betrayed his increasingly perfectionist nature. 'I don't feel that I played any better than mediocre in the final,' he said, 'but this was because Graham never put me under pressure. I don't feel the elation that I felt at winning last year.'[10] Elation or not, Reardon had acquired the winning habit; in the 1975 World Championship final in Melbourne, he had little right to beat Charlton from 29–25 behind, but somehow engineered a 31–30 victory to take the £4,000 first prize.

Reardon's fourth successive world title win in 1976, the first year that Embassy sponsored the event, was once again secured in controversial circumstances. The tournament was ill conceived from the start, with the competitors split between two venues, one in Manchester and the other in Middlesbrough. Reardon was based in the latter and found conditions far from ideal. The venue possessed a disconcerting draught, while spectators were allowed to smoke and drink during the match, as well as get up from their seats in the middle of shots. Nevertheless, Reardon's progress to the final was serene, as he sailed past John Dunning, Dennis Taylor and Perrie Mans.

His opponent in the final was Higgins, who had sweated buckets in Manchester to secure final-frame victories over Cliff Thorburn and Spencer before an equally sapping 20–18 semi-final win against Charlton. Prior to the first session, in order to prevent the Northern Irishman gaining an unfair advantage due to his familiarity with the Manchester table, the slate and cloth were changed by the organisers, but the result was a playing surface that was somewhat less than level.

Again, just as in 1973, Reardon voiced his concerns at the glare caused by the television lights. While the champion dwelled on such discomforts, Higgins seemed unconcerned, producing some sparkling snooker to open up a 4–2 lead.

Reardon, by now visibly irritated, succeeded in getting the lighting adjusted to his satisfaction and hit back to lead 8–5, however another streak of good form by Higgins moved him back into the lead 10–9. According to the Northern Irishman, Reardon then stepped up his complaints about the state of the table. Adjustments were made in the interval and Reardon proceeded to romp through the next session and take a 15–11 lead. Meanwhile, match referee Bill Timms had been replaced by John Williams. The official reason given for the switch was illness, although some believed it was a strategic decision to try and defuse Reardon's ongoing disagreements with Timms.

Whatever the truth, Higgins, wearied by Reardon's antics and his own long march to the final, grew increasingly lackadaisical. On the verge of cutting the deficit to 15–14, Higgins crucially elected to play a simple red left-handed and missed it. Reardon cleared up and eventually clinched a 27–16 victory when a mentally spent Higgins conceded a frame he could still have won. All in all, it was a disappointing final and it was probably a good thing that the BBC only screened selected highlights on *Grandstand*.

Many felt Reardon's behaviour had skirted dangerously along the boundaries of gamesmanship. 'I was accused of histrionics, but I won the £6,000 first prize,'[11] was his own plain assessment of the match, although he admitted that Higgins's behaviour had been beyond reproach – which could be read as a tacit admission that his own had not. Higgins himself later expressed his frustration at Reardon's behaviour. 'I had every right to say, "Look, you may be world champion, but I'm playing you for your title now. This is the table we've elected to play on and I don't want this table touched,"' he wrote. 'But like a fool I let him have his own way.'[12] In retrospect, despite the controversy, the 1976 final can be seen as Reardon's finest hour. For one thing, it remains one of the few times that anyone, by sheer force of personality, succeeded in intimidating the usually fearless Higgins.

Reardon's status as world No. 1 was rubber-stamped after the tournament when he topped the first official world rankings. However, his supremacy was about to be challenged. The 1977 World Championship was a special occasion – not only did it represent the 50th anniversary of the very first championship, but it was also the first to be staged at the Crucible. At the time, no one would have imagined how synonymous the Sheffield venue was to become with snooker, but its superior elegance and comfort were obvious from the start – smoking was even forbidden in the audience. There was also the small matter of an increased prize-money pot of £17,000.

Reardon prepared for the tournament with dedication, losing about a stone in weight by sticking to a diet and not drinking too much alcohol. However, after a first-round victory against Patsy Fagan, he fell to an anti-climactic quarter-final defeat against Spencer. 'I'm not disappointed because I did not deserve to win,' a resigned Reardon explained after the match.[13] Such listlessness was not surprising: Reardon had been engaged in a punishing schedule for several years by this stage.

As well as exhibitions and a number of overseas trips, Reardon's status as world champion and his easygoing sense of humour had made him into something of a television personality. He seemed to relish feeding off the energy of light-entertainment-show audiences as much as he thrived during big matches in front of large crowds of snooker fans – appropriate, really, for a man whose nickname alluded to the most famous bloodsucker of all – 'Dracula'.

While some people would have baulked at such a sinister sobriquet, Reardon took it in his stride, playing up to his image by occasionally sporting a pair of fake fangs and gamely appearing on a succession of television and radio programmes including *The Generation Game, The Paul Daniels Magic Show, The Russ Abbot Show, A Question of Sport, The Little and Large Show, This Is Your Life* and *Desert Island Discs*. On *Parkinson*, he confidently regaled chat-show host Michael Parkinson with jokes and a trick-shot routine.

Regaining the world title was his top priority, though, and he did just that in 1978 with a comfortable 25–18 victory against Mans. By now 45 years of age, it was to prove Reardon's last great triumph. For the next few years, he struggled, almost entirely as a result of the gradual disintegration of his beloved cue. Towards the end of 1978, the end of the cue finally split and two inches broke off. Cue doctor Tony Wilshaw performed drastic surgery on the instrument Reardon regarded as his 'Excalibur', but it was in vain.

The years from 1979 to 1982 were barren indeed for Reardon. Major tournament successes eluded him, his World Championship form was disappointing and, in 1981, he suffered an unceremonious drop from first in the world rankings to fourth. Several further attempts to reconstruct his cue also failed and Reardon found it hard to accept falling short of the exceptional standards he was accustomed to meeting. At one point, he even publicly pondered the possibility of retirement – prompting a rash of letters from fans around the world offering him their own cues as potential substitutes.

Eventually, in 1982, Reardon picked up a cue in a club in St Albans and rediscovered his form almost instantly. Confidence renewed, he reduced his number of exhibition engagements ahead of the World Championship, hoping to conserve his energy for an attempt to win a seventh world title. Aided by a fairly sedate draw – and a brutal cull of several seeds in the early rounds – he progressed regally to the semi-finals.

Youngsters such as Jimmy White and Kirk Stevens had been dominating the headlines throughout the tournament, so it was left to Reardon, at 49, and his 52-year-old semi-final opponent Charlton, to fly the flag for experience. The 32-year-old Higgins, who was something of a bridge between the two generations, beat White in one semi-final, while Reardon saw off Charlton 16–11 in the other.

Back in the final for the first time in four years and assured of a return to the No. 1 slot in the rankings, Reardon was a strong betting favourite, although sentiment and the majority of fans favoured Higgins. It was an extremely tight encounter and when Reardon fought back from 15–12 down to level the match at 15–15, the title looked to be in his grasp. Suddenly, though, his form deserted him, and Higgins recovered his poise and flair to secure an iconic 18–15 victory. Reardon was disappointed but philosophical, embracing his conqueror at the end of the match. 'I think the game got to me in the end for I had so many lapses of concentration,' he reflected.[14]

Such lapses had never afflicted Reardon in his heyday and, although his revival continued the following season with tournament victories in the Professional Players Tournament and the Yamaha International Masters, and a final appearance at the Masters, his career was slowly winding down. Naturally gregarious and always willing to share a joke with spectators, Reardon was also not entirely comfortable with the commercial direction snooker was taking, voicing the opinion that the game had become too serious. 'There's too much money in it now,' he said in 1983. 'All the fun's gone out of it. We're in a world of agents and managers now.'[15]

Reardon's eyesight was also suffering and he struggled to adapt to wearing glasses whilst playing. His vast experience helped him reach the World Championship semi-finals in 1985, but at the end of 1986–87, he dropped dramatically in the rankings from 15th to 38th.

At the same time, the disintegration of his marriage also brought some unwelcome tabloid headlines. Reardon remarried not long after and finally retired in 1992, moving to Devon to play golf and enjoy the financial fruits of his considerable labours, while maintaining his links with snooker by making the odd appearance in television documentaries and on *Big Break*, as well as serving on the WPBSA board.

In retirement, Reardon was able to reflect on a formidable record. Although he never won the UK Championship and lifted the Masters just once, his World Championship record was extraordinary and testament to the consistency of his all-round game. Reardon's potting, safety and temperament were all extremely solid, but what elevated him to greatness was that he possessed the strength of character to force opponents to bend to his will. 'I have always been prepared to challenge anything with which I disagree . . . I like to have a go,' he once noted[16] – a succinct summary of the way his easy charm hid the cold heart of a truly intimidating competitor.

The one spectre that hangs over Reardon's career is that of Higgins. The Northern Irishman is the man Reardon is always asked about in interviews; as well as the man whose 1982 world-title triumph is replayed on television far more often than the Welshman's own 1978 victory. Understandably, Reardon's irritation at such a situation has occasionally boiled to the surface: 'All you [journalists] talk about is him, it's pathetic,' he complained to Higgins's biographer Bill Borrows.[17] For the most part, though, he remains sanguine about the fact that Higgins is regarded as a folk hero, while his own fate is to be remembered in more simple terms as a great snooker player. You could argue forever about how Higgins's two world titles, won a decade apart, compare with Reardon's six in seven years, yet, in the final analysis, such comparisons are self-defeating. With or without reference to Higgins, Reardon bears up to scrutiny as one of the greatest snooker players who ever lived.

During the 2004 World Championship, Reardon, at 71, made an unexpected return to the limelight when it emerged that he was acting as a mentor to Ronnie O'Sullivan. The spur for this unlikely association came when O'Sullivan's father, serving a life sentence, telephoned Reardon from prison to request his help. Although Reardon's professional, polished demeanour might seem diametrically opposed to O'Sullivan's rawness, the combination worked a treat. Early in the tournament, 'The Rocket' had courted controversy with several obscene gestures around the table. Reardon, while publicly admitting he 'deplored' such antics, succeeded in relaxing and concentrating O'Sullivan's frequently troubled psyche, helping him march off with a second world title. For his part, the 2004 world champion said of his new mentor, 'They talk about great people, Muhammad Ali and that, but I would put him in a room with anybody. He is a great man.'[18]

O'Sullivan, bless him, is entitled to overstate the case: Reardon is no Ali (and I bet that's a sentence you never thought you'd read), but he was without doubt the most successful snooker player of the 1970s. He proved that playing to win consistently and remorselessly doesn't necessarily mean you have to sacrifice your personality, but, more importantly, he set new standards for mental fortitude which showed those who hoped to follow in his footsteps just how testing the path to snooker greatness is.

EIGHT

ALEX HIGGINS

The People's Champion

Alex Higgins was electric. No snooker player engendered so much passion and excitement or provoked as many newspaper headlines as the Northern Irishman. Today, decades after his wondrous peak, the 'Hurricane' remains a compelling figure; in the last five years alone, two new Higgins biographies have hit the bookshelves, an award-winning play about his life has been running in London and New York, while a television biopic is also in the pipeline.[1]

The Belfast-born maverick tore through the professional ranks, inspiring fear, loathing and adulation in roughly equal measure. A resolute non-conformist, Higgins became the youngest world champion in 1972 at the age of 22 (a record that stood until the emergence of Stephen Hendry). This achievement barely rated a paragraph in most national newspapers at the time, but, over the decade that followed, he helped transform snooker from a sport on the margins of public consciousness into a multimillion-pound industry – triumphantly regaining the world title in 1982 in front of 14 million television viewers.

Meanwhile, Higgins's tumultuous private life – incorporating two marriages, a head-butt, a death threat, a suicide attempt, bankruptcy, a 25-foot dive from a flat window and 17 arrests – was played out very publicly in the pages of the tabloids. With so many discarded chip wrappers devoted to his life already, is it truly possible to find something new to say about Higgins? 'He came, he saw, he conquered, he went off the rails' is the traditional assessment of his career. End of story? Not quite, for Higgins was a far more complex character than the broad brushstrokes of tabloid journalism ever gave him credit for. As he himself said, 'When I look into the mirror, I see the indistinct outline of an enigma. A man who's been misunderstood for most of his life, and presumably always will be.'[2]

Alexander Gordon Higgins was born on 18 March 1949 in the heart of Belfast's working-class Protestant community. Rationing was still in force after the rigours of the Second World War and the Troubles were fast approaching. Higgins was one of three children born to Alexander senior, a railway labourer, and Elizabeth, a formidable woman whom Higgins credits with supplying his survival instinct. At the age of nine, he discovered the Jampot, a snooker hall just off the Donegall Road, where 'the tobacco smoke hung thick . . . and the light was so dim it could have been night'.[3]

Snooker gradually became his obsession. Whenever he could slip away from the protective gaze of his sisters, Ann and Isobel, or from school, it was to the Jampot that he was drawn. He would observe the older players and their techniques forensically, absorbing the strategies and skills he would later revolutionise.

The bare resources of his pocket money, supplemented by what he earned scoring games for other players and selling firewood door to door, allowed Higgins to subsist on a diet of Coca-Cola and Mars bars. He rose up the rigid hierarchy of the Jampot from the sixpence-a-game tables to hallowed table eight, where the stakes were higher. By the time he was 12, Higgins was building breaks of 35 or 40. Some older members resented the schoolboy upstart and weren't averse to trying to intimidate him by bashing him on the back of his head with their cues. Consequently, Higgins was always ready to make a getaway – a possible reason, he once speculated, for his breakneck playing speed.

Higgins's dreadful attendance record at school did not go unnoticed, but his unconventional lifestyle won the tacit approval of his mother, who consoled herself that he was better off in the snooker hall than on the streets. His prodigious abilities soon outgrew the Jampot and he began to practise at the more challenging Shaftesbury Hall, where prominent amateurs such as Maurice Gill were to be found.

Although Higgins's hustled winnings were useful, the idea that he might make a professional career out of snooker remained absurd.

'Snooker didn't appear to offer a way out,' he later claimed. 'If anyone had suggested I could make a career out of it, I'd have said they were mad.'[4] His family were equally unsuspecting of the future star in their midst; when a fortune-teller visited the Higgins household and foretold that a member of the family would become famous, they presumed the prophecy referred to Alex's sister, Ann, a talented singer. It was hard to imagine that her brother would ever amòunt to much, especially after he left school in 1964 before taking his O levels.

After a brief spell as a messenger, Higgins's life took a dramatic turn when he answered an advertisement seeking stable boys for Northern Irish trainer Eddie Reavey in Berkshire. Leaving Belfast, a city blighted by a lack of opportunities, seemed the only option for a youngster without qualifications. In typically grandiose fashion, Higgins regarded the job as the first step towards becoming the new Lester Piggott despite, by his own admission, having never ridden a horse. Leaving his tearful family behind, he travelled to England on the Belfast–Liverpool ferry on which he had his first, though far from last, alcoholic drink – a half-pint of beer.

The stable lad's routine of 5 a.m. wake-up calls and mucking out did not suit Higgins, while the generous fry-ups offered at the stables saw him put on several stone, ending those dreams of stardom as a professional jockey. His habit of bunking off to the bookmakers saw him fired and reinstated several times, although he earned the affection of Eddie and his wife, Jocelyn, during his two-year stint in Berkshire. 'I could see the same self-destruct instinct in Alex that I'd noticed in Eddie,' Jocelyn said. 'Ulstermen seem to have a terrible death wish about them.'[5]

After playing barely a frame in two years, a move to London and a job in a paper mill reacquainted Higgins with the green baize before, a little over three years after leaving, he returned to Belfast. In his absence, the city had changed for the worse. 'Snooker players didn't mingle so freely any more,' he commented. 'Before the Troubles, both religions could walk into any billiard club in Northern Ireland and play what we called "sticks".'[6] Shrugging off the political ferment, Higgins immersed himself in local-league snooker and as he neared his 18th birthday he hit his first century – by the end of the same week, he claimed, a further 34 tons had followed.

Higgins's progress in 1968 was dramatic: he beat Gill in the final of the Northern Ireland Amateur Championship and then defeated Gerry Hanway for the all-Ireland amateur title; in 1969, he lost the Northern Irish title to Dessie Anderson, but a superb performance in the UK Team Trophy final in Bolton drew excited local-press attention, notably from a reporter named Vince Laverty.

Smitten by Higgins's potential, Laverty suggested to John Spencer, the reigning world champion, that an exhibition between the world No. 1 and the new whizz-kid from Belfast would be an attractive proposition. Spencer and Higgins accepted the proposal and, for the princely sum of £30, as well as a 14-point start per frame, Higgins beat his vastly more experienced opponent several times over the course of a week at locations across Lancashire.

The ecstatic response of local fans to Higgins's crowd-pleasing talents convinced him Lancashire was the place to ply his trade and he settled in Blackburn, where he was taken under the wing of local businessmen Dennis Broderick, Jack Leeming and John McLaughlin. It was McLaughlin who came up with the nickname 'Hurricane'. Higgins preferred the somewhat grander tag of 'Alexander the Great', but it didn't catch on. 'What does "Hurricane" mean?' he protested. 'It just means tornado-like or what have you. But Alexander the Great was a person in history, and I want to be remembered.'[7]

He lived the life of a hustler to the full, playing and drinking hard. As word of his talents and break-building capacities spread (a three-and-a-half-minute century in a Walsall exhibition did no harm), it became inevitable that he would become a fully fledged professional. However, with the organisation of snooker in disarray and Higgins himself unsure whether it was to his benefit to turn pro or not, he suggested to the governing body that he serve a probationary term on a wage of £35 per week, plus a further £25 per exhibition. He turned down his sister Isobel's invitation to lend him the entrance fee for the 1971 World Championship, but was already plotting his assault on the snooker world. 'I was honing my game to match sharpness. I was getting ready,' he said.[8] The following year, he took the plunge, cobbling together the £100 entrance fee himself.

The 1972 World Championship was played over a period of 12 months, from March 1971 until February 1972, with the rounds taking place at assorted venues across the country at dates and times arranged at the participants' own convenience. As a young professional in his first year on the circuit, Higgins had to negotiate two qualifiers to even reach the first round.

His first qualifying-round match saw him sweep past Ron Gross 15–6, while Maurice Parkin fell swiftly 11–3 in the next. Lying in wait in the first round proper was the Irish professional champion of the past two decades, Jackie Rea. In a symbolic match, Higgins saw off the old master 19–11 to usher in a new era for Irish snooker. The transition was completed in January 1972 when Higgins also relieved Rea of his Irish title with a breathtaking 28–12 victory. Rea, whose famous routines of trick shots and impersonations heavily influenced the likes of John Virgo and Dennis Taylor, was effusive in his praise of his unconventional conqueror. 'He's a fabulous player when he's going well,' he said. 'He does everything wrong. And yet he knocks such a lot in.'[9]

Higgins's quarter-final opponent was one of the snooker greats – former world champion John Pulman. Although no longer the player he had once been, Pulman was still good enough to have been a losing finalist in 1970. Undaunted, Higgins attacked his ageing opponent's percentage game with brute force – a tactic that reaped an impressive 31–23 victory. Next up was a classic semi-final showdown against Rex Williams, chairman of the game's governing body and the reigning world billiards champion. After the tie was rescheduled three times to accommodate Williams's commitments, Higgins entered the match determined to make his older opponent pay for what he perceived as gamesmanship. He played relentless attacking snooker, treating Williams's more measured play with disdain.

The tactic nearly backfired: at one stage, Higgins's recklessness saw him lose nine consecutive frames to trail 14–8. He fought back fiercely, though, and at 30–30 the match moved into a decider. Higgins won it, but not before his opponent, on the verge of the final, missed a crucial and pottable blue. 'That blue could have changed the direction of both our careers,' Williams observed regretfully later.[10]

All of a sudden Higgins was in snooker's showpiece final. Unsurprisingly, his hard-drinking lifestyle had made the sport's establishment deeply uneasy, as journalist Gordon Burn recalled: 'They were literally praying that this hooligan wasn't going to win.'[11] Higgins, relishing his role as a rebel with a cause, had other ideas.

Considering it was such a key event in snooker history, the setting for the final against reigning champion Spencer was somewhat incongruous and emphasised snooker's small-time status. Scheduled across six days at the Selly Park British Legion in Birmingham, the spectators were perched on wooden boards lying on beer barrels, while emergency lighting, necessary due to power cuts caused by miners' strikes at the time, cast awkward shadows on the table. The backstreet ambience, coupled with the support of the majority of the fans, gave Higgins plenty of confidence.

Nevertheless, the match was desperately tight. Neither man

managed to take full control as the score progressed from 9–9 to 18–18, and then 21–21. Higgins then struck, reeling together a seven-frame winning streak to lead 28–21. Going into the final day, Spencer narrowed the deficit to 32–28, but Higgins held his nerve, accelerating past the finishing line 37–32 with a 94 clearance, his highest of the match.

The momentousness of the victory was not lost on him, despite paltry winnings of £480. 'I wanted to do a Cassius Clay and shout from the rooftops, "I'm the greatest,"' he admitted, 'but for once in my life I bit my lip.'[12] By the time he met the small media corps, he was in a more grandiloquent mood, declaring that he would keep hold of the title for five or six years before retiring at thirty.

At the time, it seemed possible. Raw, unpredictable and full of inventive brio, Higgins had the star quality snooker needed so desperately. His victory against Spencer only attracted limited column inches in the national press – the *Times* report extending to a mere 90 words – but gradually the media began to take note of this unique new sporting character. In March, he was profiled in the *Sunday People*, but the biggest factor in bringing his name to the wider public was when ITV broadcast a half-hour documentary on his life and career entitled simply *Hurricane Higgins* on Monday, 4 September 1972. Aided by being scheduled on prime-time TV straight after *Coronation Street*, the half-hour programme reached 25th place in the all-channel ratings for the week and, although somewhat bleak in tone, proved terrific exposure.

Viewed today, the most striking aspect of the documentary is the sheer speed and flair with which Higgins played at this age. Sadly, no footage of the 1972 final against Spencer exists, but from watching Higgins knock in a century in 2 minutes 55 seconds in the documentary, one gains a vivid idea of how revolutionary his arrival in snooker must have been. Many television critics who reviewed the programme admitted they had no idea who Higgins was beforehand. *The Time*s was particularly awestruck by the way he potted balls at a speed its writer claimed would have made Paul Newman's hustler 'Fast' Eddie Felson flinch.[13]

As world champion, Higgins duly received an invitation from Ted Lowe to appear on snooker's televised showcase, *Pot Black*. However, Higgins hated the one-frame format, the Pebble Mill studio and the way the players were treated by the programme-makers. He later claimed he urinated in the dressing-room sink because the toilets were too far away, possibly an apocryphal tale, but he certainly made a nuisance of himself on-set. Although Lowe denied any conspiracy to keep him out, a return invitation was not forthcoming.

Higgins might have been moving snooker further into the mainstream than ever before, but his image did not sit comfortably with the professional, courteous and refined environment the WPBSA desired. Snooker had sought to escape from the backstreets into the cosiness of BBC television coverage, but Higgins was a living reminder of the thesis that a flair for snooker was invariably indicative of a misspent youth. In an interview with the authors, Bill Borrows, his unauthorised biographer, commented, 'He disregarded anyone or anything that got in his way. He stood up to the WPBSA when others acquiesced.'

Fearful of the uproar that would ensue if they cast Higgins into the wilderness, the snooker establishment instead tried to limit his influence with quiet acts of suppression. The *Pot Black* 'ban' was one such example and frequent fines for 'inappropriate dress' were another; Higgins's green velvet suits, white shoes and fedora added colour to snooker more than anything, but the WPBSA did not see it that way. Of course, Higgins did not help his cause with a series of other misdemeanours. Soon after becoming world champion, his boozing and tantrums during trips to Australia and India – where he offended spectators by playing topless – quickly ensured his tabloid fame spread, but also earned him a fine on his return to England.

More worryingly for the young Northern Irishman, the consistent excellence he demonstrated in winning the title soon evaporated, although it did not help that the cue with which he won the world crown had been broken by a careless hotel porter. When it came to defending his title in 1973, the growing interest in snooker ensured the championship was now a one-venue event held over two weeks with televised coverage of the closing stages and a top prize of £1,500. Higgins was slaughtered 23–9 by Eddie Charlton in the semi-finals, leaving the way clear for Ray Reardon to overcome the Australian in the final and restore the status quo. Pulman articulated the feelings of the establishment when he declared he was glad Higgins had lost because he was dragging the game down.

Throughout the rest of the 1970s, Higgins failed to shake off his inconsistency. An exhausting lifestyle of drinking and gambling, coupled with travelling the length and breadth of the country on public transport (he had never learnt to drive), did not help. An ill-fated marriage to Australian Cara Hasler in 1974, which struggled on for five years and produced a baby girl, Christel, whom Higgins has reportedly only ever seen once,[14] also did little to give his career a solid foundation. Meanwhile, his once-unshakeable confidence was being dented on the table with defeats to Fred Davis in the quarter-finals of the 1974 World Championship and Reardon in the last four of the 1975 event. Outrageously, Higgins did not receive an invitation for the latter and had to pay his own way to Australia for the tournament, which was organised by Charlton.

By now, inspired by Muhammad Ali's victory over George Foreman in 1974, Higgins was often tempering his attacking style with his own version of Ali's 'rope-a-dope' tactics – essentially soaking up an opponent's pressure with bouts of safety before striking back when they were worn down. In 1976, such fighting qualities helped Higgins reach the World Championship final again, but his progress was tortuous, encompassing 15–14 victories against Cliff Thorburn and Spencer as well as a 20–18 semi-final triumph over Charlton.

By the time of the final against Reardon, Higgins was exhausted and succumbed 27–16. He seemed strangely subdued and his play was highly erratic; he missed many easy pots, often conceded frames he was still able to win and even played, and missed, a frame-winning shot left-handed. At the same time, he allowed a bullish Reardon to get his own way when he made frequent complaints about the television lighting and table conditions.

As Higgins's form oscillated wildly, snooker continued its rapid expansion. In 1977, the championship began its residence at the Crucible – but the star attraction failed to even negotiate the first round, suffering a demoralising 13–12 defeat against Doug Mountjoy. Despite such disappointments, Higgins's cult-hero status was continuing to grow, largely because, unlike many other players, he never sought to hide his emotions at the table, which made it easy for fans to identify with him. Coupled with his flamboyant playing style, and disregard for accepted dress and social codes, he brought many new young spectators to the sport.

When Higgins hit form, he could still handsomely reward his growing army of fans. The 1977 Pontin's Open in Prestatyn was a perfect example and cemented his status as 'The People's Champion'. The tournament pitted 8 professionals against 24 survivors from a qualifying series involving 864 amateurs, veterans and youngsters. Higgins was not among the 8 pros invited to take part – mainly because the tournament's prime consultant was Lowe. Undaunted, and encouraged by his new girlfriend, Lynn Robbins, Higgins took advantage of a rule allowing professionals to take part in the qualifying competition – if they conceded a 21-point deficit per frame.

With matches being settled by aggregate scores over two frames that amounted to a 42-point disadvantage on poor-quality tables that nullified many of Higgins's natural advantages.

Relishing his underdog status, Higgins surged through the qualifiers, recovering a 104-point deficit in a match against Billy Kelly to reach the quarter-finals. As his campaign gathered pace, the crowds grew. After whitewashing Reardon and Fred Davis, he then saw off Terry Griffiths 7–4 in a final watched by a huge crowd of 2,000 who chanted his name relentlessly. Perhaps more than any of his other triumphs, the Pontin's Open demonstrated Higgins's ability to connect with ordinary fans. At the prize-giving, with Lowe watching, the crowd began yelling for Higgins to be allowed back onto *Pot Black*. In the face of such public disquiet, an invitation to return to the programme was soon issued.

Nevertheless, World Championship success continued to elude Higgins. In 1978 and 1979 he won a total of just one match at the Crucible and a 1978 Masters crown was scant consolation. Marriage to Lynn at the beginning of 1980 appeared to galvanise him, though, and he began to recapture something approaching his best form. Three tournament wins and two further final appearances saw him enter the 1980 World Championship in great heart. A 13–9 quarter-final victory against fast-emerging Steve Davis, in which Higgins was on for a maximum 147 only to run out of position and miss a double on the green, was followed by a semi-final triumph over Canadian Kirk Stevens.

To the public's delight, Higgins was back in the only final that really mattered, where he would face another Canadian, Thorburn. As well as a turbulent relationship off the table, which once led Thorburn to kick Higgins in the groin, the contrast between the two men could not have been greater. This was the Hurricane versus the Grinder – a battle of conflicting snooker philosophies as well as a personal rivalry.

Higgins, who throughout the tournament had wowed the crowd by entering the arena wearing a purple fedora, raced into a 9–5 lead with some irresistible attacking play. Fatefully, he began to play to the gallery with some extravagant pots – unfortunately he also produced some extravagant misses, giving Thorburn the chance to haul back the deficit and ultimately edge the match 18–16. After the match, a heartbroken Higgins, barely able to suppress his torment, admitted, 'My old crowd-pleasing bit came back a bit. It's hard to live with, but I'll bounce [back].'[15]

The defeat intensified the public's affection for Higgins. However, when Davis crushed him in the 1980 UK Championship final many thought he was effectively finished. The prophecies appeared to be borne out in 1981 when Davis also knocked him out en route to winning his first world title. Worse was to follow for Higgins, though. A miserable performance in the 1981 UK Championship, coupled with management problems and gathering storm clouds in his marriage, left him reeling. The birth of his daughter, Lauren, the year before had initially stabilised Higgins, but with his game disintegrating, the demands of fatherhood weighed him down. Lynn went on holiday without him and it was not long before Higgins was checking himself into a nursing home in Rochdale.

The media had a field day speculating that he had suffered a breakdown. On his return to snooker, Higgins was ritually slaughtered by Davis in York, only to pick up a microphone and announce to the crowd, 'In the words of Muhammad Ali, my greatest hero, I want to say that I can return! I shall return! I will return!' Most people dismissed it as empty defiance – how wrong they were.

Entering the 1982 World Championship as a 25–1 outsider and eleventh seed, the fact that Higgins went on to lift his second world title solidified his legend. Fate was certainly on his side that year, what with Davis's shock opening-round defeat against Tony Knowles and the early exits of Taylor, Thorburn and Griffiths. But while other results may have opened the door to the title, it was Higgins's forceful play that broke it down. With Lynn and Lauren back by his side, the crowd urging him on and a collection of superstitious knick-knacks in his possession, Higgins built up irresistible momentum. After dismissing Jim Meadowcroft in the opening round, close-fought wins against Mountjoy (13–12) and Willie Thorne (13–10) set up a semi-final showdown against Jimmy White – Higgins's spiritual heir – which proved one of the finest duels in British sporting history.

Each player produced consistently compelling, attacking snooker and as the match entered its final stages White was 15–14 ahead, needing just one more frame to become the championship's youngest-ever finalist. After carving out a 59 lead in the next frame, White looked home and dry, only to miss a relatively easy, potentially match-winning red. With the balls awkwardly placed, the challenge for Higgins was simple – pot them all to stay alive.

What followed next was to enter into snooker folklore as arguably the greatest clearance of all time, and certainly the gutsiest. Despite frequently running out of position, Higgins knocked in a mesmerising break of 69. Mixing superb potting with some disastrous positional play, the 18-shot break came close to disintegration several times, only for Higgins to somehow rescue the situation every time with astounding bravery and skill.

The highlight was a mind-bending blue which he potted into the top-right pocket before spinning the white off the side cushion, back to near the black spot and in position on a red when there looked to be no hope of the break being sustained. After watching Higgins sink the final black, White was virtually paralysed for the deciding frame, which Higgins won courtesy of a 59 break to move into his fourth World Championship final.

Even today, that 69 break is still talked about in awed tones. '[It was] one of the worst breaks I've ever seen,' commented Spencer. 'But one of the most entertaining breaks and courageous breaks.'[16] Lowe, no great Higgins disciple, observed, 'Every shot was a trick shot. No sane person would go for the shots he went for.'[17] If nothing else, the break demonstrated Higgins's ability to perform to the highest standards under extreme pressure. As Davis argued, 'When you look at what was at stake and the balls potted under pressure, it remains to this day the greatest clearance you're ever likely to see.'[18]

Higgins's opponent in the final was a daunting one – Reardon, who had never lost in six world-final appearances. Higgins led a tight game – 10–9, 13–12 and 15–12 – but Reardon continually clawed his way back into contention. At 15–15, many thought Higgins would implode, but it was Reardon who blinked first, making two errors that enabled Higgins to wrap up the following two frames. In a magnificent *coup de grâce*, Higgins secured the frame he needed for victory with a wondrous 135, his highest-ever break at the Crucible. The emotion of the 18–15 victory, and his first world title in ten years, was too much for the Northern Irishman to bear and, as he called for Lynn to bring baby Lauren to him, the tears flowed. 'The People's Champion' had reclaimed his crown.

Even given Higgins's mercurial nature, the next 18 months were extraordinarily turbulent. His marriage crumbled again and the world title was lost after an unceremonious 16–5 thrashing by Davis in the 1983 semi-finals. An attempted reconciliation with Lynn in Majorca then ended in disaster when Higgins tried to kill himself. After swallowing a bottle of pills, he was rushed to hospital and lay in a coma for 48 hours. Although he checked himself out of hospital after a miraculous recovery, he still looked terrible when he arrived in Preston for the UK Championship later that year.

What happened next was arguably an even greater feat than that 1982 world title. Having scraped his game together, Higgins reached the final against Davis, who was world champion again and had looked invincible all year. Lynn and Higgins were back together, but initially it had little effect as Davis sprinted into a 7–0 lead. Somehow, he roused himself to trail just 9–7 and the match see-sawed one way and then the other before Higgins edged it 16–15.

This remarkable victory was one of Higgins's last great hurrahs as his career drifted into a gradual downward spiral. Moving from one crisis and scandal to another, his occasional against-the-odds victories became far outweighed by shattering defeats. Such reverses usually ended with Higgins complaining about some perceived injustice or other, usually relating to the referee or officials.

After the end of his marriage to Lynn, Higgins had little luck with relationships and his run-ins with authority grew as his ranking fell. In 1986, after objecting to a routine drugs test, he head-butted a WPBSA official, earning a ban from five tournaments. His response when being asked what he had learnt from the incident was hardly a picture of contrition – he merely claimed that next time he would have to head-butt harder.

With his finances in growing disarray, Higgins somehow managed to turn on the style after returning from his ban. Despite a recent 25-foot plunge from a flat window, he succeeded, while still limping from his injuries, in beating Stephen Hendry 9–8 in the final of the 1989 Irish Masters. The Irish fans mobbed him and celebrated wildly, but it was to be his last major tournament victory.

Higgins hastened the end of his career during the 1990 World Team Cup when he allegedly threatened to have Taylor, his Northern Ireland captain, shot. He compounded his sins by punching a press officer after being knocked out of the World Championship in the first round by Steve James and then gave a rambling, drunken speech to the media in which he announced his retirement from snooker, declaring, 'You can shove your snooker up your jacksie.' By then, the WPBSA's patience was exhausted – a year-long ban, as well as ranking points deductions followed and, although he returned to the game after serving his sentence, the magic was long gone, if not the customary grit.

Remarkably, Higgins fought his way through the qualifying stages of the World Championship in 1994 to earn one more appearance at the Crucible, only to be defeated 10–6 by Ken Doherty. The following year, he failed to qualify for the final stages of any ranking tournament for the first time in his career. To add insult to injury, having lost a considerable amount of money through poor management, he was now virtually broke. A 5–1 defeat against Neil Mosley in the 1997–98 qualifying school proved to be his final match on the professional tour

– the next day Higgins was attacked by a stranger wielding an iron bar and later that summer his on–off girlfriend Holly Haise stabbed him. The Hurricane seemed to be all blown out . . .

Although Higgins's dramatic rise and fall is one of the most compelling narratives in snooker history, his ranking in the pantheon of the game's greats is hard to quantify objectively. Certainly his total of two world titles pales when placed next to Hendry's seven or Davis's and Reardon's six apiece. If you take the view that sport is purely about achievement, then it is tempting to view Higgins as a talented but temperamental maverick who failed to live up to his potential. The opposing view holds that his flair and charisma engender his two world titles with more emotional depth than any number of Davis or Reardon triumphs.

Interestingly, Higgins's contemporaries, the majority of whom had painful run-ins with him during the course of his career, have been more than willing to subscribe to the 'Higgins as genius' theory. Davis described Higgins's abilities as 'Like pinball wizard in *Tommy* – he was at one with the table.'[19] White rates him as the greatest player that ever lived, while Pulman credited him with the quickest snooker brain of any player. Rea, Higgins's predecessor as Irish champion, even said, 'At the peak of his form, I'd put Alex up there above every one of the modern stars, including Stephen Hendry and Steve Davis', while adding the caveat that Joe Davis was the greatest of all.[20]

Higgins's assets as a cueman, popularly believed to revolve mainly around his spectacular potting ability, were certainly far more wide-ranging than often claimed. His technique, like his personality, was defiantly unconventional. 'Technically, he is just a phenomenon,' Thorne once observed. 'He does everything wrong: his stance is square, he lifts his head, his arm's bent, he snatches at some of his shots. Of all the pros, Alex would be about the last one you'd want to copy technically.'[21] Higgins himself admitted his style was virtually impossible to imitate, but his snooker brain compensated for any technical shortcomings. He could, in the words of Clive Everton, 'read the table like a chess grand master'.[22]

When Higgins first emerged, his attacking fury was completely untouched by safety, but, as his career progressed, he showed an admirable adaptability by developing a more measured, though still unique style. Throughout the 1970s and early '80s, his tactical awareness was outstanding. Indeed, his safety has never been given the credit it deserves, while his positional play was highly innovative. 'Nobody plays position like him,' Thorburn said. 'He was one of the first players to break out reds from potting the red, which is a very difficult thing to do.'[23]

Higgins's lighter-than-usual cue grip and loose adherence to technical convention were key to his popular appeal. His casual, languid method of playing delicate shots contrasted with the primitive savagery of his power play. However, as he aged, Higgins's technical shortcomings became burdensome. In the early days, he could throw his whole body into shots because his hand–eye coordination was so good, but later he began to miss more of these extravagant shots. The tiny margin for error within Higgins's game, as well as his reckless lifestyle, makes his longevity all the more astounding – his World Championship career spanned 22 years in all, with his two titles coming a full decade apart.

When establishing the extent of Higgins's greatness, it is also essential to recognise that he enjoyed fame and popularity far beyond the traditional sphere of snooker's influence. Along with Joe Davis and the advent of colour television, he was one of the three defining forces of the modern game, but it also runs deeper than that. Long after leaving the snooker circuit, his unquenchable spirit and hedonistic excesses see him worshipped to this day as a counter-cultural icon by many people who have little or no interest in the sport. 'Higgins is the ultimate anti-hero,' Borrows told the authors. 'A man of both the '70s and '80s – pre-punk, punk and post-punk. Every era needs heretics, non-conformists and weirdos.'

Comedian Johnny Vegas also summed up his appeal succinctly. 'Alex Higgins is the inspiration to every pub drunk everywhere who's trying to convince their wife that they can still make it big. I'd dream about him being my real dad.'[24] As a tribute to Higgins, the band Oasis even included his image on the inner sleeve of their 1995 single 'Roll With It', lead singer Liam Gallagher remarking, 'All that money and fame and shit and he's blown the lot. What a fucking way to go. I hope that happens to me. One big fucking blow-out.'[25]

While his hell-raising exploits earn Higgins regular homage from lads' mags, the more recent twists in his life are inspiring for a different reason. After being diagnosed with throat cancer in 1998, obituary writers' pens were at the ready, especially after he made a painfully gaunt appearance at the funeral of his friend Oliver Reed. But the Hurricane fought back. An appearance on the BBC television programme *Tobacco Wars* in 1999 saw him spitting defiance and back to his best non-conformist form. 'The tobacco companies and snooker were as thick as thieves,' he declared. 'Obviously I think that they have got their advertising for a song for 25 years . . . It's easy to stop smoking. I have strong will-power. What chance has cancer against me?'[26]

The answer was provided by the succeeding years. After over 40 courses of radiotherapy, Higgins entered remission and his health started to improve dramatically. He even began to make the odd appearance again in pubs and clubs, as well as dipping his toe back into competitive snooker. An appearance in the Benson & Hedges Championship in Mansfield was cancelled because he required urgent dental work, but he returned to competitive action with a (losing) appearance in the unsanctioned Irish Open in 2003.

The following year, Higgins's return to public life gathered pace when he cooperated with actor/writer Richard Dormer on the one-man play *Hurricane*, which unflinchingly and brilliantly recreated the triumphs and tragedies of his career. After winning acclaim at the Edinburgh Festival, the play had a West End run and a UK tour before transferring for a short run in New York, where rumour has it Higgins was seen drinking with Robert De Niro. Suddenly in demand again, Higgins gave several newspaper and television interviews, as well as performing a series of exhibitions with White. With a flash of the bravado of old, he was even ejected from one performance of *Hurricane* for smoking a joint in the audience.

Outwardly, Higgins's life and times might conform to the traditional pattern of the tragic hero, but the time for reassessment is nigh. 'The essence of the man remains the same,' argues Borrows. 'He can still play, he can still make money and he will back his talent against anybody . . . He was playing frames for £10 a time in the arse-end of Manchester when he was the world champion. He is still doing the same thing in 2004. On that level, at least, there has been no decline.'

On his greatest days, Higgins would have beaten any man that ever wielded a snooker cue, and if his inconsistency prevents him from serious consideration as the greatest snooker player that ever lived, then he was certainly the most compelling figure the sport ever produced and perhaps the most inspirational. As Borrows told us, 'He refuses to go down and stay down. He has lost it all: his family, his money, his health. But he goes on fighting.'

While not enjoying the lifestyle his successes should have brought him, Higgins remains, defiantly, 'The People's Champion', even to those who never saw him at his peak. Having fought off cancer and returned to the limelight, it is also clear that, far from a pathetic figure of newspaper legend, the Hurricane has come to some kind of fragile peace with himself. After everything he has been through, that might just be his greatest achievement of all.

NINE

TERRY GRIFFITHS

Finding the Right Balance

Terry Griffiths put his heart into snooker without ever selling his soul. Although he won the World Championship just once, it was one of the most stirring triumphs in the game's history and his career was one of integrity and excellence. Fans identified with Griffiths's dry but genial humour and appreciated the manner in which he wore his heart on his sleeve. 'The family has always been very important to me and one of the greatest pressures I have felt throughout my playing career has been the struggle not to sacrifice this one vital principle,' he once noted.[1] Such sensitivity tortured him for years, but ultimately enabled him to balance his two greatest loves – snooker and his family.

Snooker stardom was a far cry from Griffiths's working-class childhood in Llanelli, South Wales. The youngest of three children, he was born on 16 October 1947 into loving but tough circumstances. His father worked in the tin mines, while his mother suffered from ulcerated legs which often incapacitated her, forcing Griffiths's elder siblings to take on much of the responsibility for looking after the household.

Griffiths spent much of his childhood hanging around with his brother, Barrie, and his friends, collectively forging a reputation as tearaways. He was undoubtedly bright and won admission to the local grammar school, but was soon expelled for persistent truancy. To his delight, this meant he could join his friends in the local secondary modern, where he excelled at rugby union, playing alongside future Welsh international legends Phil Bennett and Derek Quinnell on the school team.

It was on the snooker table that Griffiths found his true vocation, however. From the age of 14, he was a regular in local club Hatcher's and was soon hitting breaks of 50. In 1962, he left school and took a job in a colliery mine, physical work that he relished. After two years playing regularly for Hatcher's team, Griffiths became the youngest winner of the Llanelli snooker title – a record his son Wayne would break years later. It is interesting to note how Griffiths, who went on to become a master tactician, characterised his play in the early days of his career: 'I would try and pot everything, safety was non-existent.'[2]

After two years in the mines, Griffiths took a better-paid job as a bus conductor, which gave him more time to practise snooker. By then, he had also won the West Wales Championship and raised his highest break to 90. He was oozing confidence on the table, but the idea of turning professional seldom entered his head. In the 1960s, the pro-snooker circuit was dormant while the amateur scene, particularly in Wales, was buzzing. Griffiths was content to play for the love of the game and the joy of competing.

In 1969, Griffiths married Annette, a local girl he had met while she was working in a Llanelli delicatessen. He took a job as a postman and soon settled into family life, even giving up snooker for a while. However, in 1970, by which time the couple had moved into their first house, Griffiths was back at the table, often long into the night, to the exasperation of his wife. 'We might easily have split up,' he admitted. 'And there is no doubt had that happened, it would have been the snooker that was to blame.'[3]

There were other problems, too. The death of Griffiths's mother shortly before Wayne's birth hit him hard. However, out of this adversity, Griffiths became closer to his father and his snooker began to thrive as never before. In 1971, he finally made his first century, a 130, then dashed home excitedly to tell a bemused Annette, 'I've just got 130!' Her deadpan reply was, 'Oh, God, I thought we had won some money or something!'[4]

A new job as an insurance agent gave Griffiths more time to spend at home and he began racing up the amateur snooker ladder. He entered the Welsh Amateur Championship in 1972 and reached the final, losing to Geoff Thomas. He learnt from this defeat and by 1973–74 was representing Wales against Ireland in Dublin. Around the same time, he made his television debut in the HTV *South Wales Echo* Event, beating Mario Berni in the final.

He finally won the Welsh amateur in 1975, overcoming old adversary Thomas 8–7. This earned him a berth in the 1976 World Amateur Championship and he travelled with countryman Doug Mountjoy to South Africa. Finding himself terribly homesick, Griffiths fell in the quarter-finals, while Mountjoy went on to lift the title.

Slowly the realisation that he would have to turn professional to achieve his ambitions was crystallising in Griffiths's mind. The process was accelerated by victory in the 1977 English Amateur Championship and competing in front of big crowds at the Pontin's pro-am, where he lost to Alex Higgins in the final, but was consoled by a cheque for £1,000.

Griffiths retained the English amateur title in 1978, but fell in the quarter-finals of the Welsh equivalent, meaning he would miss the World Amateur Championship. This failure forced his hand – he was now in his 30s and if he wanted to make a decent fist of life as a professional, he could delay no longer. The pro circuit was becoming highly lucrative, which was a factor in his eventual decision to move into the paid ranks, but his primary motive was to satisfy his competitive urges. 'I didn't want to finish playing and wonder how I would have done against the best players in the world,' he explained in an interview with the authors. 'That's why I turned pro. I didn't really fancy being away a lot, I didn't fancy the glamour of being successful – I just wanted to compete at the highest level.'

And so it was, after lengthy consultations with Annette, that he took the plunge in 1978, although with a caveat. 'I set myself a target of three years,' he told us. 'If after three years I hadn't had success, I would have gone back to work, which wouldn't have bothered me at all.'

Griffiths was accepted as a professional in June and made Llanelli Conservative Club his training base. His first tournament as a pro was the 1978 UK Championship and everything appeared to be going to plan when he led Rex Williams 8–2 in the qualifying round, only for nerves to get the better of him. He lost 9–8, prompting a tearful post-mortem on the phone home to Annette.

In the qualifying rounds of the 1979 World Championship, he held himself together well, though, beating Bernard Bennett and Jim Meadowcroft to earn a place at the Crucible – and a guaranteed

£1,000, enough to pay off a few debts. While watching the first-round draw on television, he received another boost. 'There were two players left in the hat that I could play – No. 1 seed Ray Reardon and No. 2 seed Perrie Mans,' he recalled. 'I drew Mans and I jumped up in the air because, if I'd drawn Reardon, I would have lost. He would have overwhelmed me. He was a hero of mine.'

Mans was no pushover, but he had been somewhat flattered by reaching the final the previous year. Griffiths raced into a 10–4 lead and, although Mans rallied to trail 10–8, the Welshman won the next three frames to close out the match. This victory also helped Griffiths establish a strange superstition. On the first day of the tournament, he had come out of his hotel only to find that his car, which he had parked under a tree, was covered in bird droppings. After beating Mans, he ensured he parked under the same tree every day – the growing collection of droppings paying tribute to his progress in the competition.

The victory against Mans meant that, in just his second professional tournament, the unknown Griffiths was preparing to face Higgins in the World Championship quarter-finals. 'Now I was in the place where I turned professional to be,' he said. 'I was up against one of the best players in the world, on the biggest stage.'

It proved a bona fide classic. Higgins knocked in two centuries to lead 6–2, but Griffiths fought back heroically to level at 8–8. The final session was a dramatic masterpiece. With the score 11–11, Higgins moved 55–0 ahead in the next frame and looked certain to go one up with two to play, but then missed an easy black. Griffiths cleaned up with a superb 61 and, although the 1972 champion forced a decider, the underdog held his nerve splendidly, a 107 clinching the match and a semi-final berth.

Those who have only ever seen the stately safety expert that Griffiths later became would barely recognise the ruthless break-builder that beat Higgins that heady night – and the key was his mental approach. 'The difference between us was I had nothing to lose and everything to gain, and he was the opposite,' Griffiths explained to us.

With a semi-final against Eddie Charlton looming, Griffiths's thoughts were racing. 'I was thinking, "I can do all right in this. I'm here, I'm competing against the best."' However, Charlton, three times a losing finalist, was vastly the more experienced player. 'He was like a dog, he just ground you to death,' Griffiths recalled. 'I struggled in that match. I struggled to win it. I was very tired. I'd never played that long a match before.'

At one stage, Griffiths led 10–4, but Charlton hauled him back and led 16–15 and 17–16, before, at 1.40 a.m. on the third night, a drained Griffiths finally edged to a painstaking 19–17 victory. 'Somehow or other, I won. I found something late on to win,' he recalled later. At the time, overwhelmed, exhausted and exhilarated, he uttered those famous words in his distinctive Welsh brogue to television presenter David Vine, 'I'm in the final now, you know!'

His opponent was Northern Irishman Dennis Taylor, who hadn't been in the final before either, but whose greater experience ensured he started as favourite. 'Everyone was saying about me, "Who's this guy? He was an amateur last week!"' Griffiths told us. 'Nobody knew me, so all the pressure was on Dennis.' From the start, Griffiths was the front-runner, but Taylor plugged away and at the end of the penultimate session the match was level at 15–15.

'Really, I thought he should have beaten me,' Griffiths admitted. 'I went through a spell when I couldn't see the balls, I was so tired. In the last but one session, he just pegged me back. He should have gone ahead, but I managed to stay with him.' Somehow, Griffiths found the mental strength to rouse himself for one last effort. 'I think you're meant to win these things sometimes,' he said. 'I'll never forget it. I thought, "Well, this is it – I'm either going to win and be world champion, or I'm going to lose," and I thought, "Bollocks to it, I know which I want it to be!"' Remarkably, he demolished Taylor 9–1 in the final session to win the match 24–16.

It was one of the most unexpected triumphs snooker had ever seen. Although Griffiths's feat in winning the title at the first attempt was not without precedent – Joe Davis, John Spencer and Higgins having all done the same – he was the first, and thus far only player to do so at the Crucible – a record which will probably never fall. Nor could his route to the title be explained by a fortuitous draw, for he had to overcome former and future world champions in Higgins and Taylor, as well as previous finalists in Mans and Charlton, to lift the title.

Returning to a hero's welcome in Wales, Griffiths found his sudden fame hard to comprehend. 'God alive, I didn't realise the effect it would have,' he said. 'I was the working boy come good, so there was huge interest.' There was jealousy, too. When he returned to the Llanelli Conservative Club for the first time after winning the title, he wrote his name up on the board as usual to indicate he wanted a game. One of the members audibly took exception to what he saw as the world champion throwing his weight around, the exact opposite of what Griffiths intended, and a deathly hush fell over the club. A heartbroken Griffiths walked out and never returned.

The increased amount of exhibitions and personal appearances that being champion brought with it also proved a culture shock for him. 'I hit a brick wall halfway through the year,' he told us. 'I couldn't see my children. I couldn't see my wife. I was away all the time and my diary was full. I'd look at it and I'd cry because for six months in advance I'd know I was never going to be at home.' At times, he felt utterly overwhelmed. 'I would rush out after playing in exhibitions, sneak out the stage door and run back to my hotel and cry. Looking back now, I was told I had a slight breakdown.'

Despite these pressures, Griffiths's form initially held up well. He reached the final of the 1979 UK Championship, losing to John Virgo, and won the 1980 Masters with a 9–5 victory over Higgins, clinching the match with a 131. However, his defence of the world title ended in the second round at the hands of Steve Davis, who rapidly became his personal bogeyman. In the semi-finals of the UK Championship later that year, the Romford man slaughtered Griffiths 9–0 and also denied him in the quarter-finals of the 1981 World Championship. In the UK Championship final that December, it was the same old story as Davis handed out a 16–3 drubbing.

Griffiths's dilemma when he played Davis was that their games were very similar – both men were instinctively cautious, with formidable safety prowess. In terms of natural talent, there was little between them, but Griffiths was slightly inferior in every other department, as well as being ten years older. The 1985 World Championship final against Dennis Taylor aside, Davis usually looked at his most vulnerable against extravagant performers, while players similar to him in style and temperament (such as Griffiths and Thorburn) found it hard to stay in touch.

Nevertheless, in 1982 Griffiths gave Davis a good run for his money, beating him in the final of the Lada Classic and the Irish Masters, although Davis had the edge in the finals of the B&H Masters at Wembley and the Yamaha International. Such was the duo's dominance of the domestic circuit that, although the world rankings did not reflect it, most observers viewed them as the world's two best players. It was therefore a mighty shock when both fell to underdogs in the first round of the 1982 World Championship – Davis to Tony Knowles and Griffiths to Willie Thorne.

Soon after, Griffiths accepted manager–promoter Barry Hearn's overtures and joined his stable of players alongside Davis. With Hearn doubling Griffiths's income and halving his work, his form was initially galvanised. He defeated Davis in the quarter-finals of the UK Championship en route to winning the sport's second most prestigious title with a nail-biting 16–15 win over Higgins. Despite this success, Griffiths's abiding ambition was to overhaul Davis's supremacy, to which end he began to study the intimate mechanics of his own game and unpick his technique.

'[Davis] had set another standard and I didn't fancy being No. 2,' Griffiths told us. 'The mistake I made was I did it by myself, but then there wasn't much coaching about then.' Griffiths made countless adjustments to his grip, spending hours practising each one. He also experimented with his eyesight, minutely adjusting when and how he looked at the object and cue balls, and tinkered with realigning his body. However, paralysis by analysis soon set in. Although his technical knowledge expanded, and in practice he often played flawlessly, Griffiths's tournament results deteriorated. 'I lost my instinct for playing,' he admitted. 'I found that changes to technique take away your natural ability.'

Griffiths was no closer to consistently beating Davis than ever before, losing to him at the Crucible in the quarter-finals in 1984, 1985 and 1987. He had also stopped winning smaller tournaments, a decline reflected by his fall in the world rankings from an all-time high of third in 1981–82 to fourteenth just a year later. As his technical obsession grew, Griffiths's play became slower and more deliberate. He seemed to size up every shot for an age before committing.

By 1985, despairing of the gradual disintegration of his form, Griffiths sought advice from coaching guru Frank Callan. An objective viewpoint helped and Griffiths's form stabilised, although ranking trophies remained elusive. In 1988, Griffiths, by now the proud owner of his own snooker club, felt far more settled and enjoyed his best form in years at the World Championship. Since lifting the title, he had failed to get beyond the quarter-final stage, but, playing with the fluency of old, as well as some sublime safety, he ambushed Jimmy White in the semi-finals to reach his second final. His opponent, inevitably, was Davis.

Having won just four of his previous nineteen meetings against the reigning champion, Griffiths was a huge underdog. At the end of the first day, though, he fought back from 7–3 down to level at 8–8 and a close match looked in prospect. However, he made too many mistakes when the match resumed, ultimately losing 18–11. 'My long potting let me down badly,' he reflected. 'I had to go for them under pressure because his safety game is so good.'[5]

Although he was not to win another major title, Griffiths remained a member of the top 16 until 1994–95, longevity he attributes to the technical reshaping of his game in the mid-'80s. 'What it did do for me is that it kept me playing another ten years,' he commented. 'I was a much better technical player than I was before, but I couldn't win events because I didn't have gears to go up. I just played tidy all the time.'

In 1997, Griffiths enjoyed a World Championship swansong when he qualified for the televised stages, losing to fellow Welshman Mark Williams in the first round after a final-frame decider. By passing the torch to the standard-bearer for a new generation of Welsh players, it proved a highly appropriate way to bring down the curtain on a splendid career.

Had he not toyed with his technique, Griffiths's career might well have been even more successful, for in going for broke by trying to challenge Davis's 1980s dominance, he arguably sacrificed the chance of many more trophies. However, he is not a man to harbour regrets. 'I don't really regret anything I've done in my life or my professional career,' he said. 'You make your bed and you've got to lie in it. I still had a very successful career, so I'm very happy with that.'

Off the table, Griffiths has also been a superb ambassador for the sport. An integral figure in Wales's distinguished snooker history, he has always been conscious of giving back to the game the respect, experience and success he gained from it. In 1999, he helped launch the world's first Junior Snooker Academy in Wales, while today he is a highly accomplished coach. As well as devotedly encouraging junior and amateur players of all ages, Griffiths also advises many professional players, Hendry and Williams among them.

He might be in his late 50s, but Griffiths's enthusiasm for snooker remains infectious. 'There's always so much to learn, I find it fascinating to coach,' he told us. 'To have the opportunity to coach two of the best players in the world – well, that is the ultimate. I've been fortunate.'

On the contrary, it is snooker that has been fortunate to have Griffiths represent it. In 1979, his sudden transformation from unknown amateur to world champion captured the imagination, but it is the knowledge he has imparted to others, and the grace with which he has always conducted himself, that are his greatest legacy.

TEN

CLIFF THORBURN

Grinding to Glory

His pragmatic approach may have irked many viewers watching in the arenas or on their television screens, but there's no doubt that Cliff Thorburn's contribution to snooker history was a valued and welcome one. Having a Canadian player – and a supremely talented one at that – challenging for honours gave the World Championship a much-needed global flavour in the 1970s and '80s. With the exception of Horace Lindrum, Eddie Charlton and Perrie Mans, few overseas players had made a significant impact on the sport at the highest level before him, but Thorburn proved non-British players could rise to the very top.

As well as winning the World Championship in 1980, he was world No. 1 in the official rankings a year later and in 1983 compiled the first maximum 147 break in a World Championship match, a significant step in the standards of the game's toughest competition. However, his triumphs were just as memorable as the time it took to complete them. The average man on the street would invariably refer to his long matches if asked what Thorburn would be most remembered for. One session with Terry Griffiths in the 1983 championship lasted 6 hours 25 minutes and finished at 3.51 a.m., making the final session of his next match that year against Kirk

Stevens – a 6-hour, 11-minute job, wrapping up at 2.12 a.m. – seem like an early night.

But there were no rules about adopting a certain playing style to suit everybody else. Thorburn may have taken what seemed like a lifetime to knock in a simple pot, but he had every right to make sure he felt comfortable and confident at the table, and give each shot the attention to detail he thought it deserved. As long as the referee was happy he wasn't wasting time, there were no rules against it. The methodical Thorburn made slowness an art, but then, if everyone played like Alex Higgins, there would be nothing to talk about. The defiant Canadian personified many qualities that were different to other world champions, but none that should be looked down upon. After all, few players made more sacrifices to get to the top of the snooker ladder than him.

Born on 16 January 1948, he was handed a tough start when his parents separated when he was just one and a half. Abandoned by his mother, his father and grandmother eventually took custody of him and brought him up in Victoria, British Columbia. The young Thorburn had a mischievous streak, often playing truant from school, and was more interested in sport than his education, taking up baseball and lacrosse. One night at a bowling alley, he heard the clicking of pool balls on the crowded floor above and went upstairs to take a peek. He later decided to have a go for himself and his interest in pool, and later snooker, intensified during his mid-to-late teens.

He quit school at 16 and a year later was the best player in Victoria, which meant one thing: if he wanted to continue making money, he had to start playing out of town. Betting was the name of the game and Thorburn once went as far as stealing some money from his grandmother, cashing her $70 pension cheque, to go to Vancouver. There he played John Bear, the best player in town, who promptly beat him and took all his money, although he did have the decency to give the youngster $10 to get back home.

Trips to Montreal and Winnipeg followed and soon Thorburn was constantly touring the pool halls of Canada, and later the US, playing such illustrious names as 'Oil Can' Harry and 'Suitcase' Sam. Most of the time he was either hitch-hiking or hopping on a freight train in order to get from A to B, while accommodation often comprised Salvation Army hostels or cheap hotels. When he returned to Victoria, he earned a bit of spare money washing dishes on the Victoria–Seattle shuttle, which in turn opened up the opportunity to bet over a few frames in Seattle and make some more cash. After that, he picked up another part-time job, working on a garbage truck in Vancouver for three months, but travelled whenever he had the opportunity – or the money. Once he'd found his way to a city, he'd walk into dozens of pool halls every day, making $10 in one, losing $5 in another.

Playing for money also taught him at an early age about the harsh consequences of losing. If he lost his money playing snooker, it meant he had nowhere to stay for the night, which added a steely competitive edge to his rapidly improving game. Once he was up against a player called Paul Thornley, who had a reputation for making crazy bets. Thorburn thought he'd turn the tables and challenged Thornley to give him a 70 start while he would play every shot with the rest, even if the cue ball was tucked up against a cushion. The crafty Thorburn beat him and even made an 85 break, despite his self-imposed handicaps.

Thorburn had by this stage built a reputation for himself across the country, which occasionally forced him to change his approach. Although he was an established road player competing for money, this hardly ever involved hustling (concealing your ability in order to make significant winnings later in the evening). After his picture was printed on the cover of a Canadian snooker magazine, Thorburn was wary of being recognised and once tried to disguise himself for a match in Texas. On his way to the pool hall, he changed into an old mechanic's uniform and stopped at a nearby petrol station to put some grease over his hands and costume. He also noted the name of the station so later on he could pretend he worked there. After winning about $700 in a match, the losing player asked where he was from and where he worked. Thorburn remembered the name of the petrol station and told him.

'No, you don't,' said the man.

'Sure I do,' replied Thorburn.

'No, you don't. I own the place.'[1]

On another occasion, when playing a guy called Bill Medlum for $30 a game, he thought he was in even more trouble. After 30 hours, Thorburn had cleaned out Medlum, who then took a gun out of his pocket. 'He walked towards me and I thought I was going to die,' Thorburn later recalled. 'He passed me and I thought he was going to shoot me in the back. When I turned round, he was selling the gun for another $30.'[2]

Despite the odd hiccup and firearm incident, Thorburn's game was improving each time he criss-crossed the continent. In 1968, he entered his first official competition, the Canadian Professional Championship, but lost to Don Maybee. During the same trip, he won the Toronto City Championship, pocketing the $200 first prize.

Towards the end of 1969, he heard some surprising news that hit him hard. He had always been told by the relatives who brought him up that his mother was dead, but he got a call from his Aunt Marge who told him that his mother had in fact abandoned him when he was a baby and now wanted to contact him. Thorburn reciprocated and briefly stayed in touch, but was angered not just by being abandoned, but also about the lies the rest of his family had told him over the years. 'The biggest effect it had on me, I guess, was to make me try even harder to make something of myself,' he wrote years later.[3]

He was introduced to members of the snooker scene from across the Atlantic the following year when Fred Davis and Rex Williams toured Canada, exhibiting their skills in front of big crowds. Thorburn got to spend time with them and learnt a lot about the status the professional game was enjoying in Britain, a marked contrast to that of Canada, where the sport was looked down on as a pastime for rogue hustlers with nothing better to do with their time. After Davis and Williams had returned home, Thorburn was asked to become a resident professional at a club in Toronto, giving him the chance to earn a regular income. It was at this club, the House of Champions, that he made his first 147 break. He also married his girlfriend, Susan Byatt. His life was beginning to look more settled, on and off the table.

Reigning world champion John Spencer was touring Canada and, after playing Thorburn in Calgary, Edmonton and Vancouver, was so impressed by the Canadian that he recommended him to the WPBSA. Thorburn was now keen to come to England and prove himself alongside the likes of Spencer. He'd had enough of reading about the World Championship in magazines – he wanted to sample it for real. Thorburn's marriage had broken up after a year and a half, and it seemed as good a time as any to travel to England and turn professional. Staying initially in a London hotel, he didn't have to wait long for his first match on British soil. Alex Higgins challenged him for a fiver a game, with Thorburn given a 28 start. The Canadian cleaned up and the relationship between the two was off to a bad start – one from which it never recovered. 'All I remember is Higgins at the top of some stairs; I'm running down the stairs, I still haven't been paid, and he's got a ball in his hand, threatening to throw it at me,' he wrote.[4]

However, adapting to English conditions was a struggle. The balls were a lot heavier than those used in Canada and the States, while the pockets were tighter, but he still managed to make a winning start to his first World Championship in 1973. Playing Dennis Taylor in Manchester with 700 spectators watching, the vast majority supporting the Northern Irishman, Thorburn edged a final-frame thriller to win 9–8. His second-round match against Williams also went to a decider, but this time Thorburn suffered defeat, going out 16–15. Considering his previous match experience amounted to about half a dozen official tournaments, it was a very creditable performance. 'I didn't know what a good referee was,' he later admitted. 'With his white gloves, I automatically assumed the guy was a poofter. It was all so prim and proper.'[5]

Thorburn fell in the opening round of the following year's competition when, after leading Paddy Morgan 3–1, he lost his concentration and eventually went down 8–4. Although he now had hardened competitive experience under his belt, Thorburn was finding it difficult to handle the different kind of pressure that came with tournament play. If he ever lost money in a game back home, he could return the next day and try to win it back, but if he lost in an official event, that was it for another year.

He still travelled to other countries to take part in tournaments. In 1974, he won an event in Toronto, beating Taylor in the final, and a year later enjoyed his best run yet in the World Championship, which was held in Australia. He got his revenge over Morgan, beating him 15–6, before seeing off Graham Miles 15–2 to reach the quarter-finals. In the last eight, he was up against home favourite Eddie Charlton and was level at 11–11 before Thorburn wilted in the intense Brisbane heat and Charlton, who would go on to reach the final, ran out a 19–12 winner.

Thorburn was finding it difficult to kill off matches when he was in front, something that was highlighted perfectly in his first-round match against Higgins in the 1976 World Championship. The Canadian had produced an immaculate performance to edge ahead 14–12, but Higgins, with the crowd behind him, made the most of some beneficial flukes to win the last three frames for a thrilling 15–14 victory. Thorburn wasn't to be denied for much longer, though. The following year, he thrashed Williams 13–6 in the first round before gaining a confidence-boosting win over Charlton in a lengthy quarter-final match-up. Tied at 12–12, an assured-looking Thorburn knocked in a composed 40 break that sealed the decider and his first appearance in the world semi-finals. He needed his bottle to win that too – at 16–16 against Taylor, Thorburn made a century in the penultimate frame before winning the next to book his place in the final. He was up against Spencer, the inspiration behind Thorburn's decision to join the pro circuit after his Canadian tour five years previously.

Thorburn, however, didn't enjoy the best preparation for the biggest match of his life when a friend back home in Canada, getting the time difference the wrong way round, called him at five in the morning, disturbing his sleep. He promptly lost the first three frames. Thorburn fought his way back into the match, but Spencer wore him down in the final stages, carving out a 25–21 win and earning the title of the Crucible's first champion.

Thorburn was still playing good snooker and, despite his dogged approach, had proved to the British public that he should be taken seriously. However, after beating Patsy Houlihan in the first round in 1978, he ran into an old weakness – losing on the verge of victory. At three up with four to play against Charlton in the quarter-finals, Thorburn buckled under the pressure. He started taking on risky shots that were out of character and fell to an agonising 13–12 defeat that hit him hard. John Virgo knocked him out at the Crucible in the opening round the following year, but Thorburn restored some confidence with back-to-back Canadian Open trophies.

It had been nearly seven years since he first arrived in England and Thorburn was starting to realise that he had seen it all. He had been through so many experiences, played various types of opponents, and won and lost from an array of leading or losing positions.

In the build-up to the 1980 World Championship, Thorburn was beginning to reach his peak form, while off the table life couldn't have been better – his relationship with girlfriend Barbara Meaney was blossoming and he was about to marry for the second time. Before the tournament, a friend who owned a club near the Crucible let Thorburn base himself there in order to get in some regular practice. Barbara stayed with him for the duration of the tournament and Thorburn was finding a perfect rhythm in both his game and his lifestyle. He was so relaxed, he even quipped in an interview on the eve of the tournament that he'd win it. For many players, this would have been putting unnecessary pressure on themselves, but Thorburn hardly thought twice about saying it – he was as dedicated as ever, but this time cooler in his mind.

The week before the tournament, he refused to smoke or drink, but after the first session of his opening match against Doug Mountjoy, he found himself 5–3 behind despite the teetotal approach. That night, he stayed up playing cards with friends until 5 a.m., putting away ten rum and Cokes for good measure. The following day he came out and won the next five frames, setting him up for a 13–10 win. Victories over Jim Wych and David Taylor then put him in his second world final, this time against his old nemesis, Higgins.

The Northern Irishman claimed early on in the match that Thorburn was standing in his line of sight. At one point, Thorburn didn't have the chance to get back to his seat after missing a shot because Higgins was up to the table so quickly. The Canadian stood well behind the action, by the television cameras, but even this didn't stop Higgins turning round and glaring at him after missing his shot.

At 9–5 ahead, Higgins played a few rash shots which helped Thorburn level at 9–9. The peace of mind that had been carrying Thorburn through the previous few weeks came into effect when the match got to 16–16. He made a 119 break, and a half-century in the next frame ensured an 18–16 win and a new champion. 'In the last frame . . . I was so numb I didn't feel any pressure,' he said later. 'I seemed to be very tall, very high as I looked at the table. I could work everything out without thinking.'[6]

The achievement was, and still is, widely recognised as the first time a non-British player lifted the world title, Lindrum's tarnished success in 1952 rarely being mentioned. Afterwards, Higgins labelled Thorburn 'The Grinder', a phrase which has stuck with the Canadian ever since, particularly in Britain. Many people had been trying to come up with the ideal nickname for him based on his dogged style and Higgins hit the nail on the head.[7]

Shortly afterwards, Thorburn bought a house in Walton-on-Thames in an attempt to cut down on his transatlantic commuting and base himself more permanently in Britain, but this put a further strain on his lifestyle and the pressure of being world champion was telling on the table. Also, his success didn't have as big an impact in Canada as he had hoped, the game's reputation still struggling to improve. Even in Britain he didn't get as much recognition for winning the title as Terry Griffiths had the year before. A devastating 6–5 loss to Higgins after being 5–1 up in the semi-finals of the Masters in 1981 then shattered his confidence, while he lost his grip on the world crown when Steve Davis beat him in the semi-finals at the Crucible. Barbara gave birth to their son Jamie that July, but Thorburn's game took a while to pick up. He had a set-to with Higgins in a bar following their match at the Irish Masters, which Thorburn had lost 5–4 after leading 4–0, while a first-round exit at the Crucible to Jimmy White encouraged him to move back to Canada with his family.

The 1982–83 season was a much more successful one now that he wasn't restricted to a home in the UK. He won the B&H Masters before going on a monumental run at the World Championship. In his second-round match against Griffiths, he pulled off the impossible – a maximum break on the biggest stage of all. It began with a fluked red and he took his time, naturally, but when Thorburn rolled home the final black fifteen and a half minutes later and sunk to his knees, he had created another piece of Crucible history. 'There was not the slightest shake or tremor in my whole body,' he said.[8] 'It brings tears to my eyes every time I watch it.'[9]

After that session, he rang up Barbara in Canada to tell her all about it, but she had some very sad news of her own. She had just suffered a miscarriage and the joy of Thorburn's magnificent achievement was cruelly cut short.

That 147 had put him 3–1 up and he managed to put the bad news from home behind him to hang on for a 13–12 win in a marathon match that eventually finished at nearly 4 a.m. the next morning. It was another late finish in his quarter-final, in which he beat Kirk Stevens by the same score. It didn't get any easier. In one of the longest and toughest paths to any world final, Thorburn edged out Tony Knowles 16–15 in the semis, but had no energy left to take on Davis, the Essex man strolling home 18–6 to lift his second world title.

In the summer of 1984, Thorburn was awarded the Order of Canada in recognition of his services to snooker[10] and a year later won his second Masters title, but further success at the Crucible eluded him. Quarter-final losses to White in 1984 and Taylor the year after were followed by a last-four defeat to Davis in 1986. A third Masters win that year, along with a Scottish Masters title, had softened the blow, but they turned out to be Thorburn's last tournament victories in Britain. He won an event in Canada a year later, but in 1988 was suspended for two tournaments and fined £10,000 by the WPBSA for bringing the game into disrepute by failing a random drugs test. Traces of cocaine were found in a urine sample taken during the British Open in Derby. 'It was a one-off and I'll regret it for the rest of my life,' he later said.[11] The incident sparked an alarming slide down the world rankings and it wasn't long before he lost his place in the top 32. He battled for a few years in an attempt to get back in, but the results got worse and he eventually quit the circuit after the 1995–96 season.

Thorburn has often said he felt he was the player with the least natural talent to lift the world title. In terms of the more fashionable qualities such as sensational potting or fluid scoring, he may have a point, but the virtues he did have – steadiness, stern concentration and will-power in adversity, to name but a few – don't come easy either. Few players have travelled such a long and rugged path to get their hands on that trophy. Developing a thick skin during a series of vigorous on-road adventures in the wild pool rooms of North America at a young age certainly stood him in good stead, as did his impregnable self-discipline and desire to adapt to British playing conditions. A man who wanted it all and got it, Cliff Thorburn is a splendid example of how far dedication can take a player.

ELEVEN

STEVE DAVIS

Snooker Superstar

It was once claimed that Steve Davis was on television more often than Prime Minister Margaret Thatcher during the 1980s and it could well be true, for he ruled snooker during an era in which the sport dominated the nation's television schedules. Along with Alex Higgins, Davis's fame transcended snooker's boundaries more than any other player in the game's history. While Higgins was regarded as 'The People's Champion', Davis came to be seen as the clean-cut man of the establishment. He has been awarded an OBE and an MBE, while in 1988 he became the only cueman to win the BBC Sports Personality of the Year award. Indeed, he appeared in the top three an amazing five times, more than any other sportsperson. Davis's iconic status was sealed by that ultimate affirmation of 1980s British superstardom – a *Spitting Image* puppet.

Davis's extraordinary fame sprang from consistent professional achievement, rather than the flashy, occasional brilliance and bad-boy behaviour that made Higgins a household name. From 1980 until 1989, he reached the final of the World Championship an astonishing eight times, winning six, while also picking up countless other trophies. He held the world No. 1 slot for seven years, was for a time the highest-paid sportsperson in Britain and had, up until the end of the 2003–04 season, accumulated £5,235,103 in prize money alone. His nickname, 'The Nugget', was highly appropriate, for whatever he touched seemed to turn to gold.

A superb technician whose safety play was peerless, Davis may have lacked the natural genius of Higgins or Ronnie O'Sullivan, but he perfected the art of remorseless tournament victories. 'My style of play was based on Ray Reardon,' he once admitted. 'He'd slowly strangle them to death like a boa constrictor. And I did that.'[1] When he was at his peak, there was a significant body of opinion that Davis was the greatest snooker player of all. His only real rival for this accolade seemed to be his namesake, Joe Davis, whose dominance was, if anything, even greater. Joe never had to operate under the unremitting glare of the media microscope in the way that Steve did, however, nor contend with nearly as many talented contemporaries.

Today, Davis's public image is far removed from how he was perceived in the 1980s. Then he was Steve 'Interesting' Davis – a man popularly held to be as dull as dishwater, whose only interest was snooker. In truth, it was the perfect persona. Not only did it intimidate opponents by creating an aura of indestructibility around him, it also ensured that media interest was largely restricted to his professional acumen and expertise, rather than his private life. In turn, his impeccably respectable image put him in an ideal position to secure a series of lucrative endorsement and sponsorship deals. While critics lampooned his 'boringness', Davis laughed all the way to the bank.

Although now inexorably linked with Romford in Essex, Davis was actually born in Plumstead, south-east London, on 22 August 1957. His father, Harry, universally known as Bill, was a good amateur snooker player and his interest in the sport piqued that of his son's. 'I had a direct influence, as it was my father's hobby,' Davis told us. 'Had my father not been interested in the game, I wouldn't have been interested at such an early age, so effectively it was in my blood.' Although his mother Jean bought Davis a toy snooker table when he was just two, and a bigger five-foot table when he was eight, it was not until he was into his teens and played on a full-size table for the first time at a holiday camp that the sport took hold of his imagination.

'I spent the week in a snooker room rather than doing anything else,' he recalled. During this week, Davis worked under his father's tuition on the basic techniques of the game. When the family returned home, Bill gave Steve a copy of Joe Davis's book, *How I Play Snooker*, to use as his technical bible and the youngster got to work. From the beginning, Davis's approach exemplified the perfectionist streak which would later distinguish him from his peers. While talents such as Higgins and Jimmy White were largely self-taught, Davis had the perfect tutor in his father. Snooker strengthened their bond and, to this day, they remain extremely close. Davis recalls:

> He made sure I kept to the book. And there was never any scoring. Just coaching, coaching all the time. Dad reckoned that trying to score points would be a distraction. As always, he was a stickler for absolute and undivided concentration. He was determined to see that I first learned the correct physical techniques before I went on to the much harder departments.[2]

Bill's single-minded determination rubbed off on his son, whose patience and calm concentration doubtless owed something to his mother, a primary school teacher.

Davis was not a prodigy, but he possessed excellent raw material to gradually shape into a top-class snooker player. Physically tall and lean, his left arm, which the right-hander used for bridging, was two inches longer than his right, giving him an advantage in reach, while his double-jointed thumbs enabled him to form a strong 'V' to his cue bridge. Meanwhile, his aptitude for mathematics and physics helped him master the mysteries of the snooker table's angles and the subtleties of positional play – swerve, stun and screw. Interestingly, given his later mastery of strategy, Davis is also an extremely proficient chess player.

Most important of all, he had an appetite for practice and self-improvement that was never sated. 'I spent my weekends in the working men's club,' he told us. 'My father was a member of their snooker team and he had a certain amount of sway, so I was allowed in the snooker room more often than other 14 year olds were in those days. I fell in love with the game.' From the start, poor technique was Davis's mortal enemy. 'Dad was adamant that I should not develop bad habits,' he noted. 'He was obsessed with technique. It was the basis of my game.'[3]

In order to gain further insight into the construction of his technique, Davis's father arranged for him to have a few lessons with billiards player and television commentator Jack Karnehm, who noticed that Davis was striking the white without actually being aware of exactly where he was making contact. Karnehm prescribed more billiards practice to improve Davis's cue-ball control and the diligent apprentice duly got to work on the billiards table at Plumstead Common Workingmen's Club.

A couple of years of unrelenting practice honed Davis's technique, but he remained short of competitive experience. To assess his progress at the age of 16, he entered the British Under-19 snooker and billiards championships, losing early in both tournaments. Aware of how far he still had to go, he returned to practice in Plumstead and promptly registered his first snooker break of 50. A cluster of 60s and 70s soon followed before he registered his first century in January 1975 at the age of 17. By then, Davis had a part-time job in a supermarket, while he was also studying for A levels in maths and physics. However, he soon saw little point in staying on at school and quit. His mother was keen for him to apply for a position at the local council, but Davis's father agreed to give him a year to prove he could make it as a snooker player.

The man who was to provide Davis's career with the launch pad it needed was Barry Hearn, a key figure in snooker's expansion throughout the 1980s. The son of a Dagenham bus driver and a chartered accountant by trade, the charismatic Hearn began his career in the fashion and textiles trades. In 1974, he bought the 20 billiards and snooker halls in the Lucania chain as a property investment only to fall under the spell of their atmosphere and colour. Davis arrived on Hearn's doorstep in 1976, after being advised to visit the Lucania in Romford to test his abilities against the club's best player, Vic Harris. Although Hearn did not immediately identify Davis's full potential, the two men became close as the youngster practised and competed regularly at the club.

Davis was soon enjoying some notable successes in the amateur ranks. 'It was a fairly swift rise from the age of 18 to 21,' he told us. He won the British Junior Billiards Championship in 1976 and a host of pro-ams followed, the most significant a 1978 Pontin's Open final triumph against Tony Meo. Equally important, the hitherto shy Davis had quickly developed a more savvy and streetwise personality. The atmosphere in Romford was frequently raucous and Davis learnt to give as good as he got. He was soon an accepted member of the Essex snooker scene and in later years this status would encourage crowds of local fans to follow him up and down the country, greeting his many triumphs with the deafening 'Romford roar'.

In 1978, Davis's triumph at the CIU amateur tournament crowned a series of good results – although the English amateur title had eluded him – and armed with a five-year managerial contract with Hearn, he decided to turn professional. His application was duly accepted by the WPBSA and Hearn gave him quite an introduction at the press conference to announce his arrival in the pro ranks. 'He doesn't smoke, drink or gamble,' he declared. 'He's single-minded. His relaxation is playing mental chess. No board. No pieces. Everything in his head. He's the most dedicated professional you could hope to meet. He's a certainty.'[4]

The relationship between Hearn and Davis developed into a deep friendship that bordered on brotherhood. Although Davis's father remained his coach and technical confidant, it was with Hearn that Davis planned the course of his career. From the start, the intention was to upgrade snooker's seedy reputation by projecting a whiter-than-white image that would attract a family audience and sponsors. 'Barry and I agreed that courtesy, politeness, smart presentation and always being on time for an appointment would help me make it to the top,' Davis commented.[5]

Hearn possessed a natural flair for promotion (he would later mastermind the rise of boxer Chris Eubank), but it was with Davis that he learnt his trade. The two men would pore over the minutiae of Davis's career, discussing potential challenge-match opponents with the same precision as the details of his clothes, hairstyle and press interviews. The strategy even extended to psychology. Davis toughened up his formerly weak handshake and worked hard to eliminate emotion from his facial expressions during matches so opponents could never quite tell what he was thinking. Like Joe Davis and Reardon, he sought to maintain a confident, controlled demeanour at all times in order to intimidate opponents before a match began.

Hearn and Davis's ultimate aim was highly ambitious. 'Steve and I often talked about the world title, and we agreed that while being champion of the world was essential, we were aiming at something on a far higher level,' Hearn said. 'For Steve to become a legend in his sport.'[6] Nevertheless, success on the pro tour was not immediate, as Davis adjusted to the big-match arena. To help him, Hearn arranged a series of matches in Romford against top pros such as Reardon, Higgins and Cliff Thorburn. Played over championship distances, they enabled Davis to get acquainted with his rivals' styles and the rigours of long sessions and matches. It helped that, aided by the benefit of home baize, Davis usually won, scoring a few psychological points along the way.

Although Davis successfully negotiated the qualifying rounds of the 1979 World Championship, he fell in the first round to Dennis Taylor and his thunder was stolen somewhat by another Crucible first-timer, Terry Griffiths, who lifted the title. In November, a narrow loss against John Virgo in the quarter-finals of the UK Championship represented a rapid improvement, while in the 1980 World Championship he knocked out reigning champion Griffiths 13–10 in the second round. 'I had broken a great professional barrier,' Davis said. 'From now on, I was established as a true, top-class player.'[7] Davis ultimately lost a dazzling quarter-final 13–9 against Higgins, but he was ranked thirteenth after just two seasons on the circuit and his matchplay education was virtually complete.

Davis's great strength as he rose through the ranks was his fearlessness. 'I don't think you necessarily feel the pressure when you're younger,' he told us. 'I genuinely believe it's easier to handle the pressure when you're younger. Experience is bollocks. It's a completely misunderstood concept that experience can help you out. It might help you out in business, but it doesn't help you out in sport. It's just whether you've got the nerve to do it.'

The following season, Davis manoeuvred himself into a position of overwhelming supremacy in the snooker world. The move into the highest class came during the UK Championship in November when he demolished Griffiths 9–0 in the semis before an equally dominant 16–6 victory in the final against Higgins. Such was the unshakeable confidence in the Davis camp that, at 15–6 ahead, he practised his post-match victory speech with Hearn in his dressing-room. This triumph catapulted Davis into the public eye and his polished, professional demeanour was a hit. 'His potting is now remorselessly exact, his manner calm and reassuring,' noted Sydney Friskin in *The Times*. 'Overall he has brought to the game a boyish freshness and enjoyment.'[8]

Hearn immediately went into managerial overdrive. The day after lifting the UK title, Davis signed a cue deal with E.J. Riley, reportedly worth £25,000, the first of many lucrative endorsements he would put his name to over the next decade. He arrived at the World Championship in April with £30,000 of tournament winnings for the season under his belt and was a short-priced favourite to win the tournament. Considering the pressure resting on the shoulders of the twenty-three year old, as well as a route to the title that placed three former world champions in his path, Davis's ensuing coronation was masterful.

The phenomenally talented youngster White was beaten 10–8 in round one before Higgins was felled 13–8 and Griffiths dismissed

13–9. In the semi-finals, Davis faced reigning champion Thorburn, one of the toughest matchplayers of all time. A tense game almost boiled over when Davis took a 12–10 lead. The Canadian lost his temper and subjected his opponent to a verbal attack for what he perceived as his arrogance. The display of hot-headedness only served to inspire Davis – the following day he won the first four frames with ease to clinch victory. 'I played hard, methodical snooker,' Davis said. 'I ground him out of sight.'[9]

Whenever he felt the pressure between sessions, Davis would unwind on the Space Invaders machines Hearn had installed in his hotel suite – and return to the table relaxed and ice-cool. Welshman Doug Mountjoy emerged from the other half of the draw to face Davis in the final, but proved no match for 'The Romford Robot'. Early on, it looked like it might be a slaughter, as Davis reeled off breaks of 59, 52 and 56 to move 6–0 ahead.

Mountjoy fought back and only trailed 14–12 going into the final session, however Davis's ability to boss the early stages of a session proved crucial as he won the first four frames of the evening to close out an 18–12 victory. It was the affirmation of several years' planning, and if Davis kept a relative lid on his emotions, Hearn did not, charging triumphantly into the arena. 'He hit me like a tank, grabbing me hard around the shoulders, and almost knocking me to the floor,' Davis recalled. 'I remember thinking I was lucky to have such a good stance.'[10] The beaten Mountjoy declared that the Davis era was only just beginning. 'He is at least a black ball better than any of us,' he said.[11]

By the end of 1981, Davis's domination looked total. In the final of the UK Championship in December he saw off Griffiths 16–3 and such was the severity of the beating that even Hearn appealed to the rest of the circuit to challenge Davis more forcibly. The beaten Griffiths, a man not given to hyperbole, felt Davis had already established historical pre-eminence, declaring in a post-match interview that he now rated Davis as the best player to ever pick up a snooker cue.

In January, Davis added another major achievement to his CV when he made snooker's first televised 147 break against John Spencer in the Lada Classic. 'This is the one ambition I wanted,' he said afterwards. 'My legs were like jelly, and I was in a daze afterwards.'[12] For a player who had always chased perfection, it was a major milestone, but when it came to the 1982 World Championship, Davis looked drained and distracted. Some estimates had put his earnings in his first year as champion at a staggering £600,000, but these riches came at a price. Suddenly, the travails of a long season of tournaments, exhibitions and personal appearances caught up with him and he fell victim to one of the Crucible's biggest shocks – a 10–1 first-round reverse against the then little-known Tony Knowles.

Chastened by this loss, and a fall from second to fourth in the world rankings, Davis was back at his best the following season, peaking perfectly for the 1983 World Championship. He beat reigning champion Higgins 16–5 in the semi-finals and then came face to face with Thorburn. As shown in the 1981 semi-final, there was little love lost between the Davis and Thorburn camps, but the tense, drawn-out battle many had anticipated never materialised. The Canadian was exhausted after a marathon series of matches which had seen him play 14 more hours of snooker than his opponent on his way to the final. Davis was merciless; on the first day, he moved 12–5 ahead and on the second he knocked in a 131 en route to putting a grateful Thorburn out of his misery 18–6.

'The best feeling I had in the match against Steve was when he got to 17,' Thorburn acknowledged. 'It was a relief to know he only had one frame to win. I know now what purgatory is all about.'[13] The Knowles stumble the previous year was forgotten as Davis revelled in the glory of becoming the first man to win the world title twice at the Crucible. Finally, he also moved into the No. 1 slot in the world rankings – in truth, he had been snooker's outstanding player for well over two years by then.

The year ended with Davis seeing a 7–0 lead unexpectedly evaporate into a 16–15 defeat to Higgins in the final of the UK Championship. Despite suffering his first major setback in over a year, Davis was gracious in defeat. 'The game would become very boring if I kept on winning all the time,' he said. 'I needed someone like Alex to make me sweat. It is the only way I can improve.'[14] Although it was a sensational result, no one seriously thought the match demonstrated a deterioration in Davis's long-term career any more than it heralded a long-lasting renaissance in Higgins's fortunes. And so it proved at the 1984 World Championship: while Higgins lost in the first round to Neal Foulds, Davis marched to a second successive world-title win despite a spirited display by White in the final. Now a three-time world champion and an undisputed world No. 1, the Davis industry was in full swing and his timing could not have been more perfect.

In 1978, when the BBC began extensive daily coverage of the World Championship, 35 hours of snooker had featured in television schedules in the space of 12 months. As the 1970s had drawn to a close, snooker could boast several players – Griffiths, Reardon and Spencer among them – who were household names, as well as a genuine mainstream star in Higgins, but there was no figurehead for the sport. By 1985, with the World Championship alone now accounting for 130 hours of television, Davis had established himself as the sport's undisputed king.

After the hippy and punk excesses of the 1960s and '70s, Davis's image was also perfectly in tandem with Thatcher's Conservative Britain. Clean-cut, dedicated and successful, he was the embodiment of the yuppie dream as filtered through the nouveau riche ambitions of south-east England. The fact that he was equally comfortable in working-class or middle-class environments also made him the ideal front man for advertising campaigns and corporate endorsements.

A flow of Davis-related products flooded into shops, including a series of autobiographies and technical guides, a tongue-in-cheek book entitled *How to be Really Interesting*, computer games and special ranges of cues and snooker tables. Hearn even collaborated with perfumers Goya on a range of men's toiletries named after the Matchroom promotional company he had built on his and Davis's successes. Davis also regularly snuck into the television schedules when not competing: if he wasn't appearing on *A Question of Sport*, then he was hosting a Channel 4 chat show, being the subject of a documentary (*Pot of Gold*) or popping up on the cover of *TV Times*.

Although Davis was snooker's standard-bearer, Hearn was acutely aware of the importance of building a supporting cast of characters to complement him. So it was that other players were gradually enticed into the Matchroom stable. Meo and Griffiths were the earliest to sign up, with Dennis Taylor, Willie Thorne, Foulds and White eventually following. There was always sound reasoning behind the presence of every new Matchroom member – Meo was there for his jack-the-lad appeal, while Griffiths covered the family market – and Hearn's ultimate aim was to cater for every possible demographic. This approach did not win universal popularity, though, and some of snooker's old guard, such as Spencer and Reardon, criticised the increasing commercialism in snooker.

Similarly, for a substantial number of fans who did not approve of Davis's dominance on the table and his commercial activities off it, the way he embodied Thatcherite ideals led to him being seen as something of a hate-figure. It did not help that, in a rare public-relations miscalculation by Hearn, Davis appeared at a Conservative Party youth rally in 1983 alongside such alumni as Kenny Everett and

Jimmy Tarbuck. Davis's diametric status as one of Britain's most successful, but also unloved, sportsmen soon drew comment in weighty articles by political heavyweights like Brian Walden – Davis wasn't just a snooker player, he was a socio-political phenomenon.

Much of the mystique around Davis was maintained with carefully planned interviews and pronouncements. 'If I had a choice between sex and snooker,' he famously told one women's magazine, 'I'd choose snooker. Snooker is my justification, my fulfilment.'[15] Whether it was true or not, it certainly rammed home his image as an unbeatable automaton. Another classic line was dropped to *The Times*. 'If you are suggesting that I become a people-pleaser like Alex Higgins, forget it,' he said. 'I would much rather be regarded as a machine for the rest of my days if that is the price I have to pay for winning.'[16]

Then, with Davis's fame and the industry surrounding him at its height – and against all rational judgements or predictions – the inexplicable happened. In 1985, Davis lost the World Championship final to Taylor 18–17, having led 8–0. The course of this match is examined in full in the next chapter, so for now we will confine ourselves to examining the effect it had on Davis's career.

He had experienced losing a big lead in the past – the 1983 UK Championship final against Higgins and the 1984 World Championship final against White, which he nearly lost from a similarly commanding position – but the 1985 defeat was different. For starters, the match was decided on the very last black and Davis had spurned a good chance to pot the winning ball before Taylor sunk it. Most worrying of all, though, for a supreme rationalist like Davis, was the fact that he had not been outplayed by a natural talent like Higgins or White, but beaten in a battle of nerves by a doughty, but limited opponent. Davis's public reaction to the defeat was pragmatic. 'It's all there in black and white,' he commented wryly. Inwardly, though, he must have been in turmoil, as he hinted in a recent interview, 'I don't think I've ever been so devastated.'[17]

Davis displayed no signs of losing his nerve at the beginning of the following season. He slew the Taylor demon with a tight 10–9 win against the Northern Irishman in the final of the Rothmans Grand Prix and his rehabilitation seemed complete in November when he recovered from 13–8 behind to beat Thorne 16–14 in the UK Championship final, a comeback that he declared made him feel 'more like a man'. However, despite progressing to another World Championship final, Davis was once again beaten, this time by an even longer-priced underdog, Joe Johnson.

It seemed inexplicable that Davis had again come up short against an opponent patently not in his class. Two such confidence-sapping losses could easily have spelt ruin for his career and it speaks volumes for his greatness that this did not prove the case. Filled with renewed determination, he reasserted a vice-like grip on the World Championship in 1987 by gaining revenge on Johnson in the final with an 18–14 victory. An 18–11 win against Griffiths followed in the 1988 final and Davis's omnipotence seemed fully restored.

This impression was reinforced at the end of 1988 when Davis was named BBC Sports Personality of the Year, arguably the most prestigious individual award in British sport. The honour cemented his superstar status in Britain, but Hearn had higher targets in mind. Matchroom tours over the previous few years to Brazil, Hong Kong, Thailand and China had enabled the sport to gain tentative footholds in new territories and attracted plenty of positive publicity. However, Hearn's ultimate aim was an audacious assault on the United States market.

Today, the idea of a British snooker player attempting to conquer America might seem absurd, but Davis was such a huge name at the time, and snooker so popular, that Hearn made it sound feasible. He had some success, too. Davis appeared in the pages of *Time* magazine and the *International Herald Tribune*, while in July 1987 he faced American pool legend Steve Mizerak in St Moritz in a special snooker–nine-ball pool challenge match. It was a canny idea – Davis was a British star while Mizerak, who had been at his peak in the 1960s and '70s, had been enjoying renewed celebrity courtesy of appearances in a series of commercials for Miller Lite beer and a small role in Martin Scorsese's *The Color of Money*, starring Paul Newman and Tom Cruise, a sequel to the classic pool movie *The Hustler*. Promisingly, highlights of the Davis–Mizerak encounter were shown by ESPN in the United States and a dozen other countries also showed the programme.

Soon after, Hearn announced his biggest endeavour to date – a World Series snooker circuit with planned prize money of £600,000 to be played over five continents, including a four-day stint in Las Vegas, as well as trips to Hong Kong, Tokyo and Toronto. However, despite Hearn's energy, the great dream never came to fruition and the ambition of selling the stubbornly British pastime of snooker to the United States died when financing for the World Series collapsed.

The United States might have resisted Davis's charms, but in the 1989 World Championship he was simply untouchable, conceding a measly 23 frames as he won a third successive world title, and sixth in all, with a crushing 18–3 win against John Parrott in the final – the most comprehensive World Championship final victory ever. Today, Davis rates this match as the most satisfying triumph of his career. 'When I went into the tournament, I was not feeling as if I was in the best form,' he told the authors. 'So, to actually win the tournament by beating John 18–3 – that was probably the best I've played in a final, even if I completely ruined the event as there wasn't even an evening session. Obviously, you can't beat the excitement of winning it for the first time, but the sheer achievement of winning 18–3 in a final against another great player is something I'm proud of.'

It is ironic, then, that in the wake of his most dominant World Championship triumph, Davis's career almost immediately headed into decline. His 1989 and 1990 UK Championship losses to Stephen Hendry symbolised a monumental power shift in the game and, no matter how hard he tried, Davis could not return to his former glory. He unpicked and reassembled the fundamentals of his game countless times, with deteriorating results, and from his World Championship victory in 1989 until a Mercantile Credit Classic triumph in 1992, he failed to win a single ranking tournament. One happy consequence of this slump was that Davis at last generated the support and sympathy he had been denied in the past, yet his talents so richly warranted. Defeat humanised him and, at the same time, his arch sense of humour, which had always been in evidence, began to work its charm on previously sceptical fans.

In the 1980s, it was thought that when Davis's game declined he would simply walk away from snooker, that his pride would not allow him to suffer by comparison with his previously peerless self. It was a theory he himself had given credence to. 'If, for instance, I ever reached the stage that John Spencer is at, I would walk away from the table forever and never look back,' he said in 1982. 'John makes me feel sad. He was a champion, now he is an "also ran".'[18] However, when it came to it, rather than retire with his substantial earnings, Davis stayed and fought for every result possible, even when terribly out of touch.

'It takes a strange person to give up,' he declared in 1994. 'It's much more natural to stay and fight.'[19] His play became over-negative at times, but in the wake of capturing the 1992 Mercantile Classic, Davis regained something approaching his best form between 1992 and 1995. During the 1993–94 season, his form was so good he arrived at the Crucible with a chance of regaining the world No. 1

ranking he had lost to Hendry in 1990. In the end, though, he lost to the Scotsman in the semi-finals.

Thereafter, Davis slid slowly down the rankings, although he did enjoy one of the most emotional nights of his career in 1997 when he lifted the B&H Masters with a vintage 10–8 triumph against O'Sullivan. The crowd's reaction to the old stager's victory over his younger opponent proved how popular Davis had become and as a bonus he picked up the biggest single pay cheque of his career – £135,000.

However, when Davis dropped out of the top 16 at the end of the 1999–2000 season, and slumped to 25th place in 2002, career obituaries were being prepared. Stirringly, though, a more relaxed approach to practice saw Davis enjoy a splendidly consistent 2002–03 season and he shot back up to No. 11 in the rankings. A 29th ranking title nearly arrived in 2003–04 when he reached the final of the Welsh Open. He was just a frame from victory, leading 8–5, only for opponent O'Sullivan to snatch the contest 9–8. 'I feel like an angler who had a big one on the hook and failed to land it,' Davis reflected.[20]

Despite being the oldest player on the main circuit after Joe Johnson's departure from the rankings in 2004, Davis, at 47, is as defiant as ever. 'It would be nice to still be in the top 16 when I'm 50,' he said in 2004. 'I have set myself a target rather than just going out there and enjoying my snooker. I'm going to do what Paul Newman did in *The Color of Money* and get myself very fit.'[21]

The Color of Money reference is particularly apt for, in recent years, Davis has also carved a reputation on the nine-ball pool circuit, where he is known not as 'The Nugget' or the 'Ginger Magician', but 'Romford Slim'. Davis's old friend Hearn turned to promoting pool in the 1990s after reducing his commitments in snooker, feeling disaffected with the game and its political infighting. The centrepiece of Hearn's interest in pool is the Mosconi Cup, a US versus Europe team event based on the Ryder Cup, which was staged at the MGM Grand Hotel in Las Vegas in 2003. In 2002, Davis potted the decisive ball to give Europe a rare overall victory in the competition. For Davis, pool is a sideline, but for Hearn, along with darts, it has largely supplanted snooker in his affections.

Davis's intention to be in the top 16 at the age of 50 guarantees he will be on the circuit for several years to come, although it remains unlikely that he will add any more major trophies to his substantial list of achievements. Nevertheless, his legacy is secure. To younger snooker fans raised on the exploits of Hendry, O'Sullivan, Mark

Williams et al., it might seem strange that Davis, the current elder statesman of the game, with his thinning hair, wry smile and sideline in television presenting, was once the most feared competitor on the circuit. However, even by today's high standards, the Davis of the 1980s was a fearsome snooker player. Although his safety-conscious philosophies now appear outdated, in terms of technique he is probably unrivalled in snooker history. The fact that this ability did not come naturally to Davis – that he had to work at refining and crafting it, not merely when he was growing up but constantly throughout his career – also speaks eloquently for his dedication and determination.

Despite suffering several famous reverses while under pressure (Higgins in 1983, Taylor in 1985), Davis possessed a supreme temperament and will to win, fighting back from those most shattering of defeats to win multiple world titles. In common with Hendry, Davis relished the pressure of the big occasion, even once commenting that he never felt the same player if television cameras and lights weren't in the arena.

Although he did not match the number of world titles Joe Davis claimed, and his modern-day tally has since been surpassed by Hendry, Davis's triumphs raised the profile of snooker to uncharted heights, endowing him with fame and influence the likes of which Hendry and Joe never experienced. His professionalism forced other players to raise their own standards and that is why, quite simply, the development of modern snooker without Steve Davis is unimaginable.

TWELVE

DENNIS TAYLOR

Seizing the Moment

By the mid-1980s, snooker was a very big business indeed. Huge numbers of viewers were tuning in to watch the action on television and if the emotional drama wasn't enough to keep them gripped, the game's seemingly never-ending line of bubbly characters certainly was. The likes of Alex Higgins, Jimmy White, Kirk Stevens and Tony Knowles ensured the game's bad-boy tag was thriving and kept the housewives happy, while the rise of Steve Davis added another element. The undisputed king of the baize, the *numero uno*, who, on the few occasions he did lose, provided a sensation to treasure for fans rooting for the underdog.

How fitting it was, then, that the greatest match in the history of the sport, the 1985 World Championship final, would unfold during the peak of the game's popularity. The fact that Davis was involved, and, of course, eventually beaten, contributed significantly to this act of perfect drama. But who would have thought that a 36-year-old Northern Irishman, who once left home for England in search of work without a thought for snooker, would be the central figure in the game's pinnacle moment?

Dennis Taylor, born on 19 January 1949, grew up in Coalisland, County Tyrone, in a Catholic family home, sharing a bedroom with his four sisters and two brothers ('We had to put a curtain up between the boys and girls'[1]). He enjoyed a healthy appetite for sports as a youngster, taking up Gaelic and Association football as well as boxing, in which he won two schoolboy bouts. At the age of nine, he started to learn snooker by playing with marbles at home and followed up this interest when he learned that the local billiards club, Gervin's, allowed children in between 5.30 and 7 p.m., before it got too busy.

Supplemented by his part-time job selling ice cream in the local cinema, Taylor spent his youthful hours and money at the club, perfecting his technique while standing on a lemonade box in order to reach the table. He played billiards in an effort to learn how to control the cue ball better and by the time he was 15 had won both the senior snooker and billiards competitions at Gervin's. After leaving school, he got a job at the town's pipe works, but was sacked along with a handful of other employees after a faulty set of pipes got through. He was later offered his job back when the manager discovered Taylor wasn't to blame, but the teenager, by then 17, had already decided what his next step would be. Job opportunities in Coalisland were scarce and, in 1966, he headed to England in search of work.

So focused was he on earning money at first, Taylor didn't even pack his snooker cue. He stayed with his uncle and aunt in Darwen, near Blackburn, and got a job cutting patterns for the carpets that went in cars. When his first wage packet arrived, he thought he'd sample the local competition and wandered into the nearest snooker club.

'I imagined that the level of play on the mainland would be much too sophisticated for a young lad from Gervin's who had never played outside the area where he lived,' admitted Taylor, whose top break up to then had only been 54.[2] However, he soon discovered that he could more than hold his own against the Lancashire amateurs and splashed out on a new cue. He started playing in the local Blackburn league and within a few months scored his first century. He also gained the respect of Lancashire's biggest player of the day, John Spencer, after beating him 3–0 in an exhibition and in 1968 won the British Junior Billiards Championship in Birmingham.

Not only was his snooker vastly improving, Taylor's off-table life was taking a dramatic upturn in fortunes. He met Trish, who also came from a Catholic family, and the pair clicked straight away. By 1970, by which time they were both 21, they married. Trish was later to play a supportive and significant role in Taylor's career, taking on the job of diligently organising his exhibition dates and negotiating his appearance fees.

Taylor was a sales director for a television rental firm at the time, but was finding it difficult balancing a full-time job with his snooker. In 1972, the opportunity arose for him to turn pro. He was offered a job as manager of the Elite Snooker Club in Preston, which guaranteed a decent wage and plenty of practice time. With the advent of the popular *Pot Black* television series and the World Championship enjoying a renaissance having recently returned to the knockout format, Taylor realised snooker was on the up and decided to hop on board. Although his CV was on the thin side, especially having failed to win the English Amateur Championship (seen as the standard stepping stone into the professional ranks), his friend Spencer spoke up for him at the WPBSA and they accepted his application.

There were few tournaments around at the time, which meant an impressive performance at the World Championship was crucial in order to boost a player's profile and, with it, their invitations to exhibitions. Taylor's first appearance on that stage was in 1973. In the first round, he was drawn against another World Championship debutant, Cliff Thorburn, but the Canadian triumphed 9–8. In seven of the nine frames he lost, Taylor had led by 40 or more points, but failed to make it count. 'I clearly still had something to learn about coping with the stresses of a big event,' he admitted.[3]

Now with a wife and two children to support, it was a big defeat for Taylor and things got even worse the following year when he lost in the qualifying round 8–1 to Marcus Owen. That defeat proved to be a turning point. He ditched the job at the snooker club to focus solely on his game and took a chance by travelling across the Atlantic to play in the Canadian Open. Having to pay his own travelling and living expenses, Taylor figured he would need to reach the semi-finals at least just to break even.

As it turned out, he went one better, beating Higgins in the last four, which included a personal-best 138 break, however he lost to Thorburn 8–6 in the final. During the interval, Taylor had lost his concentration when he went to buy a soft drink. After waiting patiently in the queue and coming back with his refreshment, an official accused him of taking too long and keeping people waiting. This upset Taylor enormously. 'I didn't like the idea of keeping people waiting, and I didn't like being ticked off by an official,' he said.[4] The incident broke his rhythm and he went on to lose the match.

Nevertheless, the trip (in which he also scored a remarkable 349 points without missing a shot during three successive frames of a practice match) had been a success. The BBC invited him to take part

A legend at work: Joe Davis, the only player to win every World
Championship he entered, lines up a pot. He controversially retired
from the competition undefeated in 1946.
(billiardsandsnookerarchive.co.uk)

Fred Davis (right) celebrates winning the first of his eight world
titles with his mother, Elizabeth, and older brother, Joe, in 1948.
(billiardsandsnookerarchive.co.uk)

Where a genius learnt his trade: the old snooker hall used by Joe Davis and, later, by his younger brother, Fred, in Whittington Moor, Chesterfield. The building on Sheffield Road now houses a health club. (Nick Johnson)

The Lindrum Hotel on Flinders Lane in Melbourne, Australia, commemorates one of the great billiards and snooker families. A young Horace Lindrum refined his skills at the Lindrum billiard room on this street. (Roana Mahmud)

John Pulman, winner of eight World Championships between 1957 and 1968, was unfortunate to reach his peak during snooker's wilderness years.
(Eric Whitehead/Snookerimages)

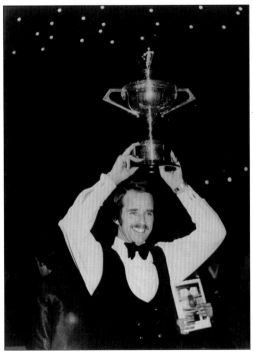

John Spencer lifts his third World Championship in 1977, the year the event was first staged at the Crucible Theatre in Sheffield.
(billiardsandsnookerarchive.co.uk)

Alex 'Hurricane' Higgins, arguably the most popular snooker player of all time, achieved the notable feat of winning his second world crown a decade after his first.
(billiardsandsnookerarchive.co.uk)

Six-time world champion Ray Reardon showing typical concentration at the table. The Welshman struggled to maintain his form when his eyesight began to fail.
(Eric Whitehead/Snookerimages)

Dennis Taylor holds the World Championship trophy aloft after defeating Steve Davis 18–17 on the final black in the deciding frame in 1985. It remains arguably the greatest match in snooker history.
(Eric Whitehead/Snookerimages)

Steve Davis, winner of six World Championships, proved age was no barrier when he broke back into the world's top 16 at the age of 45.
(Domenic Aquilina)

Jimmy White during his renaissance season of 2003–04. He reached the final of the European Open and won the Players Championship.
(Domenic Aquilina)

Seven-time world champion Stephen Hendry, the most successful
player in the modern era and, for many, the greatest of all time.
(Domenic Aquilina)

A familiar pose: Stephen Hendry, the game's most prolific
tournament winner, had won a record 35 world-ranking titles by
the end of 2004. (Domenic Aquilina)

Welshman Mark Williams: twice a Crucible champion and the first left-hander to lift snooker's greatest prize.
(Domenic Aquilina)

Ronnie O'Sullivan in action during 2003–04. He ended a hugely successful campaign back in the world No. 1 spot and world champion for the second time.
(Domenic Aquilina)

in *Pot Black*, thus raising his profile, and he later won his first tournament since turning professional, albeit a non-ranking event in Bristol, beating Spencer and Higgins on the way. The prize money came in handy, helping Taylor to save up the funds needed for a trip to Australia, where the 1975 World Championship was being held. He eliminated Perrie Mans 15–12, Fred Davis 15–14 and Gary Owen 19–9, but suffered an uncomfortably choppy flight from Sydney to Brisbane for his semi-final with home favourite Eddie Charlton and had little time to recover before the match, which he lost 19–12.

For the next few years, Taylor, recognised throughout the circuit as a skilled player with ample charm, found it difficult to shrug off his 'nearly man' tag. By his own admission, he lacked a killer instinct at vital moments. He reached the quarter-finals of the 1976 World Championship, another semi-final a year later and was knocked out in the first round in 1978 by Fred Davis.

A final appearance in the 1979 Bombay Open and his best run in the UK Championship – to the semi-finals – lifted his spirits before another attempt on the world title that year. He knocked out Steve Davis, Ray Reardon and John Virgo to reach his first world final. His opponent was Terry Griffiths, a Crucible debutant and comparative unknown who had lit up the tournament with his composed and gutsy snooker. Many of Taylor's relatives came over from Northern Ireland for the occasion and things looked to be going according to plan as he edged ahead 15–13. Taylor had chances in both of the following two frames to go 17–13 up, but wasted them, allowing Griffiths to hit back and level at 15–15.

Taylor, who has suffered from poor eyesight from a very early age, had up to then always worn glasses during matches, but this was the first major tournament in which he had tried contact lenses. Although they improved his sight significantly, he found them very sore, and had to take one of them out during the final. With this problem, and his confidence badly hit by the loss of those two crucial frames, he had a disastrous second day. He tensed up, gripped his cue too tightly and went on to lose nine of the ten frames played that day, allowing Griffiths to take the title at his first attempt 24–16.

The critics who claimed Taylor's game went to pieces under pressure were again in full voice and the defeat clearly hurt him. 'The trouble with that kind of comment is that it gradually saps your confidence. You begin to half believe it yourself, no matter how hard you tell yourself it isn't true,' he admitted.[5] The silver lining was that he had made it to No. 2 in the world rankings. That year he also won the Irish Championship, previously held by Higgins, and in 1981 was runner-up in the Wilsons Classic and Jameson International, losing both finals to Davis.

He decided to drop his contact lenses in 1983 and approached snooker coach and former television commentator Jack Karnehm, also an optical instrument manufacturer, who suggested the idea of a specially designed pair of glasses for him. Working away in his garage one weekend, Karnehm put the main part of the lens at the top, rather than the bottom, ensuring that when Taylor bent down to address the table, he was looking right through the optical centre of the lens. The glasses, once he had adjusted to them, were a revelation that changed Taylor's game. He didn't need to worry about either sighting up a shot or contact lenses burning his eyes again, while he could also eliminate his eyesight as a factor when trying to analyse any problems with his game.

However, one problem he could do little about was Davis. The Nugget was dominating the game, meaning there was less to go round for everybody else. Taylor retained the Irish Championship, but slipped to No. 13 in the rankings. Things improved in 1984 when he reached the semi-finals of the Irish Masters and at the Crucible, enough to keep himself safely in the top 16 for the 1984–85 season, and this seemed to settle him down.

He won the Costa del Sol Classic that summer and started using a new cue which was two inches longer and slightly wider at the tip. He was in good form going into the Jameson International and won his first two matches, but on the eve of his quarter-final, Taylor received some devastating news – his mother had died of a heart attack back in Coalisland. In a daze, he scratched the tournament and went home for the funeral. At the encouragement of his family, he returned to the circuit in time for the Grand Prix in Reading, but many felt it was too soon for him to come back after such a tragic interlude.

Taylor, still grieving behind closed doors, looked surprisingly sharp in his first-round match against Ray Reardon and won it 5–3. He followed that up with victories over Kirk Stevens and Neal Foulds to reach the final, and many commentators realised his upturn in form was more than just mere coincidence. His mother's death had obviously had a major impact on him and, unconsciously, it had stripped him of the nervous anxiety that had previously plagued his game on the big occasion. Taylor was realising that snooker was by no means the most important thing in his life, and overnight this had resulted in him taking a far more relaxed approach to the game. He faced Thorburn in the final and refused to let the Canadian have a sniff, an array of aggressive scoring helping him register eight frames in a row for a 10–2 win and his first ranking tournament victory.

He was 40–1 at the bookies to lift the World Championship on the eve of the tournament and he illustrated the same momentum shown at Reading by breezing through his first two matches, 10–2 against Silvino Francisco and 13–6 against Charlton. His match with the slow, pragmatic Australian ended up being good practice for his quarter-final against the similarly styled Thorburn. Taylor dominated the contest, despite it lasting more than ten hours, going through 13–5. 'After beating Cliff, I felt quietly confident and ready for anything,' he wrote.[6]

He out-potted a frustrated Tony Knowles in the last four, seeing him off 16–5, to book his place in what turned out to be the most famous snooker match of all time – the final against Davis. The Essex millionaire, world champion for the previous two years and three times in all, had won eight of the nine matches between the pair, one of them 9–0. To say he was an overwhelming favourite would have been a glaring understatement.

It was a perfect clash of styles and personalities – the affable also-ran against the unstoppable machine – and the purists were fearing a mismatch. So was everyone else eight frames into the contest, having seen Davis win all of them. The odds of a whitewash were cut from 300–1 to 100–1 as Taylor, red-faced and slumped in his chair, looked a sorry sight. 'I was more embarrassed than anything,' he admitted.[7]

It looked like the match would finish a session early, but before the watching millions could make plans for their now spare Sunday evening, Taylor rallied. Perhaps the awareness that defeat was apparently imminent relaxed him, but he was now cueing freely. He racked up his first frame six hours into the match, but once he had that under his belt he won six of the next seven to end the day trailing just 9–7. Taylor remembered seeing Davis's face 'stiff as a mask' as they walked off that night. 'That late surge on the Saturday evening was crucial, because Steve could never feel safe again . . . I knew which of us would sleep better that night.'[8]

The prospect of having such an assured victory yanked away from him was beginning to affect the favourite. On top of that, the crowd's support for Taylor was increasing, the fans preferring the vulnerable battler with a big heart to the invincible winning robot. The following afternoon, Davis looked as apprehensive as Taylor was brave, and the underdog pulled it back to 11–11, before Davis won a couple of crucial frames on the black to lead again 13–11 at the interval. Now the pundits had another chance to explain why Taylor wasn't going to win – the fact that he was still behind after such a hardy recovery would surely only dampen his spirits, while Davis had begun to take frames despite playing nowhere near his best, a bad sign for the Northern Irishman. Whatever the reason, he failed to seize the initiative after the break, Davis extending his advantage to 15–12. But suddenly Taylor was at it again, pulling it back to 15–15. Surely Davis was done for now? But the favourite displayed some courageous fighting skills of his own to open up a 17–15 lead with just three frames to play, only for Taylor to level it up again at 17–17 as midnight approached.

Davis opened up a slight lead in the decider before potting the yellow and fluking the green to go 62–44 ahead, meaning Taylor required all four remaining colours for victory. He potted a risky long-distance brown into the yellow pocket, then dispatched the blue and pink, which were also in the baulk area, to leave the championship resting on just one ball – the black.

Instead of attempting a safety, Taylor went for broke and tried to double it into the middle pocket, only to see it clip the jaw. After another three shots between the pair, Taylor found himself with a possible long pot into the green pocket. There wasn't much distance between cue ball and object ball, and any professional would have expected to bury it – except under these circumstances. He went for it full-blooded once again, with the Irish fans in the arena and all those across the sea watching it on television ready to jump for joy, but the black missed, rebounding back towards the top of the table, where the cue ball was waiting.

Taylor couldn't bear to look at the carnage he had left as he walked back to his chair. Davis got up to see that a thin cut into the corner was all that stood between him and the title. The shot was straightforward, but no gimmie. Not difficult, but not easy. The cue ball was close to the side cushion, while the pocket in which he was attempting the pot was out of his line of vision. Still, it was the best chance either of them had had up to then. It was a shot Davis famously said afterwards he would get seven times out of ten, but perhaps only three times out of ten under such pressure. He overcut it and the crowd gasped. Taylor's hopes were still alive.

The black was now hanging over the corner pocket and the cue ball hadn't travelled too far. It was a simple chance, but, considering Davis had already missed a decent opportunity of his own and it had been so long since any ball had been potted, Taylor couldn't afford to snatch at it. 'I'd done it thousands of times before. But never like this,' he recalled.[9] He clipped it in and thrust his cue aloft with both hands as the crowd cheered not only in recognition of a stunning comeback victory, but also for the climax of a game that had delivered maximum levels of drama.

It was 12.23 a.m. (the final frame had lasted 68 minutes) and 18.5 million viewers, the largest British television audience ever for a sporting event at the time, had stayed up to watch Taylor's – and snooker's – greatest moment. The *Irish Times* held back its presses in order to carry the result, while the people back in Coalisland, many wearing their pyjamas and dressing gowns, took to the streets in celebration. A week later, 10,000 people gathered for a civic reception in the town square to welcome him home. In the wider public domain, Taylor was an overnight success. Terry Wogan invited him on his chat show twice in as many weeks to talk the nation through his magnificent victory. The public couldn't get enough of him.

There are many reasons why the events that night unfolded the way they did. There's no doubt that Taylor summoned superior levels of courage and skill which he had never shown before in order to fight back to win, but perhaps Davis was not as unbeatable as many believed at the time. In the 1983 UK Championship final, he led Higgins 7–0, only to lose 16–15. The memories of this savage defeat would have come flooding back after Taylor launched his own recovery at the Crucible.

There was also the 1984 world final in which Davis led Jimmy White 12–4 and nearly let it slip before prevailing 18–16. With these past experiences weighing on his mind, Davis knew that even with a big lead he was not untouchable, and this inner weakness may well have played a part in his downfall. Taylor's form going into the final must also be taken into account. He thrashed all of his opponents on the way, winning 52 frames and losing just 18 from his 4 matches, while Davis lost 23.

It would have been too much to ask for any more from Taylor the following season, but he gave it a good go. With his schedule now exploding, Trish was relieved of her organisational duties and Taylor signed a deal with manager Barry Hearn. The world champion reached the final of the Grand Prix where, attempting to retain his title, he lost to Davis, but he did bounce back to win the Canadian Masters. A young John Parrott, whom Taylor beat 5–1 in the first round in Canada, vividly remembered the pounding he received:

> That was the best snooker I had come up against at the time
> . . . I made a 90-odd break in the one frame that I won. In
> fact, I hardly played a bad shot, but he was too good . . . he
> was really having a good spell during this period.[10]

Taylor, however, openly admitted afterwards that his preparations for his return to the Crucible were far too intense. He arrived in Sheffield early to soak in the atmosphere and, looking for inspiration, watched videos of himself in action. As it turned out, like so many other returning first-time Crucible champions, he went out in the first round, Mike Hallett beating him 10–6.

He pipped Higgins to the post 9–8 to win the Wembley Masters in 1987, the same year in which he recaptured the Canadian Masters title, but after that the trophies dried up. His rivalry with fellow Northern Irishman Higgins, however, which had been bubbling under the surface for some time (started when Higgins had taken a liking to Taylor's sister, Molly, when they were teenagers and had asked her to marry him), was hotting up. During the World Team Cup in 1990, Higgins hit out at his rival in tumultuous fashion, as Taylor relates:

> He lost his first frame and he wasn't very happy about it . . .
> He was in a bit of a paddy as he came off the table and that was
> when he threatened, in front of other people, to have me shot
> the next time I went back to Northern Ireland.[11]

That was just part of a verbal tirade and Taylor, who made an official complaint, was still seething when the pair met shortly afterwards at the Irish Masters. 'It wasn't that [the shooting threat], it was a very personal thing that Alex said about a member of my family,' he said. 'I had so much to prove because of what had gone on.'[12] Taylor won the match 5–2 and said of the result later, 'That, for me, settled the argument.'[13]

He managed to maintain a level of consistency which ensured he kept his place in the top 16 until 1994, but, always a man to bask in the limelight, Taylor didn't enjoy the constant grind of low-key qualifying matches. He retired in March 2000 and by that time had already established himself as a valued member of the BBC's snooker commentary team.

Until April 1985, Taylor was known as a decent but limited snooker player and a likeable chap. But overnight he became one of the most instantly recognisable faces in the industry by playing the leading role in a piece of sporting theatre presented in its purest form. The image of him holding his cue aloft in celebration is probably the most evocative snooker memory of all, and one still imitated in pubs and clubs across the country when someone downs a crucial black. Taylor wasn't another nice guy who came second, he was the man who won the mother of all matches.

THIRTEEN

JOE JOHNSON

Ordinary Joe

Joe Johnson was the most unlikely and unexpected world snooker champion of all. When he arrived at the World Championship in 1986, he had never won a match at the Crucible, let alone a ranking tournament, and was rated by bookmakers Coral as a 150–1 shot. By making a mockery of these odds and going on to beat Steve Davis in the final, the likeable family man provided snooker's blue riband event with its second rags-to-riches climax in as many years.

Born in Bradford on 29 July 1952 and raised in the Yorkshire city, Johnson's biological father, Malik Farooq, was of Pakistani descent, while it was his adoptive father Ken Johnson who introduced him to snooker as a youngster. A talented break-builder and excellent long potter, Joe was largely a self-taught talent. 'When I was learning the game, all I could do was copy the best player in my club because snooker wasn't on the box,' he recalled.[1]

He enjoyed a highly successful amateur career, winning three Yorkshire championships, as well as the national Under-19 title in 1971, and represented England on ten occasions in the Home International Championships. His breakthrough year was 1978 when, by finishing runner-up to Terry Griffiths in the English Amateur Championship, he qualified for the World Amateur Championship in

136

Malta. He lost in the final to Cliff Wilson, but the confidence gained from this performance, as well as a then record amateur break of 140 made the same year, persuaded him to forsake his full-time career as a gas fitter and enter the world of professional snooker in 1979.

Johnson's initial performances proved disappointing for a player of his undoubted ability. He acquired a reputation for being unable to cope with the pressure of playing under the heat and intensity of television lights and it seemed no coincidence that the most impressive displays of his first few years on the circuit came in the untelevised Professional Players Tournament in 1983. He carved out victories against Jimmy White, Eddie Charlton, Cliff Thorburn and Tony Meo to reach the final, where he met Tony Knowles. After falling 6–1 behind, Johnson mounted a magnificent fight back, including a crisp 135 break, before being denied 9–8.

This performance helped him rise up the world rankings from 35th to 23rd. Meanwhile, behind the scenes, he had an effective support network to guide his career. When he had first met local businessman John Cocker, Johnson was driving an old banger and had holes in his shoes. The two men soon became firm friends and when Cocker opened Morley Snooker Centre, he offered Joe the role of resident professional, providing him with a base for his practice sessions. Another figure who brought stability to his career was Wally Springett, owner of Springett Welding in Batley, who became his manager.

Johnson's World Championship form was proving consistently poor, though. In his first four attempts to reach the tournament, he had fallen short in the qualifiers on every occasion. Finally, in 1984, he succeeded in reaching the first round proper, only to maintain his unenviable record of never winning on television by being summarily dispatched 10–1 by Dennis Taylor. Nevertheless, when the end-of-season rankings were calculated, Johnson had advanced a further four places and was now skirting the fringes of the top 16.

The following season provided the final push he needed. First, Johnson broke his television jinx to reach the semi-finals of the Mercantile Credit Classic. He then qualified for the World Championship for the second year in a row, courtesy of a 10–6 win against Geoff Foulds. He gave a far better account of himself than the previous year, but was edged out 10–8 in the first round by Bill Werbeniuk. While the nation stood agog as Taylor beat Davis on the final black, Johnson was able to celebrate having done just enough to edge into the coveted world No. 16 slot. Little did he know that, in 12 months' time, he would be providing the championship with an even more outrageous finale.

The 1985–86 season, which would change Johnson's life forever, began inauspiciously enough. He might have forced his way into the game's top bracket, but he remained pretty much unknown to the wider public and by the time the World Championship came around, a couple of quarter-final appearances were the biggest successes his season could boast. He had still never won a match at the Crucible and was not even considered a dangerous dark horse. While contemptuous odds were slapped on Johnson, Davis, still smarting from his defeat the previous year, was installed as the overwhelming favourite to regain the title.

However, several factors were working in Johnson's favour, notably how content he was in marriage to second wife Terryll. Furthermore, he was determined to put a smile back on the faces of his fellow Bradford residents, who had suffered the agony, almost exactly a year before, of the fire at Bradford City's Valley Parade stadium, which killed 56 people. With nothing to lose, Johnson exploded out of the blocks in the opening round, beating Dave Martin 10–3. He then dispensed with Mike Hallett, Taylor's conqueror, 13–6 in round two.

Suddenly, he was in the quarter-finals and beginning to attract media attention. His varied employment history – including part-time crooning in a local band called Made In Japan – and witty Yorkshire patter made for good newspaper copy even if, as journalist Gordon Burn observed, 'The thing that was becoming clear about Joe Johnson as the competition proceeded was that he had no interest in pumping himself up and turning big-time.'[2]

At one stage in his quarter-final with Griffiths, it looked as though Johnson's challenge was at an end. After trailing 9–7, the Welshman rallied and went three frames up with just four to play. However, with the pressure off, Johnson once again began playing with freedom and flair, seizing his chance when Griffiths rushed a shot on the green in the next frame and missed. Over the next fifty-two minutes, Johnson reeled off two centuries and four additional breaks of thirty-plus to snatch the match 13–12. 'I knew I could win [the tournament] when I beat Terry Griffiths,' he said later. 'I'd never beat him before. It was then I knew I were a good player.'[3] Griffiths himself, ever perceptive, declared that Johnson reminded him of himself back in 1979.

Waiting for Johnson in the semi-finals was the housewives' choice and Bolton bad-boy Knowles. As well as a classic Lancashire versus Yorkshire match-up, it was also a showdown that offered an intriguing mix of personalities – the underachieving jack the lad versus the overachieving family man. In the event, demonstrating the same carefree attitude and formidable long potting he had shown throughout the whole tournament, Johnson was simply too good for the world No. 3, winning 16–8. Meanwhile, in the other semi-final, Davis ground down Thorburn's resistance after several lengthy safety-filled sessions to take his place in his fifth World Championship final. Bookmakers installed Davis's Goliath as 2–9 favourite, with Johnson's David at a wider 5–1.

As the final approached, the underdog didn't even need to feign insouciance. 'What's the worst that can happen? I can lose,' he declared. 'That's the worst that can happen.'[4] Beneath the one-liners, however, Johnson was beginning to sense that fame might prove a double-edged sword. 'Sometimes I'd like to be an ordinary gas man again, playing the game for fun,' he reflected at one press conference.[5] When the match began, he was perhaps too relaxed, while Davis was, for once, visibly hyped, steaming 3–1 ahead after rattling off breaks of 108 and 107. Johnson rallied well, though, and at the end of the first evening, the players were deadlocked at 8–8.

The following day, as Johnson skipped down the steps into the Crucible arena for the final day's play, there was definitely magic in the air. Ever stylish, he was sporting a pair of red, pink and white leather shoes. 'They glinted and sparkled in the lights and looked like shoes from a fantasy story which are believed to be imbued with magic, talismanic qualities,' noted Burn.[6] Whether it was down to the shoes or merely a sense of his own destiny, Johnson played like a man possessed, taking the first four frames to move 12–8 ahead. Davis hit back and only trailed 13–11 at the end of the afternoon session, while the first two evening frames were shared. At 14–12, Johnson's lead was slender, but he remained nerveless, closing out the next two frames to go into the mid-session interval just two shy of victory.

Backstage, the press corps and players' lounge were aflutter with excitement and the prevailing opinion was that the scars of Davis's defeat to Taylor the previous year had been reopened. Davis was certainly below his best against Johnson, negative and stilted and devoid of his usual seductive rhythm, but how much of that was due to psychological damage from the Taylor defeat, and how much was the result of the excellence and fluency of his opponent's play is open to debate.

Whatever the truth, Johnson wasted little time clinching the match. With no visible tension in his cueing arm, he wrapped up the next two frames and was champion of the world. The emotion of a second Crucible fairy tale in as many years was too much for some to take – tears visibly welled in the eyes of fellow players John Spencer and Willie Thorne as they stood and watched.

Johnson's own reaction was more prosaic. 'I were just going to play snooker,' he commented. 'That's why I didn't feel any pressure.'[7] When asked at what point he knew the title was his, he replied, 'In the last frame, when I were in among the balls. I were determined not to miss.'[8] He also paid fulsome tribute to Davis. 'I felt sorry for Steve. He's a great player and a perfect gentleman, in and out of snooker. I learnt a lot from playing Steve today. How to keep cool.'[9]

Viewed today, Johnson's victory can be seen as the final twist in the narrative of snooker's most popular era. It built on the drama of Taylor's victory the year before and the rise of Davis to superstardom. From its roots as a bastardisation of billiards, snooker had now travelled via the smoke-filled backstreets of working-class life to become an integral part of the British sporting and cultural establishment. As if to reinforce the point, soon after Johnson lifted the trophy, novelty single 'Snooker Loopy', compiled by the Matchroom Mob in association with chirpy cockney singing duo Chas 'n' Dave, climbed to number seven in the singles chart.

The maelstrom of fame hit Johnson hard. 'Even in the first week, my wife, my friends and my family were treating me different,' he reflected.[10] Journalists besieged his house and he was forced to reveal the complexities of his parentage and upbringing in an exclusive interview which the *Daily Star* crassly headlined 'My Two Dads'. Although he signed an agreement with Howard Kruger, a manager who also looked after Higgins, Johnson declined many commercial deals. He appeared on *This Is Your Life*, but found the attention his feats had created hard to comprehend. 'I knew how to react to the people of Bradford,' he noted. '[But] when I fly to somewhere like Hong Kong and there's press and television everywhere it blows my mind.'[11]

Unsurprisingly, his form soon disintegrated. Despite starting the 1986–87 season ranked eighth in the world, he failed to progress beyond the last 16 of any major tournament. By the time he was back at the Crucible to defend his title, he was a no-hoper again. A year earlier, when asked when his triumph would sink in, he had replied, 'Next year when I get beat in the first round.'[12] His words almost came true before he squeezed past Eugene Hughes to get his defence under way.

Suddenly, his form returned and victories over Murdo Macleod, Stephen Hendry and then Neal Foulds propelled him back into another final against Davis. There was to be no repeat of the previous year, though, as the 'Ginger Magician' reasserted the natural order with an 18–14 victory. Nevertheless, in mounting one of the sturdiest-ever defences of a first Crucible title, Johnson had proved he

140

was no one-season wonder and nudged up to five in the world rankings.

Thereafter, despite a Scottish Masters title in 1987 and the European Grand Prix crown in 1989, he gradually slipped down the rankings, dropping out of the top 16 in 1990–91 after five seasons' residency. More worryingly, he suffered a series of heart attacks and eyesight problems. Ever-resilient, Johnson continued playing throughout the 1990s and formed a business partnership with friend Dave Shipley. Snooker clubs based in Barnsley, Bradford and Wakefield were acquired and Johnson also established a successful youth academy for young players. His professional career finally came to an end in 2004 when he slipped off the main tour, an ankle break the summer before having impeded his game even further. Ironically, his departure meant that his status as the oldest player on the circuit passed to old rival Davis.

When looking back at his 1986 triumph, Johnson voices few regrets. 'I still watch [my] victory almost every night,' he said. 'It seems like yesterday when it happened. Unfortunately for me it came at the tail end of my career – I was 34 and it's hard to compete in the game nowadays when you're that kind of age.'[13] Through his business interests, as well as a spell as a director of the WPBSA, Johnson has remained intimately involved with the game. 'I couldn't survive without snooker,' he freely admits.[14]

As one-time 'fairy-tale' champions and two-time World Championship finalists, comparisons between Johnson, Taylor and Griffiths are inevitable. In the case of Taylor, they certainly stretch beyond the superficial. 'They were both homely, chubby, modest unassuming men,' Burn analysed. 'They had always been regarded as having very secure futures as spear carriers in snooker's classic dramas.'[15] Johnson's overall record may not bear comparison with either man, who both operated in the game's highest class for much longer, but for creating one of the sport's most indelible memories, he will be long remembered. He seized the chance fate offered him with both hands and was a far better player than he is usually given credit for.

His attacking style and ability to crash in long pots also prefigured the tactical approach that would dominate snooker from the 1990s into the new millennium. More importantly than that, though, his greatest triumph was the apotheosis of every schoolboy daydream ever played out on a 4x2-foot snooker table. Johnson taught us that if you dare to dream, fairy tales do sometimes come true. As he declared that heady night in May 1986, 'I've been world champion every day . . . I have visions, dreams, of being world champion . . . Dreams no longer.'[16]

FOURTEEN

STEPHEN HENDRY

Winning the Brave Way

Some sports are lucky enough to have them – phenomenal talents who burst onto the scene, fulfil their early promise and end up raising the standard by a country mile. They're so good and they come around so rarely, but without the likes of Don Bradman, Jack Nicklaus, Michael Schumacher and Stephen Hendry, sport runs the risk of stagnating.

The abilities a player needed to win the World Championship in 1990 – when Hendry became the youngest man to ever claim the trophy – were significantly different to those required in 1999, when he won his seventh crown. Not only did he rule snooker for that decade, he also turned the game on its head. He had the skill and the desire, but what made him stand tallest, what separated him from the chasing pack, were his unmatchable levels of bravery.

Words like guts and courage have not been used often enough when describing Hendry. That's probably because he has so many strengths it's hard to get round to them all. He is the most prolific break-builder ever (his record of first-class centuries, approaching 650 at the time of writing, is unlikely to be matched), the best middle-pocket potter and the most determined player to grace the sport. He reads the game as instinctively as anyone ever has and his elegance around the table is a privilege to behold. But time and time again, his greatest triumphs were achieved thanks to his positive shot selection under the most extreme pressure – he simply had more bottle than anyone else.

Before Hendry's day, a couple of useful 40-plus breaks were often enough to win frames at the highest level. He then raised the stakes, scoring freely and potting the old tactical pros off the table. It's down to him that today's players are brought up on the theory that unless you split the pack of reds at the earliest opportunity and follow it up with a century on a regular basis, as if on autopilot, then you have no chance of taking the biggest prizes.

It wasn't until two weeks before his 13th birthday, in December 1981, that Hendry enjoyed his first taste of snooker. He had taken no great interest in the game before then, but his parents decided to buy him a 6x3-foot table for Christmas, completely unaware that this choice of present would transform their son's life. 'I'd never really watched or played snooker,' he admitted in an interview with the authors. 'My dad played a bit of social snooker, but he wasn't any good.'

Nevertheless, Hendry gave his new toy a go and within a fortnight he was making 50 breaks. Two or three months later, his dad took him along to their local club in Dunfermline to play on the full-size tables. 'It was just for fun at the start,' he explained. 'And obviously I realised I had a talent and started entering junior tournaments.' He won the 'Star of the Future' Under-16s competition at Pontin's when he was 14, while a television appearance on *Junior Pot Black* boosted his profile. Snooker fans in Scotland, bereft of top-quality players for years, were beginning to get very excited at the prospect of celebrating their first world champion since Walter Donaldson.

All this success was unfolding against the backdrop of a troubled time in Hendry's personal life. His parents separated, something that he didn't see coming and shocked him deeply, and which, some have claimed, went some way to developing his sober approach to life. The separation saw Hendry and his younger brother move with their mother to an Edinburgh council house.

On the snooker table, however, it was full steam ahead. Scottish Under-16 and British Under-16 titles were captured before Hendry won the Scottish Amateur Championship when he was 15 and became the youngest-ever entrant at the World Amateur Championship a year later. Now aged 16, he was faced with the choice of entering the competition for a second time or turning professional. 'My father and I took the decision that I couldn't learn anything else as an amateur,' he said. 'If I wanted to learn, I had to be in with the big boys.' He couldn't have been more right. History has taught us that Hendry always revelled in the big occasion and he was far from intimidated by playing the big names at an early age.

During his debut season on the pro circuit, he reached the last thirty-two of the Mercantile Credit Classic, became the youngest Scottish professional champion at seventeen and, having won five World Championship qualifying matches, made an impressive showing on his first trip to the Crucible, going down 10–8 to Willie Thorne in the opening round. Considering it was the biggest match of his career, he wasn't fazed. 'I've always played my best snooker on the biggest occasions. I've never been overawed by anything like that,' he said. 'Obviously it was the World Championship and everyone knew that was the biggest event, so once I got there it was a matter of just trying to enjoy it and not embarrassing myself, and in the end I played pretty good and almost beat Willie.'

In a further effort to throw Hendry into the deep end as quickly as possible, his manager Ian Doyle set up a series of matches against Steve Davis, still the main man around, to be played in Scotland. Davis, keen to beat the new wonder-kid being tipped to take his throne, won all six challenge matches between the pair, but it was Hendry who came out the real winner. Picking up first-hand Davis's supreme technique, shot selection and matchplaying tactics, the young Scot learnt more than enough from his 6–0 drubbing and put it to good use. On his return to the Crucible in 1987, he gained quick revenge over Thorne in the first round, winning through 10–7, before beating Steve Longworth 13–7. Hendry, 7–1 down to reigning champion Joe Johnson in the quarter-finals, staged a gutsy comeback to level at 12–12 before losing the deciding frame.

However, he was still making big progress and the following season, 1987–88, he won his first ranking event at the age of 18 – the youngest player to do so at the time – at the Rothmans Grand Prix. A last-16 victory over Davis was a particularly pleasing scalp, while he also beat Tony Knowles, John Parrott and Dennis Taylor on his way to lifting the trophy. Hendry also won the British Open later that season and played his part in arguably the match of the tournament at the Crucible. He was leading Jimmy White 10–7 in the second round, but the Londoner dug deep and compiled a fine 86 break in the final frame to sneak through 13–12. There had been 26 breaks of over 40 in a thrilling contest.

It wasn't long before Hendry reached another final. This time it was the UK Championship in 1988–89 where, after a run that included a superb 9–3 thrashing of Davis, he fell victim to a revitalised Doug Mountjoy in the final, the veteran Welshman winning 16–12. Another title victory on his debut appearance at the Masters at Wembley softened the blow and Hendry finished the season by going further than ever before in Sheffield. A cool 67 break in the final frame saw him beat a spirited Gary Wilkinson 10–9 in the first round, while more comfortable wins over Thorne and Terry Griffiths, 13–4 and 13–5 respectively, saw him reach the semi-finals, where a defiant Davis knocked him out 16–9.

Hendry was now up to No. 3 in the world rankings, with only Parrott and Davis above him. But coming into the 1989–90 season, there was an added slice of pressure – if he wanted to break Alex Higgins's record of becoming the youngest world champion, this would be his last chance. He warmed up for the Crucible in remarkable fashion. He beat James Wattana in the final of the Asian Open in Bangkok, before also winning the Scottish Masters and the Dubai Classic. He clinched his first UK Championship crown by beating Davis 16–12 in the final and followed that up with his second Wembley Masters title. Everyone knew he had plenty of natural talent, but now Hendry was combining this with the sound decision-making and stubborn matchplaying skills that would become his forte. Having already won five major events that season, and with an out-of-sorts Davis appearing to lose his way, Hendry, now 21, was favourite for the tournament as he headed for Sheffield focused on making history.

'People were starting to talk about whether I could beat Alex's record to become the youngest world champion,' he said. 'I didn't let it get to me, it wasn't something that was on my mind all the time, but certainly it was a big thing.' Parrott himself admitted at the time that he was looking over his shoulder. '[Hendry] was starting to look the complete player, and he went to Sheffield knowing he was in great form. He was a genuine favourite.'[1]

Canadian Alain Robidoux gave Hendry a fright in the first round, hanging in there at 7–7 until the Scot pulled away by taking the final three frames. Straightforward wins over Tony Meo and Darren Morgan followed, and in only his second world semi-final he came back from 4–0 and 11–9 down to complete a 16–11 win over Parrott. His opponent in the final was White, who won that epic contest between the pair in 1988, but this time Hendry controlled the match from the off. His skills had been honed, his preparation was perfect and his mind completely focused on this moment as he performed some exemplary long potting and safety play on his way to an 18–12 victory.

Davis had dominated the 1980s by showing what a dedicated professional with bags of talent could achieve. He made the skill of nudging out two or three reds at a time to accumulate a frame-winning break an art but, as the watching millions could now testify, his time at the top was over. Hendry, picking up his sixth title of that incredible season and with it completing a clean sweep of all the game's major prizes at the age of just 21, was now No. 1 in the rankings. Like Davis, he was clean-cut, sipping mineral water during matches rather than downing gallons of beer, and practised relentlessly. The new pretender, waiting patiently in the wings for the previous couple of years, had pounced.

Typically, the Scot refused to sit back and celebrate his new-found glory and instead took the sport by the scruff of the neck. He picked up another five ranking titles the following season, but the highlight of his campaign was a stunning recovery in the final of the invitational B&H Masters, where he came from 7–0 and 8–2 down to beat Mike Hallett 9–8 in front of a mesmerised Wembley crowd.

Hendry only twice failed to reach the last eight throughout the entire season, a marvellous bout of consistency. But sometimes sustained good form isn't enough and when he needed extra inspiration for the big one in Sheffield, it deserted him. Attempting to become the only first-time champion to successfully defend his crown at the Crucible, he surprisingly lost the final four frames of his quarter-final against Steve James to succumb 13–11.

However, his Crucible experience the following year would be very different. He breezed through to the final, dropping just 14 frames on the way, but White, his opponent again, was on a roll after knocking in a 147, only the second in the tournament's history, in the first round against Tony Drago. The Londoner edged into a 10–6 lead after the first day of the final and it looked as if he would finally get his hands on the trophy he craved so much. White stretched that lead to 12–6 and led 14–10 going into the final session – no player had ever come back from such a deficit at that stage to win a Crucible final.

A peak television audience of 11.6 million viewers looked on in amazement as Hendry, applying an extremely positive game plan, launched a staggering recovery. He racked up frame after frame, pouncing on White's mistakes to clean up in some, while occupying the table throughout in others. He won all eight frames of the evening, making it ten in a row overall, to storm to the title in one of the most cold-blooded pursuits of glory snooker had ever seen. There were no nerves, no chance of economical percentage play; Hendry went hell for leather from the start of the evening to the finish. White didn't do much wrong, but when he did, Hendry punished him every time. It was ironic that the Londoner, whose popularity stemmed from his status as one of the game's flamboyant risk-takers, was on the receiving end of such a brave and attacking display.

'I never know when I'm beaten and I never give up in a game,' Hendry told the authors, recalling the famous comeback. 'At 14–8, there was still a long way to go and I knew for Jimmy the hardest thing would be getting over the line. When I got it to 14–10, I knew if I could get a good start in the evening he'd be under pressure. I then won the first frame and I could tell Jimmy was really under it, and from then on it was just a matter of keeping my concentration and keeping on top of him.'

It was arguably Hendry's most spectacular achievement on the table and, in doing so, he showed just how well he could play under the utmost pressure. Going for an outrageous shot knowing it's a potential frame-winner takes plenty of mettle – it's more often than not, of course, a frame-loser if it's missed. Some of the very best players will refuse the pot, because they know they can't make them all, and produce a safety. Hendry, as he proved throughout his career, but particularly on that night, was an exception. What most players would see as a suicidal shot, he would declare a calculated risk. Trying a risky pot was the percentage shot for him, as he knew that playing a safety and opening the frame up was not always to his advantage.

Being aware of your own abilities and basing your shot selection on them is a lot harder than it sounds. Should you go for the tricky pot, say, three times out of five? Or should it depend on how you're feeling on that particular day? Hendry was so in tune with his own game and form that he nearly always made the right decision – and it was often the brave one.

While the style of his 1992 victory bewildered most snooker fans, Hendry himself was even more proud of the way he lifted the title again the following year. He had actually endured a mixed season by his high standards and was shaken after receiving death threats from a woman on the eve of the Grand Prix. She also wrote a play called *Daggers in the Billiard Room* in which Hendry is murdered in the final act, and sent it to him. The woman was later convicted, but Hendry, unable to focus on the matter at hand, went out in the first round to Tony Chappel.

His game and confidence gradually picked up, however, and by the time he arrived in Sheffield, he was firing on all cylinders. A 10–1 thrashing of Danny Fowler was followed by a 13–4 win over Morgan and a 13–7 victory against Nigel Bond. In the semi-finals, the Scot comfortably saw off an exhausted Alan McManus, who had worked hard to knock out Crucible debutant Ronnie O'Sullivan and a revitalised Davis. That set up another final against White, and Hendry reminded everyone just who the defending champion and world No. 1 was by knocking in a 136 break on his first visit to the table. After that, he never looked back as White, struggling with his long safety play, began to lose his concentration and heart for the battle. Hendry crushed him 18–5 to collect yet another title. 'I think every round up to and including the final that year I was in total control,' he explained to us. 'Even now that's probably my favourite World Championship because I played so well and dominated every opponent and, to me, that gives me more pleasure than close finals, because it just proves how well you played.'

He refused to give up the title and in 1994 had to overcome a major handicap to retain it once again. He slipped in his hotel bathroom and fractured his left arm just below the elbow on the eve of his second-round match. 'When they took the X-ray, the fracture was about half an inch,' he remembered. 'When I woke up in the morning [of the match] I couldn't get my arm straight, so obviously at that point there was no way I was able to play.' The clock was ticking and, on hearing about the accident, his opponent, Dave Harold, would have been forgiven for contemplating the chances of a bye into the next round.

Hendry was taken to a local private hospital where he was administered a painkilling injection, but he was determined not to pull out of the event and stepped through the famous red curtain at the Crucible to face Harold. 'It was quite uncomfortable,' Hendry admitted. 'It was fine when I was down on the shot, it was getting down and coming up again which was the uncomfortable thing. I couldn't pick up the rest, I had to get the referee to do it.' After losing the first frame, the other title contenders must have been thinking they were in with a chance, but Hendry refused to feel sorry for himself and recovered in astonishing fashion to earn a resounding 13–2 victory.[2]

Further wins over Bond and Davis set up a final against the ever-popular White for the fourth time in five years. Hendry, who was being forced to put his injured arm in a sling when not playing, could have done with another 18–5 and an early finish, but White was having none of it and shook the Crucible into a frenzy by clinching the 34th frame to take the match into a decider at 17–17. The Londoner got amongst the balls first and looked set to make a sizeable break, but, with the pressure at fever pitch, he missed a routine black off its spot. Hendry, who had never been pushed so close in a world final before, didn't even blink in sweeping up the remaining balls to clinch the frame, match and title for a fourth time.

If he could win the game's biggest prize with a fractured elbow, there was simply no stopping him when fighting fit. Hendry cruised to his fifth world crown twelve months later, compiling only the tournament's third 147 in the semis before disposing of surprise finalist Bond, and then made it six in seven years with a comfortable 18–12 win over Peter Ebdon in the 1996 final.

By this stage, Hendry's domination of the game was being threatened by the likes of John Higgins, Mark Williams and O'Sullivan, who were all turning their early promise into ranking victories. Hendry, having seen off the likes of Davis and Parrott years earlier, relished taking on these new challengers and was determined to keep his No. 1 ranking. His courageous fighting skills came to the fore in a remarkable final against O'Sullivan in the 1997 Liverpool Victoria Charity Challenge. Hendry was leading 8–2, but the Essex man suddenly hit top gear and rallied to pull it back to 8–8 with one to play. Any normal player would think about playing the deciding frame of a final with a fair degree of caution – after all, one mistake and both the match and title are often lost – but Hendry strolled up and knocked in a maximum 147 break to lift the trophy.

Having equalled Davis's and Ray Reardon's record of six World Championship victories in the modern era, Hendry looked on course to hit the magic seven that year. He made it to the final and was up against Ken Doherty, a first-time finalist who had played the snooker of his life to get that far. It looked a similar pattern to Hendry's previous two finals against Bond and Ebdon, where the ambitious pretenders, having used all their energy in the previous rounds, were overwhelmed by Hendry at the death. Doherty, though, was inspired by his big moment rather than daunted, and pulled off a shock 18–12 win.

Worse was to follow a year later for Hendry when the opening-round draw dramatically paired him with White, who had been forced to qualify for the showpiece event having fallen out of the top 16. It was a return to their grand duels of the early 1990s and, in front of a packed Crucible audience, veteran White took some revenge for all those final defeats by nailing a well-deserved 10–4 win. To make matters even worse for Hendry, John Higgins went on to win the title, which was enough to take over at the top of the world rankings, a position Hendry had proudly held since 1990.

Word on the street was that Hendry's powers were on the wane. Many had found the concept of him losing a world final the year before difficult to comprehend, but what could they make of a first-round exit? Had the bubble burst? Had he lost his appetite for snooker? The popular assumption was that he was so content with his off-table lifestyle that he had lost his edge. Following his marriage to long-time girlfriend Mandy, the couple had recently had a baby son, Blaine, and Hendry's family life was certainly taking up more of his time. But he was quick to dismiss the claims, suggesting that, if anything was wrong, it was perhaps a case of temporary green-baize fatigue.

He was still capable of producing moments of brilliance, but his ability to sustain peak concentration over long periods was not what it was. He suffered an inconsistent 1998–99 season, including a humiliating 9–0 defeat to Marcus Campbell in the UK Championship, and, as he headed to the Crucible, he was by no means the favourite.

A first-round win over up-and-coming Leeds youngster Paul Hunter gave him the confidence to go on and beat James Wattana and Matthew Stevens to reach the semi-finals, where he was joined in the draw by arguably the three strongest players around at the time – Williams, Higgins and O'Sullivan. Hendry was paired against O'Sullivan and, in a match of remarkable quality, the Scot proved that his break-building remained of the highest order and his desire for success unquestioned. He stormed into an early lead before the Essex player matched that with some faultless snooker to edge ahead 13–12, but Hendry then pulled away, grinding down the frustrated O'Sullivan 17–13.

In the build-up to the final, everyone was talking about the prospect of a modern-day record seventh world crown. All the pressure may have been on Hendry, but he was not going home empty-handed this time. Against Williams, he took control of the final early on and as the match wore on he got stronger and stronger, sealing an 18–11 victory. Having surpassed Reardon and Davis on the winners' list, most experts within the game believed breaking this record ensured Hendry was no longer one of the greatest players of all time, but now the greatest. 'This feels better than the other six put together,' he declared that night,[3] and years later he revealed to us how significant a step he still regarded it to be. 'It was a big thing. It was the last real record worth

150

breaking that I wanted to break. There was a bit of pressure on doing it that year too, especially in the final.'

Hendry's comeback from his apparent decline may have partly been down to his capacity to mentally switch off when at home. As mentioned before, his marriage to Mandy and the birth of Blaine had increased his awareness of a lifestyle away from the table. While many claimed this was a possible weakness in terms of his motivation for the game, in some ways it was the opposite, especially considering Mandy's hatred for snooker. The couple first met when she was 16 and he 15 at a Pontin's tournament in Prestatyn where Hendry was playing in an amateur competition. But soon after he turned pro, Doyle banned Mandy from attending tournaments with them, fearing her presence was distracting his young protégé. 'Maybe it's one of the reasons Mandy hates snooker,' Hendry told Mordecai Richler.[4] 'I'll walk through the door and she won't allow me to mention it.'[5] At least it meant that whenever he had a bad defeat on his mind or had suffered a frustrating day at the practice table, he didn't mull it over once he got home.

That historic win over Williams wasn't enough to win back his No. 1 spot, but he kicked off the following season by winning the Champions Cup and the British Open, where he made another 147 in the final. After that double success, though, Hendry's game suddenly went off the boil and he went 27 months without winning another ranking event. In 2001, he admitted in interviews that his game was getting steadily worse, practice was becoming a chore and that confidence-wise he was at a new low. The journalists who had talked up his previous 'slump' in the late 1990s now had something meatier to write about.

Ultimately, Hendry's honesty about his decline and his refusal to look for excuses helped him resolve the negative issues surrounding his game quicker than perhaps many veterans would have done. He was by now 32 and in the past many a player perceived to be over-the-hill had accepted his fate and failed to get back on the rails. In an individual sport where confidence is paramount, a seasoned player can easily get embarrassed at suffering a string of defeats, and the idea of retirement and being liberated from the chore of daily practice seems the only way out. Hendry, determined to do something about it, hired Terry Griffiths to coach him and the Scot's game picked up. Griffiths helped advise Hendry on a few technical faults that had entered his game, but more importantly improved his psychological approach, encouraging him to keep his mind clear and focused, something many players have found difficult when they get older.

The 27-month drought ended with victory in the 2001–02 European Open and by the time it came to the next World Championship, Hendry, despite having an illustrious and lengthy career to look back on, realised he still had plenty more to offer. At the Crucible, he picked up impressive wins over Shaun Murphy, Anthony Davies, Doherty and O'Sullivan in another semi-final. He was up against Ebdon in the final, a repeat of 1996, but this time the Wellingborough player was a much more resilient force. In a match that went the distance, he made the most of some uncharacteristic Hendry errors in the final-frame decider to lift the trophy 18–17.

It was a desperately disappointing outcome for Hendry, who could at least take some comfort in the fact that he had broken another record – 16 centuries during a World Championship, eclipsing the 14 managed by Higgins in 1998. A year later, Hendry was at it again, becoming the first man to score more than 100 career tons at the Crucible, but his run ended at the quarter-final stage against eventual winner Williams.

Hendry's form was still a vast improvement on what he had been producing during that 27-month barren run between 1999 and 2001, but in the summer of 2003 he was forced to overcome another tough obstacle. On his return to Heathrow following a flight home from a tournament in Thailand, Hendry discovered his cue had been accidentally snapped by baggage handlers at some point during the trip. It was the same cue he had used since he was 14, and one he was incredibly attached to. It was stolen during the 1991 Grand Prix in Reading and Doyle offered a £10,000 reward for its safe return. Two days later, a man walked into a local police station with the cue, claiming he'd found it in a rubbish tip, and took off with the reward, no questions asked. It may sound like an expensive deal considering the cue originally cost just £40 off the shelf, but both Doyle and Hendry knew it was worth it.

Ironically, the cue itself was regarded by many as fairly useless – a somewhat weak, tatty piece of wood that, by Hendry's own admission, had certainly seen better days and wasn't even straight. If it had been taken to an auction with its history unknown, no one would have bid a penny for it. His former coach, Frank Callan, once famously said, 'He's become the world's best player with the world's worst cue.'[6]

At first, Hendry tried to see if the cue, split 15 inches from the butt, could be repaired, but cue doctor Lawrie Annandale had no success. It was a disaster. Top players, as mentioned in previous chapters, usually take months to get used to a different cue and being forced to work with a new one after so many years with his trusty old faithful would be a huge psychological test.

Cue maker John Parris travelled up to Hendry's home in Auchterarder, Perthshire, to offer him a choice of three new ones made to the original's specifications. Although no two pieces of wood are ever the same, Hendry picked one of the three and liked it straight away, claiming that he had started doing things with the cue ball he hadn't done for years. 'When it happened, it was a real setback and I was thinking, "Is this the end?",' he admitted to us. 'But that was just a knee-jerk reaction. When John Parris showed me the cues, I made a decision to pick one rather than go from one to the other, and in practice it felt pretty good almost straight away.'

Many pundits thought it could well be the beginning of the end after Hendry made an early exit from the season's first tournament, the LG Cup in Preston. But they were left in no doubt as to Hendry's confidence in his new cue at the next event, the British Open in Brighton. The Scot looked in terrific form, coming from 3–1 down to beat John Higgins 5–4 in the quarter-finals before seeing off Matthew Stevens in the semis and O'Sullivan in the final. He proved that was no one-off by making his way through to the final of the UK Championship, which he lost to an inspired Stevens, but it was clear Hendry's game, far from deteriorating with the forced change of cue, had in fact improved.

He also won the Betfair Premier League later that season, but was demolished by a rampant O'Sullivan in the semi-finals at the Crucible. Hendry had looked in good shape until then, but after losing the first session 6–2 to O'Sullivan, the Essex player won the next 7–1, before going on to win 17–4 as Hendry was blown away.

As well as being a fierce competitor on the table over the years, Hendry has also been known to speak his mind about the state of the game's organisation. In an interview in 2001, he admitted he'd almost got kicked out of the WPBSA for saying a couple of years previously that snooker was 'poisoned from top to bottom'. He went on:

> It's the same story over and over again. There's been new boards, new chief executives and it's made no difference. They've not been able to attract sponsorship, the prize money's gone static . . . We're supposed to run the game, the players, but you'd go to players' meetings and we're supposed to be able to ask questions, but they'd stop us the moment anyone asked anything difficult.[7]

In 2002, Hendry, still frustrated by this ongoing problem and acting on the behalf of some players, teamed up with Davis and Griffiths to demand the resignation en masse of the WPBSA board. The trio also questioned why the WPBSA's accounts, which contained £3.1 million in June 2001, had been reduced to £800,000. However, the governing body won a vote among professional players by 48 votes to 26 at an extraordinary general meeting in Telford and lived to fight another day. Afterwards, Hendry stepped into the background, stating that he would never get involved in snooker politics again.

His frustration with such off-table matters, though, has never affected his hunger for the game or his desire for success. That British Open triumph in 2003 was Hendry's 35th ranking title, an illustrious career haul (including five UK Championships and six Masters titles on top of his successes in Sheffield) that no other player has matched. But it's more than just statistics that make him stand out, it's the way he achieved them.

Most players tend to strike a fine balance between attacking play and safety, but in his prime Hendry played a huge majority of his game in an attacking frame of mind. 'It's just the way I played,' he told us. 'I've always taken on probably one shot more than I should have a lot of times. I've always been an attacking, aggressive player. That's the way you've got to play nowadays. If you don't take a risk to get in, then your opponent's certainly going to and you can miss out.'

Hendry's positive approach to the game in general was another of his major strengths. His ability to handle pressure, considering the fact that he was by no means the most popular player of the 1990s, must not be underestimated. Four of his seven world-title wins came from beating crowd favourite White in the final, with the huge majority of the audience vocally behind the Londoner.

Hendry has never been one to play on the emotions of the crowd or to will them onto his side. Instead, he prefers to keep his thoughts, whether they be of raging passion or a battle with nerves, to himself and allows the fans to make up their own minds. As Richler wrote, 'Hendry is not a fan favourite. Scoring a century, he does not acknowledge the spectators' applause. Flubbing a simple pot, neither does he lean over the table, head hanging low, or bang his cue against the cushion, soliciting sympathy.'[8]

As well as the crowd cheering for White, Hendry has often been forced to accept the opposite when he has been at the table. Keen not to be seen as a sore loser, the Scot has let a lot go over the years and only lodged official complaints as a last resort. In the 2000 Masters at

Wembley, he was heckled by a small, unruly section of the crowd during his 6–3 defeat to Ken Doherty and filed a complaint to the tournament director. This was an exception, though, and most of the time Hendry has either put similar distractions to the back of his mind or, if they have affected him, kept them under wraps.

When playing White at the 2003 Masters, Hendry was shamefully booed by several fans as he was introduced into the arena. Referee Alan Chamberlain was forced to address the crowd immediately, warning them, 'We don't want any of that in our sport.' In the same tournament against the same opponent in 2004, a member of the crowd coughed loudly just as Hendry was about to strike the cue ball on two separate occasions, putting him off his stride. White has always strongly objected to such behaviour, which was also condemned by the commentators in the arena, who clearly felt the coughing was a deliberate technique to put Hendry off. Nevertheless, the Scot refused to complain or blame his defeat that day on the disruptions.

On top of the watching hundreds in the crowd, Hendry, when up against popular players over the years, has also had to deal with millions of television viewers at home willing him to miss. Obviously, he has always enjoyed solid support from a fan base of his own, but in many cases it was in a minority. It's entirely understandable that, in terms of White versus Hendry, the masses find flamboyance more appealing than imperturbable excellence, but considering Hendry's appetite for the attacking game, you can't help but feel his reputation for dullness is unfair as well as inaccurate.

Coping with being the villain in so many finals must have been tough, but Hendry still dealt with it, showing admirable dignity and class. A fine example of this was after the thrilling 1994 world final, the year in which he broke his elbow. A photographer asked the triumphant Hendry to put his arm in a sling and pose with the trophy, but the Scot refused, stating it would be unfair on his beaten opponents, while he also didn't want to belittle White's role in an absorbing final. It was fitting that in the same year Hendry's good sportsmanship and dedication to the game were recognised when he was awarded the MBE.

You'd be hard pressed to find any analyst of the game who doesn't believe Hendry is the greatest player ever to pick up a cue. As well as winning more titles than any other modern-day player, he has knocked in more century breaks and won by far the most prize money.

His record of seven world crowns was only bettered by Joe and Fred

Davis and John Pulman, but seven of Pulman's eight victories were played on a challenge basis where he only had to beat one player to win the trophy. Fred Davis was undoubtedly a superb player who also won the title eight times, but during those years, 1948–56, there wasn't exactly a long queue of talented opponents fiercely contesting the championship, and he didn't need to win five matches in a row like players do today. Fred, although technically sound and a great ambassador of the game, also never struck huge amounts of fear into opponents like Hendry did. The Scot's ruthless edge often meant matches were won before the first break-off.

Steve Davis won six world titles, but the number of quality opponents around even in his day was not as high as it is today. In the finals of 1981 and 1987, Davis beat Doug Mountjoy and Joe Johnson respectively. Not only that, the standard of the top 16 in general is now higher than ever, meaning that, in the early rounds of the competition, Hendry has been up against hugely talented players such as Doherty, Ebdon, Stephen Lee, Paul Hunter and Matthew Stevens – all former or potential champions, but likely opponents before the semi-final stage.

What about the mavericks whose natural talent had more of an impact on the game than Hendry? Alex Higgins, many people's choice as the greatest player ever in terms of ability, won his second world title ten years after his first – an astonishing achievement – but there's more to snooker than potting balls when you're in the groove. Hendry had superior matchplaying skills compared with Higgins and his contemporaries White and O'Sullivan, and surely the process of transforming your abilities into trophies under extreme tension is a talent in itself? Hendry, Higgins, White and O'Sullivan all grew up with heavy expectations placed upon their shoulders at a very early age. The pressure was on them all to deliver and Hendry handled that hype better than any of them, building on his early promise to establish himself as an unmoveable force for a generation.

The only other player who perhaps could stake a genuine claim to Hendry's 'all-time greatest' tag is Joe Davis. Winner of 15 titles, Davis – like Hendry – really did intimidate opponents with his peerless ability and robust personality. But there were only a handful of players around in the 1920s and '30s, and Davis was also under less scrutiny during each tournament as media coverage was basically non-existent back then. Every shot Hendry has ever played at the Crucible has been in front of the cameras, available for deep analysis, whether it be positive or negative, by the watching millions. As O'Sullivan himself once admitted, 'Under pressure, he goes up a gear, whereas most players usually go down one.'[9]

Hendry had the lot – pure snooker ability which he harnessed to perfection, a focused mind, and a selfish determination to conquer every player he came across and every record he took on. Many players in the future may come close to matching him in some aspects of the game, but the one area where he will remain unequalled is his bravery, and his knack of knowing when to exploit it.

FIFTEEN

JOHN PARROTT

Standing Tall Among Giants

Stephen Hendry's dominance in the 1990s ensured the hopes many other players had of increasing their trophy haul and prize money were somewhat limited. While the dynamic Scot cleaned up, the rest were left cursing the fact that Hendry hadn't been born a generation earlier. There's no doubt that John Parrott would have won more than his nine ranking titles had the competition at the time not been so fierce. But it was, and his record, although not as colossal as that of others, is still highly impressive.

Parrott is acknowledged by many as a player whose wit and charm played a major role in popularising snooker in an age of serious competitors with stern faces. But while his exemplary manners and sportsmanship helped him cultivate an appropriate clean-cut image (later recognised by an MBE), the Liverpudlian's on-table prowess must not be overlooked. A solid and belligerent player, with a delightfully smooth cue action, Parrott looked unstoppable during his golden year of 1991. His dedication to the game has never been questioned and even after losing his place in the top 16 in 2001, he refused to fall by the wayside and still relishes taking on the big names today.

However, the green baize of the snooker table was not Parrott's first love – as a youngster, he was into crown green bowling. One evening, though, when he was playing his favourite sport with his father, the British weather played its part in defining the young Parrott's future. 'It started to rain when we were playing bowls, so my dad took me across the road to the snooker hall instead,' Parrott recalled in an interview with us in 2004. 'I opened the door and saw this smoke-filled room with two tables and I immediately got the bug. We put our names down on the board and, when it was our turn, I got a cue out of the rack and I loved it.'

That snooker club, the Dudley Institute, was adjacent to Penny Lane and a 12-year-old Parrott found himself returning there time and time again. The opportunity to get some practice in at home soon arose when he saw an advert in the *Liverpool Echo* for a second-hand, 6x3-foot table for £25. 'My father phoned the bloke up and we went there one afternoon, strapped the table to the top of my dad's van on the roof rack and prayed it wouldn't rain on the way home,' he told us. 'We had a front room which basically we did nothing with, so the snooker table went in there and I spent many a happy hour knocking the balls around.' Within six weeks of taking up the game, Parrott had compiled a half-century break. 'I threw myself into playing all the time because I loved it and, for some bizarre reason that only "The Man Upstairs" can explain, I was quite good at it very quickly.'

Although Parrott's father was no great player himself, he was an astute observer of the game and had read many technical help books, so he became his son's coach at the Dudley Institute. He also ordered Parrott a cue from Stuart Surridge, the cricket manufacturers, and the youngster was soon selected for the club's local team. In one game, he compiled the first century break ever made in a one-frame match in the Merseyside leagues, a total clearance of 129.

He started entering individual competitions too and won the north-west regional Under-16s tournament three times. It was becoming clear that snooker was the biggest thing in Parrott's life and he decided to quit school at 17, a year into his A levels, to concentrate on it full time. A fellow member of the Dudley Institute, Phil Miller, became his manager and, recognising the youngster's need to build up some serious match experience, entered Parrott in competitions countrywide.

In 1981, he won the Pontin's Junior Championship and a year later captured the Pontin's Open and *Junior Pot Black* titles. He also reached the final of the British Under-19 Championship, but lost to Neal Foulds. In 1983, he retained his *Junior Pot Black* crown and made it through to the final of the English Amateur Championship, where he lost to Chesterfield's Tony Jones 13–9. During that season, Parrott had won 14 out of the 18 competitions he entered and was clearly one of the top amateurs around. After that English amateur final defeat, he applied to join the professional ranks and was accepted by the WPBSA.

He enjoyed an exceptional debut season on the pro circuit in 1983–84, the highlight being a run to the semi-finals at the Lada Classic in Warrington. He beat Doug Mountjoy 5–4 to qualify for the televised stages and, on his debut in front of the cameras, Parrott performed magnificently to defeat Alex Higgins, world champion just two years previously, 5–2 in front of 2,500 fans. In the quarter-finals, he saw off Tony Knowles 5–1, but a missed plant into the centre pocket in the deciding frame of his semi-final against Steve Davis cost him dear. The Nugget got out of his chair to complete a match-winning break of 71 to book his place in the final, 5–4.

However, that run gave Parrott the confidence he needed to qualify for his first World Championship. He roared through the qualifiers in Bristol, whitewashing veteran Perrie Mans 10–0 in the final round to seal his place at the Crucible. There, he beat Knowles once again, this time 10–7, to go through to the last 16, where he faced Dennis Taylor. Parrott found himself on the verge of defeat at 12–7 down, but he won four successive frames before going down 13–11 in a thoroughly entertaining battle.

Nevertheless, it had been a fine debut season for the young Liverpudlian and by the end of it he had risen to No. 20 in the world rankings. 'I think it was a case, as it is with a lot of players, where in the first season you're full of beans and you're just glad to be a professional – you can't wait to play and you don't have any fear,' he explained to us. 'It surprised me a little bit, but I think it was probably a bit of overachievement as well. But one thing I was pleased about was that I proved I could cope with playing in front of the television cameras which, I was assured by many people, wasn't easy to do.'

The next target was to make the top 16, but after the success of that initial season Parrott struggled to find consistency in his game. The 1984–85 season was a disappointment until the World Championship came around, where he reached the quarter-finals after wins over John Spencer and Kirk Stevens. In the last eight, he led 4–0 and 9–5 against Ray Reardon, but the Welshman hit back to 12–12 and laid a shrewd snooker on the last red in the decider, from which he won a free ball and then the match.

Parrott finished the season ranked 18 and could only improve by one position the following year as breaking into that elite top 16 seemed a bridge too far. Reaching the semi-finals of the Goya Matchroom Trophy – where he lost to Dennis Taylor – was the highlight of that season, while at the Crucible he was a second-round loser to Jimmy White. 'For those couple of seasons, it took me a while to settle down and I was having a bad time,' he admitted. 'I was practising and working hard, but just lost direction.'

The turning point came in 1987. In the third round of the British Open, he crashed out 5–1 to Warren King and failed to make a break of more than 30. 'It was pathetic,' he wrote. 'I was thoroughly disillusioned with my game. I seriously considered quitting snooker and going out to look for another job . . . both technically and psychologically, my game had hit rock bottom.'[1]

He was still only 23, but now he had faced up to his problems, he knew the only answer was to scrap hard to get out of the rut he was in. It was almost as if worrying about a pending crisis had been his downfall and now that the crisis had arrived, everything became clear. The defeat to King spurred Parrott into action and he finally broke into the top 16 for the 1987–88 season and reached his first major final at the Mercantile Credit Classic in Blackpool, where Davis edged him out 13–11. Parrott exacted revenge on King in the opening round of that year's World Championship, beating him 10–4, but was knocked out in the second round by Cliff Thorburn.

The next season was Parrott's second in the top 16, and automatically qualifying for all the ranking tournaments seemed to relax him – except for when playing in finals. During that campaign, he lost several of them: Davis beat him 9–5 in the World Matchplay, Hendry denied him in the Masters and Mike Hallett took the honours at the English Championship. Parrott was certainly finding it difficult to handle the pressure that came with competing in finals, but he bounced back to win the European Open, his first ranking-event success, beating Terry Griffiths 9–8 in the final in Deauville, France.

As such a consistent, not to mention long, season drew to a close, he headed to Sheffield with high hopes. But the strain of what had already been an emotional few months increased further on the opening day of the tournament, which coincided with the Hillsborough disaster, occurring just two miles away from the Crucible at Sheffield Wednesday's home ground. A crush behind one of the goals led to 96 Liverpool fans losing their lives and Parrott, as his home city mourned, wore a black armband the following day for his first-round match against Steve James.

Parrott, receiving huge sympathetic support, won 10–9 in a thriller and declared afterwards that he would do all he could to take the trophy back to Merseyside. Wins over Dennis Taylor and White were followed by a 16–7 thrashing of Tony Meo in the semi-finals and it looked like he might just do it, but inside he was shattered. 'That final was just a classic case of me having a fantastic season, and having too much snooker, and coming into the final with absolutely nothing left. I've never felt so drained,' he told us. The final turned out to be a history-maker, as Davis, showing no mercy, won by the biggest margin in a Crucible final – 18–3. 'Unfortunately, Steve had been getting a bit of coaching at the time and had got his "A" game back,' Parrott added. 'The first few frames I was fearing the worst and obviously, when it ended 18–3, I just wanted to get out of the place.'

He reached his second successive Masters final the following season, but again failed to lift the trophy. The tip on his cue split on the eve of the final against Hendry and Parrott had left his spare set of 'bedded-in' replacement tips at home, meaning he had to use a brand new one. He felt all at sea and Hendry took the title 9–4.

The press seized on the chance to poke fun at the player who was reaching so many finals, but failing to capitalise when the pressure was really on. Some of the papers were claiming he had no bottle, but he retained his European Open title, this time held in Lyon, France, beating Hendry 10–6 in the final. Parrott was trailing 6–5 at one point, but played what many regarded as the best snooker of his career up to then to win the final five frames.

Back at the Crucible, he survived a major scare in the first round. Trailing 9–7 to Mark Bennett, Parrott hit back to win the decider with a clinical 69 break that proved just how well he could perform under the spotlight. He beat Dean Reynolds 13–11 and Thorburn 13–6 to move into the semi-finals, but fell in a disappointing defeat to Hendry. Tied at 11–11, both players made mistakes in a scrappy final session, with the young Scot eventually going on to win 16–11.

In 1990–91, Parrott was suffering from cue problems. The various new butts and joints which had been added over the years had changed its balance and he was beginning to lose all confidence in it. Apart from a semi-final appearance at the UK Championship, Parrott made early exits from most tournaments. In the spring, he had a new cue made especially for him in London and liked the feel of it straight away.

In his next tournament, the Irish Masters, he got to another final, but lost 9–5 to Davis. However, his game was improving and with perfect timing – the World Championship was up next and Parrott, unlike in 1989, was the freshest horse in the race. Rated at 16–1 for the title by the bookies, he edged past Nigel Gilbert 10–6 in the opening round in a game that was closer than the scoreline suggests. He then raced to a 13–1 triumph over Knowles, which included breaks of 137 and 138, with a session to spare, giving him an extra day off to relax in the process.

He had to work harder to knock out Griffiths 13–10 in the last eight, before a high-quality semi-final against Davis, who had turned out to be something of a bogeyman for the Liverpudlian over the years. Parrott led 10–4 before they shared the next session 4–4 in a display Parrott still remembers vividly. 'In that session, every time he was making a 90, I would go and make a 90; we traded blows,' he told us. 'I don't think I've ever seen Steve play as well, but I played equally as well. To come out of that session still in the lead was a massive boost.' Still feeling fresh and able to step up a gear, Parrott overcame his old nemesis 16–10. 'My game was good and I was feeling fresh, and that was one of the best matches me and Steve ever had, so putting that baby to bed was a great result for me.'

Now that that old score had been settled, Parrott had one more thing on his mind – making up for his miserable final in 1989. Although he had beaten the man who thrashed him that year, Parrott was desperate to make the most of the occasion, something he was robbed of doing the last time due to exhaustion. Up against White in the final, he made the best possible start, taking a commanding 7–0 lead in just over 70 minutes. 'The first seven frames of that final, I've never played better,' he told us. 'I knew that I would have to silence the crowd and, once I was out there, I played some terrific stuff. In terms of quality, that was my best session ever.'

White launched a comeback, but every time he got near Parrott the latter would edge further ahead with a vital clearance. He led 11–5, which later became 13–8 and then 15–9. A poor safety shot from White when 17–11 down proved crucial, giving Parrott the chance to clear up and clinch his biggest win of all. Despite a crisis of confidence midway through that 1990–91 season, Parrott, with the help of his new cue, had picked himself up and turned his prospects around in double-quick time. His preparation for the Crucible had been less hectic than two years previously, while he handled the pressure admirably, refusing to surrender winning positions and snapping up his half-chances when necessary.

His positive response to those tense situations proved that psychologically his game had improved a level and that he was capable of maintaining or seizing control of a match, whether it be in the first round or a final. A significant factor in him achieving this was how he put to the back of his mind the public fuss surrounding his disastrous 1989 final. 'There were no thoughts in my mind of what happened in 1989,' he wrote. 'I had never felt so confident about a match in my life.'[2] He was by far the player of the tournament, with only one opponent finishing within three frames of him throughout.

Crucially, he managed to prove that his Sheffield triumph was no fluke. At the start of the following season, Parrott, at the zenith of his career, added the game's second most prestigious event, the UK Championship, to his trophy cabinet. Even with the likes of Hendry (by now very much the real article) and Davis (still an intimidating prospect and ranked No. 2 in the world) around, Parrott was standing at the top of the tree.

As with many players, Parrott's best years coincided with a settled and happy life away from the action. His wife, Karen, whom he married in 1989, was at the time travelling with him to all the events, making Parrott feel very much at home. 'For the first five years of my marriage, my wife was with me on the circuit and it was the best five years I've ever played,' he said to us. 'She came everywhere with me, travelled the world, and I was happy whenever she was with me. I had no hankering to be home, I was perfectly content and she was having a great time going away to tournaments.'

He began the defence of his world crown by making history in the opening round, beating Eddie Charlton 10–0 for the first-ever Crucible whitewash. He beat Knowles in the last 16, but lost his grip on the title in the quarter-finals, with young Scot Alan McManus knocking him out 13–12.

The 1992–93 season started well, with Parrott winning the Dubai Classic for the second year in a row, knocking in a composed 63 break in the final-frame decider to beat Hendry 9–8. He also made it through to the final of the UK Championship once again, but failed to defend his title, White beating him 16–9. A clutch of talented new professionals, young and hungry for quick success, had joined the ranks and the market was flooded with high-quality players. The likes of McManus, Ken Doherty and Gary Wilkinson were making their presence felt, while another rising star, Thailand's James Wattana, knocked Parrott out of the 1993 World Championship at the quarter-final stage. The quality of these new players meant life was getting more difficult for the likes of Parrott. Tournament victories became more and more scarce over the next few years, but he did win the Sky

Sports International in 1994, the Thailand Classic a year later and his third European Open in 1996.

It was increasingly a case of being there or thereabouts for Parrott, rather than at the very centre of things. He still had a solid game, but with the standard of competition getting higher, he was finding it more difficult to win several matches in a row. For the rest of the 1990s, his stubborn consistency helped him maintain his place in the top 16, while at Sheffield he was a regular quarter-finalist, a major boost in terms of ranking points. But at the turn of the millennium, and now in his mid-30s, Parrott began to drop off the pace. By his own admission, he preferred to spend more time with his wife and two children, Josh and Ellie, than crouched over a practice table.

The 2000–01 season started promisingly when he captained the England team to victory in the Nations Cup, but after that he lost a string of first-round matches, the only bright spot being a run to the semi-finals of the Thailand Masters. He was then knocked out of the World Championship in the first round by Michael Judge, a defeat which signalled the end of his 14-year stay in the elite 'top 16' club, falling from No. 10 to 22 in the rankings.

By 2003, he had slipped to No. 30 and many were putting this slide in form down to the increasing number of his off-table activities. Parrott was combining his snooker with a highly successful career in television. A position as team captain on the long-running quiz show *A Question of Sport* raised his profile, while he also appeared as a pundit for snooker tournaments covered by the BBC.

Along with his television work, Parrott has always been one for spending plenty of time at the races, as well as on the golf course, where he plays off a six handicap. However, in the autumn of 2003, Parrott showed that all these extra-curricular activities might have been of benefit to his game – in terms of helping him to relax – when he went on an unexpected run to the semi-finals of the LG Cup. 'I enjoy doing the BBC work,' he told us. 'Sometimes the days are long, and it's definitely harder than playing, but it's something I enjoy. As is the golf, the football and the racing, which I watch every day. It's nice to get away from snooker sometimes and have something else to think about.'

That LG Cup run saw him beat world No. 5 Stephen Lee (including a fine 137 clearance), Lee Walker and Chris Small. 'I think sometimes just a little bit of confidence has been the key,' he continued. 'This season I've played better than the last three or four, and I've basically done half the work and just took a bit of pressure off myself. The last few years, I've been beating myself up and working hard and playing pretty awful, but I can honestly say that this year, even with the games I've lost, I'm not unhappy with any of the performances.'

That confidence helped him safeguard his proud record of being an ever-present at the Crucible since turning professional. In the final qualifying round, he trailed Judge 5–0 and 8–4 before winning 10–9 to book his 21st consecutive trip to Sheffield. In the first round, he stuck with Paul Hunter until the latter stages when the Leeds player, scoring more freely when amongst the balls, pulled away for a 10–7 victory. 'I was happy with the standard of my matchplay, but I was like an old boxer. I had plenty of ring craft, but no punch,' said the former champion.[3]

Parrott, like many one-time world champions, will go down as a player who nurtured his talent into a winning formula and made it count when the time was right. His extensive television work over the years has turned him into a good-hearted, mainstream personality, but no one should forget that at one time this fierce competitor snatched his chance to rule the world.

SIXTEEN

KEN DOHERTY

The Darling of Dublin

When Ken Doherty took the World Championship trophy to Dublin in 1997, he received a welcome like no snooker champion before him or since. As he travelled through the city displaying the famous old trophy on an open-top bus, huge crowds swarmed onto the streets of the Irish capital to acclaim him.

As well as providing the Republic of Ireland with the mother of collective hangovers, Doherty brought some romance back to snooker. Despite taking the game to new heights, Stephen Hendry's dominance in the 1990s appeared so unyielding that the sport had begun to suffer in terms of public appeal. By denying the Scotsman a record seventh crown, for the time being at least, Doherty not only provided the Crucible with its biggest upset since Joe Johnson beat Steve Davis, but also convinced a new generation that the World Championship was not the exclusive preserve of one man.

Doherty's 1997 triumph was also historic – he remains the only former world amateur champion to have also won the professional game's ultimate honour and only the second player from outside the United Kingdom, after Cliff Thorburn, to lift the trophy at the Crucible. While renowned chiefly for ending Hendry's run of five consecutive championships, Doherty is also an intriguing personality in his own right. On the table, with his pale features and that characteristic scar down his right cheek, he looks every inch a tenacious and fierce competitor. Off it, he is highly engaging and unusually cultured for a sportsman, with a fine line in witty patter – he is as happy discussing the merits of Woody Allen's earlier and later films as he is mulling over technical snooker niceties.

Doherty's road to glory began at Holles Street Hospital, Dublin, where he was born on 17 September 1969. One of four children, he grew up in the village of Ranelagh. Naturally bright, his early ambition to be a policeman was soon surrendered to snooker. The trigger came at the age of ten when he awoke at Christmas to find a small snooker table at the end of his bed. He was soon hooked, although his tender years meant he had to wait until Sunday each week to be accompanied by his older brother to the local club, Jason's, to practise. With its motley collection of snooker and pool tables and space-invaders machines, it was the cool place to be.

Television also played a part in his increasing interest in snooker, as Doherty told the authors. 'I used to watch the World Championship every year on television. The one that still sticks out in my mind was the second Alex Higgins win in 1982 when he beat Jimmy White in an epic semi-final. He came back from the brink of the dead and then beat Ray Reardon in the final and the wife came out with the baby. Even now, watching that makes the hairs on the back of my neck stand up. From then on, I always wanted to be a snooker player and try to emulate what Alex Higgins did.'

Throughout his teens, Doherty spent increasing amounts of time away from school and on the practice table, occasionally being chased back to lessons by his wooden-spoon-wielding mother. Aided by club manager Andy Collins's willingness to give him free table-time, Doherty swept all before him in the amateur ranks, winning the Irish Under-16 title in 1983 and retaining it the following year. In 1985, he was runner-up in the Irish Amateur Championship and the Under-19 Irish Championship was annexed in 1986, which qualified him for the World Amateur Championship, although he fell in the group stage.

In 1987, Doherty won the Irish amateur courtesy of an 8–7 win against Richard Nolan and put in an improved performance in the world event. By now clearly Ireland's outstanding prospect, he made the decision to leave his close-knit community behind and move to England for an assault on the professional ranks. 'I had to come over and see if I could make it against the best players in the world,' he explained to us. 'It was OK being a big fish in a small pool in Ireland, but I had to see how good I really was.'

After sitting his school exams, receiving two passes and five honours, Doherty crossed the Irish Sea and found digs in Turnham Green, west London, commuting each day to Ilford Snooker Centre to practise under the gaze of the club's resident professional, Irishman Eugene Hughes. Something of a father figure to many young Irish players, Hughes helped give Doherty's career a firm launch pad.

However, it was a series of early successes that really instilled in him extra faith in his abilities. 'I never had that confidence until I got over here and won a couple of big pro-ams,' he said. 'It made me think I could make it.' The money coming in from pro-ams enabled Doherty to move nearer to Ilford, where he first encountered Ronnie O'Sullivan, then a precocious youngster, who regarded his elder with awe and affection. Although he found practice sessions against Doherty demoralising, O'Sullivan also saw him as something of a surrogate sibling.

Those early days in Ilford went a long way to forming Doherty's formidable strength of character. 'I ended up there for ten years,' he went on. 'There were a lot of special memories, a lot of good times, but a lot of bad times as well because it was quite a struggle at first.' In 1988, he captured the Pontin's Open and 1989 was another exciting year – after regaining the Irish amateur title by beating Anthony O'Connor 8–4, he travelled to Reykjavik, where he scooped the World Under-21 Championship. The globetrotting continued with a trip to Singapore, where a crushing 11–2 win over Jonathan Birch secured the world amateur crown.

His run of success was not unbroken, though. At one point, after missing qualifying for professional status, Doherty hurled his cue under his bed in disgust, declaring he never wanted to see it again. Such disillusionment proved short-lived – if anything, the extra wait to turn pro increased his hunger.

The 1990–91 season was Doherty's first on the pro circuit and one of steady progress. A Mercantile Credit Classic quarter-final appearance highlighted his potential, but it was at the World Championship that he made his biggest impact, fighting through the qualifiers to secure a first-round tie against Steve Davis. Showing steady nerves, Doherty gave the six-time champion a major fright before succumbing 10–8.

Reaching the Crucible helped him end the season ranked 51st and the following campaign was even more successful, with two ranking semi-final appearances pushing him to No. 21 in the world. Doherty's star was firmly in the ascendancy and in 1992–93 he picked up his first ranking title, the Welsh Open, with a 9–7 final win against Alan McManus. The season was capped by a 9–2 triumph over Stephen Murphy in the Irish Professional Championship and a rise into the hallowed top 16.

Over the following four years, Doherty inched up the rankings, but major titles eluded him; most disappointing of all, he lost the 1994 UK Championship final to Hendry 10–5. Many began to question his mental approach, while others felt he did not possess a big enough 'weapon' to compete with the top break-builders. These perceptions appeared to be reinforced by a 13–5 second-round exit at the 1996 World Championship to Darren Morgan. It was a poor end to the season and in the lead-up to the 1997 World Championship, after another inconsistent campaign, Doherty's manager Ian Doyle felt moved to challenge his charge's commitment.

Doherty's response, in the white-hot arena of the Crucible, was staggering. He had recently moved back to Dublin, which had raised his spirits, but he entered the World Championship on the back of a confidence-sapping first-round British Open exit. Nevertheless, after a nervy 10–8 first-round win against Mark Davis, he hit his stride in the last 16, destroying Steve Davis 13–3. It was a stunning result in which Doherty demonstrated his break-building capacities with two centuries as well as a 96 (when a missed 13th red cost him a possible maximum), and eight other breaks of 50-plus.

Davis admitted he had been 'annihilated' and, wind in his sails, Doherty prepared for a quarter-final against John Higgins, whom he hadn't beaten in four previous attempts. Long touted as the next big thing, many felt Higgins was the player best equipped to end Hendry's dominance. However, despite losing the first three frames, Doherty won 13–9, knocking in a 116 in the last frame.

With Irishman Doherty squaring off against Canadian Alain Robidoux, and Scotsman Hendry facing Thai James Wattana, it was the most cosmopolitan semi-final line-up in the tournament's history. While Doherty was never in serious trouble, moving from 4–4 to close out an assured 17–7 victory, Hendry had a tougher time of it, winning 17–13.

Despite having displayed the best form of his career to reach the final, many expected the Doherty story to end there. The statistical case for a Hendry victory was overwhelming – he had won five tournaments already that season and was on an unbroken streak of twenty-nine wins in World Championship matches. In six previous appearances, he hadn't lost a Crucible final and was on the brink of surpassing Steve Davis and Ray Reardon's modern-day record of six world titles.

All Doherty brought to the baize was a superb amateur career, six mildly disappointing seasons in the professional ranks and one ranking-tournament victory. Furthermore, in the previous two finals, Hendry had paid no heed to the collective desire for a fairy-tale finish by ruthlessly repelling the challenges of two other first-time finalists, Nigel Bond and Peter Ebdon. As if that wasn't enough, history was against Doherty, with no previous world amateur champion having also won the professional crown. 'I was conscious of that,' he admitted to the authors. 'The only one who'd come close was Jimmy [White], who'd been in six world finals and never won.'

However, to those watching carefully, it was obvious Doherty was not content with the role of sacrificial lamb. For one, he insisted his family stay away from the Crucible so he could concentrate purely on the task at hand. 'I didn't approach it like an underdog,' he went on. 'This was my chance and I wasn't going to let it go. I was playing the best snooker I could play and this was my big opportunity to win the World Championship. I realised I may not get another chance. I had to try and seize it, and play the best snooker of my life.'

If it was a surprise that Doherty took a close opening frame, then there was a sense of inevitability when Hendry knocked in consecutive centuries to lead 2–1. Gradually, though, Doherty's dogged safety and consistent break-building carved out a 5–2 advantage. Hendry blasted back with a 122, but Doherty remained unflustered. After Hendry missed three good chances on the pink, Doherty stole a psychological victory by outrageously doubling a re-spotted black to lead 7–4. By the close of the first day, he had an 11–5 lead.

A major upset was on the cards, but many observers, remembering Hendry's comeback from 14–8 down to beat White 18–14 in 1992, still expected the Scot to prevail. This belief began to evaporate as a nerveless Doherty extended his advantage to 15–7, but then came the Hendry charge – a 137 clearance was the catalyst as he reeled off five frames in a row. Suddenly, Doherty's lead had wilted to just 15–12.

The Irishman soon regained his equilibrium, though. 'He should have gone 15–13,' he told us, 'but he missed a red along the back cushion behind the black. I was never so delighted to see a red missed in my life. I was out of the chair like a greyhound. I only needed the red and another black, and that was it – it was 16–12 and from then

I knew I was going to win.' As he knocked in the winning balls, millions of Irish viewers remained glued to their televisions – for a few hours, crime figures in Dublin even fell dramatically. 'I won it pretty easily in the end, really, although there were a few hairy moments,' he recalled.

Doherty's life soon entered the surreal vortex of excitement and celebration common to all first-time Crucible winners. As the first world snooker champion from Ireland, his victory inspired a national party, with a quarter of a million people taking to the streets to welcome him home. 'The most pleasing thing was bringing the trophy back to Dublin,' he noted. 'I got a fantastic reception – they were all waiting on the tarmac at Dublin airport and then we got an open-top bus all the way through the city and back to my village in Ranelagh for a street party. It was what dreams are made of.'

A fanatical Manchester United fan, Doherty was invited to parade the trophy at Old Trafford and was hailed by Irish President Mary Robinson as an ambassador and role model for Ireland's youth. Unsurprisingly, he savoured his year as champion to the full. 'I had such a good time with the trophy that I didn't want to give it back,' he remembered. 'I kept it on my mother's television in the living room. I used to come in every day, pick it up and give it a big kiss.'

Doherty's standard of play dipped over the 11 months which followed, but he harbours few regrets. 'I didn't have a good season,' he told us. 'It wasn't that I forgot about snooker, but I felt really strange. I was world champion. I'd reached the peak and thought, where do I go from here? It took me a while to get used to it. I didn't have the best of seasons, but I didn't mind – I had the World Championship.' He also mounted a spirited defence of his title in 1998, reaching the final before ceding his crown 18–12 to Higgins. 'I gave it a good run,' he said. 'I got back to the final and had a tough match against John; he played tremendous that year.'

Since lifting the world title, Doherty has confirmed his place among the world's top players by winning a further three ranking titles. However, his finest recent achievement came in the 2003 World Championship where a roller-coaster sequence of increasingly tense victories did almost as much to cement his standing within the game's elite as his 1997 triumph, even though he fell just short in the final against Mark Williams.

After his opening match, a 10–9 black-ball victory against highly rated youngster Shaun Murphy, Doherty required another final-frame finish against Graeme Dott in round two, having trailed 7–2. His ensuing quarter-final victory against Higgins appeared to offer some relief as Doherty raced 10–0 ahead. 'The Wizard of Wishaw' then launched a stunning comeback, snaffling seven frames on the trot before Doherty steadied himself for a 13–8 victory.

However, it was his 17–16 semi-final victory against Paul Hunter, one of the most extraordinary matches of all time, for which Doherty may come to be best remembered. At one stage, he trailed 15–9, before summoning a five-frame winning streak to narrow the deficit to just one frame. Hunter nicked the next, before Doherty sealed an astonishing victory by winning the final three frames. 'It was the most incredible game I have ever played in,' he admitted. 'I always say to myself, if you dream about it, it will come true.'[1]

The final was a tense showdown between the extravagant long potting of Williams and Doherty's tactically and psychologically unrelenting approach. Obviously drained from his 98-frame slog to reach the final, Doherty appeared powerless early on as Williams raced 10–2 ahead. A minor rally saw the deficit reduced to 11–5 overnight, but odds of 50–1 on Williams and 12–1 against Doherty told their own story.

At the start of the second day, a six-frame streak containing two centuries hauled Doherty back to 11–11. From there, the game edged towards its conclusion in small steps, with deadlocks at 12–12, 13–13 and then 14–14 at the final mid-session interval. Williams knocked in a 120 as he moved 16–14 ahead, but back again came Doherty with a 112 to level at 16–16. Williams finally doused his opponent's fire 18–16, but rarely can a player have gained as much honour in defeat as Doherty.

The 2003 championship certainly offered a graphic demonstration of how Doherty has refined his mental approach. Appropriately enough, he is even married to a psychiatrist. 'I'm interested in the mind, it's so complex and so vast,' he told us. 'If you believe in yourself, you can do anything – and that doesn't only apply to snooker, it applies to life in general. Most of the guys in the top 32 can make centuries, make maximums, but it's all about doing it when you need it most. That's where confidence and psychology come in.'

From the occasionally lackadaisical attitude that characterised his early career, Doherty has developed one of the coolest temperaments on the circuit – with the odd exception, such as the missed final black in the 2000 Masters final that cost him a maximum 147. His major strength is that his game is truly rounded – as well as being a fine potter and break-builder, he possesses the capacity to slow down games and play challenging safety. Coupled with his flair for escaping from snookers and snaring crucial doubles, he has become a formidable player.

As for weaknesses, Doherty himself admits a lack of consistency is his Achilles heel. 'When you're not playing your best, having the ability to win is very important,' he noted. 'All great champions can do that. Some days I play really well and score really heavily. But some days I can't. I'm not consistent enough. I can go out and beat O'Sullivan one day, and then go and lose to someone ranked 60, 70 places below me.'

Despite a disappointing 2003–04 season, Doherty should remain a dangerous competitor for several years yet and is already assured of a place in the pantheon of great Irish sporting heroes. With the benefit of perspective, the groundbreaking nature of his 1997 world-title triumph has not dimmed one iota – especially when you consider that Hendry was in good enough form to make five centuries in the final and still lost.

'It was against the best player in the world, who hadn't been beaten there for the last five years,' Doherty said. 'I stood up to this guy, even though he's the best player that's ever played the game. It was a great triumph – a triumph of wits and confidence more than anything.' Hendry has never been quite the same player since and, while much of that can probably be explained by natural decay, Doherty certainly succeeded in shattering his aura of invincibility.

The fact that he won the world title by beating the greatest player of all time and has gone on to reach two more finals certainly ensures Doherty ranks highly among the platoon of snooker's one-time champions. A second world title would enhance his reputation yet further and it remains the motivating factor for the rest of his career. 'I can always say I had it once,' he admits. 'It's taken the pressure off completely. I'm not searching for that Holy Grail any longer. My name is on the cup and whatever happens nobody will ever take that away from me. But I want to have it again. That's what keeps driving me on.'

SEVENTEEN

JOHN HIGGINS

Following in the Master's Footsteps

When he burst onto the scene in the 1990s, John Higgins was the perfect example of a post-Stephen Hendry player. Learning the lessons laid down by his fellow Scot, Higgins – with exceptional break-building at the forefront of his armoury – knew the best way to make an impact at the highest level was to score heavily, and do it regularly.

A wonderfully fluid player around the black spot, Higgins doesn't go to the table with the aim of making a useful 40-odd break and then giving his opponent something to think about by playing a good safety shot. His intention has always been to win the frame at one visit, preferably with a century break to boot. His tenacious attitude and admirable skill in escaping snookers means he's ready for a tactical battle if required, but his main priority has always been to out-pot his opponent.

He has already made his way up to third on the list of all-time competitive century makers[1] and is second on the roll-call of Crucible centurions, while his haul of sixteen ranking event titles can, at the time of writing, only be bettered by two players – Steve Davis and Hendry.[2] If this wasn't enough to prove his scoring finesse, Higgins made history in the autumn of 2003 when he became the first player to score a maximum 147 break in back-to-back ranking-event matches.

Born and raised in the Lanarkshire town of Wishaw, central

Scotland, in May 1975, Higgins started playing at the age of nine when his father took him to a local amusement arcade. Upstairs was a bar with six snooker tables and while Higgins senior helped himself to a drink or two, his son picked up a cue and got to know and love the game that would make him famous. Higgins's desire for quick success was reflected by his speedy rise up the snooker ladder as a youngster. His major breakthrough came in the junior event at the 1991 World Masters in Birmingham. He knocked out Ronnie O'Sullivan on his way to the final where he beat Mark Williams to collect the £5,000 first prize – the biggest junior pay packet in snooker history at the time.

A year later, Higgins, who had just turned 17 and was reaping the benefits of having Hendry as a practice partner, joined the professional ranks along with O'Sullivan and Williams. However, the young Scot took time to adjust to the new level of competition. In his first year as a pro, his best result was a run to the last 16 at the Grand Prix; apart from that, he pulled up few trees and finished the season with a modest ranking position of 122. He moved up to 51st after an improved 1993–94 campaign, but the fireworks everyone was expecting finally arrived during the following season.

In only the second tournament, the Grand Prix again, Higgins went all the way, beating Dave Harold 9–6 in the final. If that didn't make everyone sit up and notice this young lad from Wishaw, the events that followed certainly did. The Scot beat Davis 9–5 to win the International Open and then saw off O'Sullivan in the final of the British Open to lift his third ranking title of the season, the first teenager ever to do so. That treble haul earned him £283,970, 12 times more than he had made during the previous season.

These achievements were all the more impressive considering Higgins had endured an acrimonious split from his manager, Ian Doyle, that season. Doyle controversially refused to give Higgins a wild card for the invitational Scottish Masters in Motherwell in September 1994. The young Scot was not best pleased and the rift widened a month later when Higgins mislaid his return air ticket from the Dubai Classic and the pair argued over the cost of a replacement, which prompted a less-than-amicable parting of the ways. Denbigh businessman Chris Williams became Higgins's new manager, but the player's father, John senior, soon took more of a hands-on role in his son's affairs and the partnership turned out to be a successful one. John senior carefully nurtured Higgins through a vital period of his career and still carries out the same duties today, accompanying his son to tournaments all over the world.

The young Scot was by no means distracted by this off-table interference or overawed by his stunning burst of success in that 1994–95 season. He finished off the campaign by qualifying for the televised stages of the World Championship for the first time in three attempts, but Alan McManus defeated him 10–3 in the first round at the Crucible. Despite that defeat, Higgins was earning plenty of plaudits, not just for his skill and promise, but also for his commendable table manners and sportsmanship. For a player so young, he seemed to have the dignity of a seasoned professional. Never losing his temper, he was polite and courteous both at the table and backstage, pleasantly carrying out his promotional duties whether it be dealing with WPBSA officials or talking to the media.

By this stage the world No. 11, Higgins managed to build on his successful campaign and quickly established himself as one of the most consistent winners on the circuit. In only two ranking events in 1995–96 did he fail to make at least the quarter-finals, while he added the German Open to his trophy cabinet and successfully defended his International Open title. He reached two other finals, at the Grand Prix and British Open, and by the time he returned to Sheffield he was being tipped as a serious title contender. He made it through to the quarter-finals where he faced O'Sullivan. The pair, who are the same age, had gone head-to-head many times as youngsters and knew each other's games inside out, but this was by far their biggest match to date.

With O'Sullivan weighed down with disciplinary issues (a hefty punishment was hanging over him after he had head-butted a WPBSA official backstage at the Crucible earlier in the tournament), Higgins built up a decent advantage and led 10–6 going into the final session. He seemed to have the game wrapped up when he was leading 12–11 and was amongst the balls in the next, but he missed the pink when clearing the colours after running out of position in potting the blue. O'Sullivan nipped in to level and the Essex man clinched the decider to earn a semi-final berth.

Despite the crushing disappointment of that missed pink, Higgins was up to No. 2 in the world and consolidated that with another impressive, if less spectacular, 1996–97 season. He won the European Open, was runner-up in the UK Championship and reached two other semi-finals, but his hopes of going further than ever before at the Crucible were dashed again at the quarter-final stage, eventual winner Ken Doherty defeating him 13–9.

Higgins stepped it up a notch the following season, reaching a staggering eight finals, six of them in ranking events. He won the German Open for a second time, the invitational Charity Challenge and the British Open, while finishing runner-up in the Grand Prix, UK Championship, Malta Grand Prix, Regal Welsh and Scottish Open. With this impressive haul of results behind him, Higgins had a slim chance of replacing Hendry as world No. 1 at the World Championship, providing Higgins won the tournament and Hendry lost in the first round. Jimmy White ensured the latter, producing a magnificent display to knock the six-time champion out 10–4 in the last 32.

Now it was up to Higgins and, unlike in 1996 when he fluffed his big chance on that missed pink, the young Scot thrived in the limelight. A 10–8 first-round win over Jason Ferguson seemed to settle him into an offensive rhythm which no other player came close to matching. He beat Anthony Hamilton and John Parrott (against whom he made breaks of 102, 143 and 139 in three successive frames) to set up a semi-final with O'Sullivan. This time Higgins didn't falter in sight of the winning post, at one point taking eight frames on the trot to steam away from his opponent and register a convincing 17–9 victory in what was supposed to be an evenly matched contest.

Higgins refused to let his momentum drop for the final and was always in control against Doherty, who, like Higgins's previous opponents, could do nothing but admire the Scot's ruthless break-building, which culminated in him making 14 centuries, a record in one World Championship.[3] His 18–12 victory in the final was a triumph for youthful, effervescent virtues over meritorious matchplay. The fact that this had all been achieved in only his fourth visit to the Crucible reflected how much class Higgins had and how quickly he had imposed himself at the highest level in the sport.

With the game's most prestigious prize safely in his locker, he went on to take the second- and third-biggest titles, with victory in the UK Championship and Masters the following season. Everything was coming up roses for Higgins and in 1999 he also announced his engagement to long-time girlfriend Denise, whom he met when he was 17 (the couple tied the knot the following December).

Back on the table, Higgins won the China Open to leave him in good shape when returning to Sheffield as favourite to defend his crown. Things looked ominous when he blitzed Gerard Greene 10–2, Mark King 13–4 and Stephen Lee 13–6 to set up a semi-final with Williams. But just as Higgins had made the most of an unstoppable tempo behind him 12 months earlier, the Welshman had it this time around.

Williams won the first session 5–3 before Higgins came back to level at 8–8, but the match was effectively sealed in the third session, a determined Williams winning it 6–2 to lead 14–10. Higgins had lost the initiative and couldn't find an answer in the final session, leaving Williams to take the three frames he needed for a 17–10 win.

The Welshman was to exert further agony on Higgins a year later. The Scot had won the Welsh Open and a second Grand Prix title earlier in the season, but once again ran out of steam in the semi-finals at Sheffield. Higgins built up a 15–11 advantage, but Williams clawed it back in fine style to go through 17–15 and take Higgins's world No. 1 spot in the process. The Scot admitted afterwards he had 'bottled it' and felt the defeat was one of the lowest points of his career.

However, he gained quick revenge by beating Williams 10–4 in the final of the UK Championship that autumn and went one better at the World Championship the following spring, edging out Matthew Stevens in a thrilling semi-final before coming unstuck against O'Sullivan in the final, losing 18–14. Earlier in that 2000–01 campaign, Higgins, as defending champion, decided to pull out of the Grand Prix at the quarter-final stage to attend his brother Jason's wedding. The appointment of his father as manager a few years earlier had proved how highly he valued his family and he refused to change his priorities, deeming the wedding far more important than ranking points and a possible trophy.

Higgins made more history in 2001–02 by becoming the first player to win the opening three tournaments of a season, a haul which included the British Open. But after that burst, there was little to celebrate and his season ended on a disappointing note when he went out of the World Championship in the quarter-finals, courtesy of a 13–7 defeat to Stevens.

Having established himself as one of snooker's most consistent tournament winners over a decade, Higgins was starting to show signs of wear and tear for the first time. Much of his success had been down to his consummate 'B' game – if he wasn't potting opponents off the table, he was digging in and picking up victories the scrappy way. His back-up plan, however, was beginning to crumble and he was losing more of the closely fought matches in which he used to employ all his know-how and cunning to win. This was at first put down to him and Denise having a baby son, Pierce, which meant more sleepless nights and off-table responsibilities to deal with. Higgins himself admitted that he did not practise as tirelessly following the birth – a major shift in focus in a player's life always has the potential to affect their snooker. Unfortunately for Higgins, his game failed to pick up in the months and years that followed and it took him until November 2004 – a wait of three years – to win another ranking event.

This unforeseen dip in form was a striking example of how psychological snooker can be. How could a naturally skilled player, with ample experience and numerous titles under his belt, lose his magic touch over a fairly lengthy period? All players endure tough spells when, for one reason or another, they lose form, but Higgins, who possesses significant mental strength, was the last person many would have expected to struggle escaping from such a rut.

When he headed to the Crucible in the spring of 2004, he was in danger of losing his place in the top four, a position he had held for the previous eight years. He survived a mighty scare in the opening round when Crucible debutant Ryan Day opened up a 9–7 lead and looked set to wrap up a shock win in the next frame, but missed a routine pink off its spot into the corner. Higgins battled back and, without looking entirely convincing, scraped through 10–9 to leave the Welsh youngster devastated. However, it proved to be no wake-up call for Higgins. In the next round, he laboured badly against Graeme Dott and was glad to finish the first session only 5–3 behind. But Dott was determined not to let the former champion off the hook and went on to complete a 13–10 victory, with Higgins failing to rediscover anything like his true form.

After the defeat, which saw him drop to No. 5 in the rankings, Higgins admitted, 'There was no way I deserved to win that match. I didn't play well enough to peg him back, I was just playing for pride at the end. I've got to do something, see a sports psychologist or something, because my concentration is just not there at all. It's not good enough if you want to win things and it's not been good enough for a couple of years. You start to doubt yourself the more you lose and out there today was torture. I didn't feel in control and it was horrible.'[4]

So, what was behind this relative slump in form that halted his trophy haul? If the challenge of fatherhood played its part in a few bad results in 2001–02, why did he fail to pick himself up over the couple of years that followed and return to anything like the high standards he set himself in the late 1990s? A few defeats certainly affected his confidence and he found it difficult to turn the tide, but the format of the current game could also have played its part.

When Higgins enjoyed the majority of his success, he had three main rivals to worry about – Hendry, Williams and O'Sullivan – but at the beginning of the twenty-first century, the game suddenly opened up and a bigger group of players, including the likes of Stevens, Doherty, Paul Hunter, Stephen Lee and Peter Ebdon, could mount serious challenges for every tournament. Higgins has therefore suffered from playing in an era where the top eight or nine players are so closely matched in ability (more so than ever before) that it purely comes down to who performs better on the day. On top of that, there is the credible threat from those outside the elite: Chris Small, David Gray and Stephen Maguire all won ranking events when they were placed outside the world's top 16 during Higgins's drought, while Dott, No. 13 at the time, made it through to a world final in 2004.

Following a semi-final defeat to Hunter in that year's Masters, Higgins, 28 at the time, admitted that his poor run of results was causing him sleepless nights, as he worried about whether his best years were behind him. Getting back to previous heights in sport is always a tricky obstacle to overcome, but even more so when you've been at the very top. Higgins spent two seasons as world No. 1 and, as a former world champion, nothing else but a repeat of that was good enough.

His barren run in terms of ranking titles wasn't all doom and gloom, though. In the final of the 2003 LG Cup, Higgins, trailing Williams 6–4, dragged himself back into the match in stunning fashion when he compiled a 147, despite the balls being far from ideally placed. He came out for the next frame with his mouth smeared in lipstick after receiving a kiss from Denise backstage, but couldn't put the maximum out of his mind as a ruthless Williams cleaned up for a 9–5 victory.

A month later, the next tournament was the British Open in Brighton and, in Higgins's first match, he knocked in another maximum during a 5–1 win over Michael Judge.[5] The final red was tucked near a side cushion, but Higgins pulled off a tremendous shot with the rest, using plenty of check side to get position on the black. Clearly, he was still showing sporadic signs of his true class. His reference to seeing a sports psychologist following that Crucible defeat to Dott also showed he was making the effort to think outside the box, that he was not prepared to just sit back arrogantly and wait for his golden touch to return. And when it did, it was back in Brighton at the British Open in November 2004. Higgins beat an in-form Maguire 9–6 in the final, compiling a crucial and brilliant 144 break when the match was balanced at 5–5. The drought was over.

There have been few players in the history of snooker who have made break-building look so eloquent as Higgins. He is a delight to watch when in full flow – the deeper his concentration, the more rapid the jigging of his eyebrows becomes as he lines up a shot. The Scot's excellence and dignity established him as a popular player in the 1990s, and fans and pundits alike have always welcomed his positive attitude and respect for the game, whether winning or losing, and never more so than in his recent struggle to return to top form. No matter how much frustration set in, his constant refusal to lash out and get snappy with opponents or the media was a greatly admired quality that has been, and will be, a key to his rightful success.

EIGHTEEN

MARK WILLIAMS

Casting Convention Aside

In a sporting context, 'unconventional' is an adjective usually applied to highly skilled, mercurial talents often set on self-destruction through drugs and alcohol. However, such performers are often as predictable as their polar opposites – it's just that they subscribe to a different rulebook. The careers of 'wayward geniuses' George Best and Paul Gascoigne, for example, both followed a trajectory from glorious self-expression to the depths of depression that was painfully predictable. The truly unconventional are a far more select group, comprising enigmatic figures who defy analysis, or give out contradictory signals. Boxer Chris Eubank was one such performer – Mark J. Williams is another.

The only left-handed world snooker champion and the first player since fellow Welshman Ray Reardon to enjoy two spells at the top of the world rankings, Williams has already made a significant mark. His virtues are plentiful: long and single-ball potting that is arguably the greatest of all time, nerves that appear to be composed of the purest Sheffield steel and a never-say-die instinct that ensures he seldom loses a major match without a fight.

Yet the Cwm-bred cueman divides fans and is as likely to arouse exasperation and indifference as respect and adulation. While many view Williams as down-to-earth and charming, others regard him as insufferably arrogant. Furthermore, the suspicion is often voiced that, for all his accomplishments, Williams merely sees snooker as a means to an end, a way of ensuring financial security. As he himself has said, 'I would be a liar to say that I am here to win tournaments; I am here to win as much money as I can out of the game.'[1]

Such comments might incur the wrath of purists, but Williams is resolutely his own man. He has little time for convention, particularly if it gets in the way of victory; hence his habit of regularly curtailing breaks with loose shots once a frame is secure. Statistics may not be motivating factors in his career, but his record is formidable nonetheless. Love him or loathe him, Williams can't be ignored.

Born on 21 March 1975 in Cardiff, he first picked up a cue at the age of ten after his father Dilwyn bought him a six-foot table for Christmas. By eleven, he was a regular on the tables of the Emporium Snooker Club in Bargoed, eight miles from his home village of Cwm. He represented Gwent at pool and often practised snooker for six hours a day, knocking in his first century at the age of thirteen. His skills so impressed Welsh factory worker Kevin Bohn that he asked a local bookmaker to give him odds on Williams becoming world snooker champion before 2001. The £140 Bohn invested at 300–1 reaped a windfall of £42,000 a decade later.

Williams was also a promising schoolboy boxer, winning 12 bouts out of 12 before he decided potting balls was a less painful vocation. His path towards a career in snooker was hastened when he followed his father down the pit for his first, and only, shift as a miner. The subterranean experience unnerved the 15 year old profoundly. 'It was pitch black,' he once recalled. 'It was the scariest thing I've ever experienced.'[2] After 12 hours in dark passageways and tunnels, getting covered in soot while rats crawled over him, Williams resolved never to return.

His experience of the pit sent him to the practice table with renewed vigour. An early taste of the big-time came at the 1991 World Masters at the National Exhibition Centre in Birmingham. An ambitious Barry Hearn endeavour with prize money of £1 million, the tournament was a snooker version of Wimbledon. There were men's and women's singles and doubles events, as well as mixed doubles. Williams reached the final of the junior event, only to fall 6–1 against John Higgins. He beat Higgins in the final of the UK Under-16 event, though, and also won the UK Under-19 title, while Matthew Stevens denied him in the Welsh Under-19 final.

The seventeen-year-old Williams turned professional in 1992 at the same time as two other future world champions – Ronnie O'Sullivan and the aforementioned Higgins. In contrast to the ultra-confident performer he later became, the teenage Williams was not averse to self-doubt. 'When I first turned professional, I dreamed of winning the World Championship, but realistically I never thought I would,' he admitted.[3]

O'Sullivan's autobiography provides a further insight into Williams's mindset at this age. He recalled how his father let the two youngsters drive his Mercedes round a car park near Blackpool, where the snooker qualifying school was held. Williams was in awe of the car, but when O'Sullivan senior told him he too would be able to afford such a luxury one day, the youngster shook his head.

The highlights of Williams's first two seasons on the circuit were a smattering of last-32 and last-16 appearances as he climbed from 119th to 58th in the world rankings. In 1994–95, he offered further hints of his potential by reaching the last sixteen of two ranking events, while on the non-ranking circuit he won the Benson & Hedges Championship, earning a wild card for the Masters. In the first round, he thrashed Willie Thorne 5–0, ensuring a healthy cheque for £11,000. The season ended with triumph in the Pontin's Open and a rise to 39th in the rankings. For all his progress, though, Williams was consistently falling short in the tournament that mattered most – the World Championship. From 1993 until 1995 he failed to qualify three times out of three, David Wilson, Billy Snaddon and Mark Davis denying him.

It was therefore something of an upset when Williams succeeded in lifting his first ranking title, the 1995–96 Welsh Open, without ever having played a competitive shot at the Crucible. His 9–3 victory against John Parrott in the final in Newport was impressive, but many critics were convinced Williams would be a one-hit wonder. Thorne even said as much from the commentary box as the Welshman lifted the trophy. Mind you, given the Leicester man's catalogue of gambling misfortunes, it was never the safest of tips.

Although defeat against Jamie Burnett ensured Williams once again failed to reach the Crucible in 1996, the Welsh Open win helped propel him to 16th in the rankings. With the grind of qualifying now over, Williams's career picked up pace. He lifted two ranking events in 1996–97 – the Grand Prix and the British Open – and was finally able to celebrate his Crucible debut. Appropriately enough, he beat his future mentor and countryman Terry Griffiths 10–9 in the first round in what was the veteran's final World Championship appearance.

Williams's challenge ended in the second round with a 13–8 defeat against Stephen Hendry, who was to become his greatest friend – and rival – on the circuit. As well as both being under the management of Ian Doyle, the two players share similar philosophies and mentalities. Both are suspicious of fame and if they are concerned about the public's perception of them, they never let it show. Williams also shares Hendry's highly competitive nature and bloody-minded determination to win on his own terms.

The two players combined to produce an electric Masters final in 1998. Williams, by now ranked fourth in the world, trailed 9–6, but fought back to level 9–9 before winning the final frame on a re-spotted black. This proved he had guts, but the consistency was not quite there yet, as was shown eight days later when he lost against the world No. 90, Peter Lines, in the Scottish Open. Astonishingly, it would be almost six years, and forty-eight matches, before he again lost his opening match of a ranking event.

Williams enjoyed his best World Championship performance to date in 1998, reaching the semi-finals before losing to Ken Doherty. The impression that he was a growing force in the game was reinforced by three ranking-tournament triumphs the following season and a first World Championship final appearance against Hendry. Swayed by Williams's impressive form – and a comparatively barren couple of seasons for his opponent – many tipped him to deny the Scotsman his coveted seventh world title. Williams certainly appeared confident; with typical bravado, he had been talking about buying a Ferrari if he won the title, and the press had a field day when they found out the car was already on order. If it was a statement of intent, it proved misplaced, as Hendry powered to an 18–11 win. Williams was never in front and the only time he was level with his opponent was when the match began.

Rather than let defeat deflate him, Williams drew strength from it. He gained a measure of revenge over Hendry the following season by knocking him out of the UK Championship in the semi-finals, a result that saw him move to the top of the provisional world rankings. His growing potency was further showcased by his 10–8 win in the final against fellow Welshman Stevens. Williams's ability to select the correct shot at the right time and win low-scoring, scrappy frames with crucial clearances ultimately proved the difference between the two men.

When Williams also progressed to the final of the Scottish Open (which he lost 9–1 to O'Sullivan), he found himself in the remarkable position of being guaranteed the No. 1 slot in the end-of-season rankings whatever happened at the Crucible. This placed him in danger of becoming snooker's first official No. 1 to have never won the sport's greatest prize, but the unflappable Welshman took it in his stride. 'All the pressure is off,' he claimed. 'Now I can give it a good go at Sheffield.'[4]

From the beginning of the 2000 World Championship, Williams oozed confidence and nonchalance. Fergal O'Brien was beaten 13–9 in the quarter-finals, then 1998 champion Higgins awaited in what proved to be a monumental semi-final encounter. At one stage, Higgins led 14–10, just three frames from victory, but Williams then showed what a tenacious competitor he is, winning four of the next five frames to cut the deficit to 15–14. The match ultimately hinged on a dramatic 30th frame. Higgins had the chance to re-establish a two-frame advantage but, having constructed a 55 break, a miss allowed Williams back to the table and he duly cleared up to draw level at 15–15.

Williams had broken Higgins's resistance and he won the next two frames with relative ease to set up a showdown with Stevens – the first all-Welsh final in World Championship history. 'I hadn't written myself off when I went 14–10 behind,' an elated Williams insisted after the semi-final. 'I played some good shots under pressure and I think I handled this a bit better than he did.'[5]

That performance ultimately gave him the confidence and will-power to fight back from an even more perilous position in the final. At the end of the first day, he trailed Stevens 10–6, a deficit which soon expanded to 13–7. However, with the title in his sights, Stevens, hitherto so fluent, suddenly saw his cue arm stiffen. Williams took merciless advantage, winning seven out of eight frames to level at 14–14. A 120 clearance in the 29th frame, his 11th century of the championship, edged Williams ahead, and from then the result was in little doubt, Williams clinching an 18–16 victory. His final shot of the championship, with which he slammed the black off the table, was a graceless conclusion, but as a defiant statement of his superiority it seemed strangely apt.

With a cheque for £240,000 in his pocket and Higgins, his nearest challenger in the world rankings, more than 10,000 points adrift, the snooker world was at Williams's feet. 'To be world No. 1 and world champion is something I have dreamed of since I was a kid,' he declared. 'It's a great day for Welsh snooker.'[6] Williams also gave an insight into the complex psychological approach that has made him such a formidable performer, adding, 'While Matthew had a big lead, I never gave up. I never thought for a minute that I was going to lose.'[7] It was a statement that appeared to directly contradict his comments the previous day when, 10–6 adrift, he had bemoaned, 'I felt drained out of my head. Somehow I have to try and stick with Matthew, but, if I feel the same tomorrow, I don't think I have much of a chance.'[8]

There is often more to what Williams says in interviews than meets the eye. Few players have been so self-critical in public as him; after his 2003 UK Championship exit against O'Brien, he declared, 'Other top players must watch me sometimes and laugh to themselves that I am world champion and world No. 1. I can play so badly at times that it is frightening.'[9]

By downplaying his own ability ('I can't be classed in the same bracket as Hendry and [Steve] Davis' was his assessment of his second world title[10]), Williams seems able to liberate his play from the pressures that force many players to crumble. Whether it is a calculated strategy or merely a subconscious mental action, such an approach goes a long way to explaining Williams's outstanding record in high-pressure situations and his ability to rescue lost causes. To quote Davis's famous maxim, he is able to play as if it means nothing when it means everything.

To extend this theory, when he plays down his own chances, Williams is also encouraging others to dismiss him, thus providing him with the motivation to confound his critics. 'I have been shutting people up throughout my career,' he said in 2004. 'When I won my first tournament, people were saying I would never win another one. Then when I won the world title, it was the same story – there were a few saying I would never win it again. It feels good that I have proved them all wrong.'[11]

In the wake of his 2000 world title, Williams's preparation for the following season was far from ideal. He was fortunate to escape injury while on holiday in Thailand, when he was crushed between two golf buggies, and after returning home was bitten several times on his left hand by his Rottweiler. They were the portents to an unhappy season. Although Williams added another Grand Prix to his list of ranking tournament victories, Higgins beat him easily 10–4 in the final of the UK Championship.

He also fell victim to the 'Crucible curse', which has seen no first-time champion successfully defend his world title, falling 13–12 to Joe Swail in the second round. Williams diagnosed his problem as too much practice. 'I'm not taking the game so seriously in future,' he said afterwards. 'I've worked hard at my game all season and I'm still playing crap. I'll spend a bit more time playing golf and fishing.'[12]

The following season he played better, but appeared to have lost the knack of winning the matches that mattered most. Back-to-back ranking-title victories at the China Open and Thailand Masters were no consolation for a 10–9 reverse against Paul Hunter in the Masters final (a match Williams had led 5–0) and another second-round exit at the World Championship, this time to Anthony Hamilton. The latter defeat spelt the end of Williams's two-year reign at the top of the world rankings and he was so demoralised he claimed he felt like crashing his Ferrari into a brick wall.

Williams's form was probably not helped by political ructions within the game, which saw him and Hendry get caught in fierce crossfire. Longstanding grudges and grievances had exploded to the surface in 2001 when the two players, together with their management group, 110sport, took the WPBSA to the high court. The governing body were ultimately found to have abused their dominant position by not giving their players the freedom to choose which tournaments they participated in. For a while, a split in the pro ranks and the establishment of a rival snooker circuit looked likely, but in November 2002 a group of players, again led by Hendry and Williams, failed in their bid to install Altium as the game's financial arm, rather than World Snooker Enterprises.

This infighting spelt the end of Williams's affection for the players' lounge and created divisions between many professionals, with Hendry and Williams on one side, and Peter Ebdon, Higgins and O'Sullivan among those opposing their views. 'A lot of players don't get on now,' Williams has admitted.[13] He seldom hangs around in tournament venues now after the completion of his matches, preferring to keep his own counsel.

Back on the table, Williams's career got a much-needed overhaul as the 2002–03 season approached, when he brought in Griffiths as his coach. The 1979 world champion had accumulated a wealth of experience concerning the psychology of snooker and his presence in Williams's corner soon helped his protégé regain his hitherto impressive mindset. At the UK Championship, Hendry was thrashed 9–2 in the quarter-finals and world champion Peter Ebdon 9–3 in the semi-finals.

In the final, Williams led Doherty 9–7, only for the Irishman to level the match at 9–9. After a prolonged safety exchange, Doherty pocketed the white and Williams took advantage with a 70 clearance to secure his first major title on British soil for 26 months. 'I kept a clear head throughout and that was mostly down to Terry and the way that he has been helping me along,' Williams said of Griffiths's influence.[14]

Doherty and Williams were to meet again in the final of the World Championship a little over four months later, with the Welshman starting the match as a hot favourite. Since the UK Championship, he had also added a second Masters title to his cabinet and his form in Sheffield had been imperious, with Stuart Pettman, Quinten Hann, Hendry and Stephen Lee beaten for the loss of just 19 frames. In his match against Hann, Williams had won an incredible 13 successive frames, a Crucible record, after falling 2–0 behind.

Doherty's more tortuous route to the final had seen him complete a marathon 98 frames, compared with Williams's 72, so it was little wonder that the Irishman looked exhausted as Williams sped 10–2 and 11–5 ahead. Nevertheless, Doherty fought back with incredible tenacity and succeeded in levelling the match at 12–12, 14–14 and then 16–16.

It was now anyone's title, but, displaying laudable composure, Williams dug in to take a nervy 33rd frame 96–28. At 43 points ahead in the next, he responded to a Doherty safety by outrageously doubling a red into the middle pocket and maintaining position for the black. A 77 break followed and the title, as well as the No. 1 ranking, were his once again. Williams's immediate reaction to the nerve-jangling victory on live television was understandable. 'I was shitting myself,' he declared. 'At 16–16, I was singing songs in my head. I think Tom Jones's "Delilah" was in my head. I was just trying to take my mind off the arena and the crowd.'[15]

The victory made Williams the third man, after Hendry and Davis, to win the triple crown of UK, Masters and world titles in one season and he later revealed that Griffiths's wise counselling had again helped usher him past the winning post. 'Terry said that if you're under pressure, the main thing is to realise it and not kid yourself,' he said.[16]

At the beginning of his next campaign, Williams lifted the LG Cup, meaning he was now holder of all four tournaments televised by the BBC. The rest of 2003–04 was a disappointment, although there were mitigating factors. A first-round exit at the UK was followed by a second-round reverse against Joe Perry in the World Championship, then the loss of the No. 1 ranking to O'Sullivan, with whom Williams is barely on speaking terms these days. Shortly before the Perry defeat, Williams had become a father for the first time, although he sportingly did not cite this as an excuse.

It is difficult to escape the conclusion that, as he enters his 30s, Williams's career is at something of a crossroads. Now firmly part of the snooker establishment (he received an MBE in 2004), Williams has already achieved enough to be considered one of the greatest players of all time and has the potential to soar higher still in the pantheon of the game's champions.

At times, though, Williams's attitude to snooker seems to be contradictory, schizophrenic even. He does not care for fame and has little time for snooker conventions, yet he would never have achieved the things he has without snooker, or a deep love for it. Nevertheless, it is possible to judge Williams too harshly. His conduct is not always impeccable and he can be graceless, but these are characteristics shared by many other champions. Besides, there is also something appealing about his rawness and the fact that he is still happy to play at his old club as one of the lads.

More than perhaps any other great cueman, Williams possesses the ability to keep snooker in perspective. This will probably make him happier in retirement than many of his contemporaries, but, with financial security and his family uppermost in his mind, will Williams's ability to achieve further great feats on the table be compromised? His coach Griffiths has admitted, 'Mark can do whatever he wants to do. He's got the skill, he's got the temperament – it's just a matter of whether he can keep the motivation.'[17]

Williams himself has declared: 'If I never win another world title, or even if I never win another tournament, I will still be happy because I've achieved more in the game than I ever thought I would.'[18] It is certainly hard to imagine a past-his-peak Williams toiling on the circuit as a veteran. However, only the brave or the foolhardy would write him off just yet; Williams is in the enviable position of being able to play free from the expectation that players who have never won the World Championship, or won it only once, often labour under. Realistically, he should remain at, or around, the summit of the sport for at least another five years. Only then, with the benefit of perspective, might snooker historians be able to distinguish the real Mark J. Williams from the enigmatic shadow that currently envelops him.

NINETEEN

RONNIE O'SULLIVAN

A Mystery Wrapped in an Enigma . . .

Ronnie O'Sullivan's timing was perfect. Snooker, although still boasting impressive television viewing figures, was suffering a dip in popularity during the early 1990s. Stephen Hendry, head and shoulders above the rest, was unstoppable and could afford to win a string of matches without producing his best until it really mattered.

The fun and eccentric characters who lit up the 1980s such as Bill Werbeniuk, Willie Thorne, Tony Knowles and Kirk Stevens were a distant memory, as was the prospect of another 'Snooker Loopy' taking the charts by storm. An era of ultra-professionalism was under way, with serious players fighting for the scraps that Hendry occasionally left behind. Crowd favourite Jimmy White kept on losing to the ruthless Scotsman in world finals, giving the tournament a predictable feel.

But before fears that the game was going stale could really settle in, a stream of young talent came bursting out of Wales, Scotland and England simultaneously, quality which the sport is still benefiting from today. Mark Williams from Cwm was making headlines with his stunning potting skills, a young lad by the name of John Higgins was knocking in centuries like there was no tomorrow north of the border in Wishaw, while in Essex there were rumours going around that a fearless teenager, hungry for success and using his cue like a magic wand, was about to take the game into a new stratosphere. Exciting times lay ahead.

White was still a serious world-title contender, but the adrenalin rush the game enjoyed when he first burst onto the scene had long gone, as had the maverick charm of Alex Higgins. Now there was a new, erratic talent waiting to make his mark, carrying a bad-boy image the snooker-loving public would later adore, but one which O'Sullivan himself was never quite sure whether to immerse himself in or keep his distance from.

The story of Ronnie O'Sullivan, despite its obvious similarities to those of the immensely popular Higgins and White, is unique. It's tempting to pigeon-hole him, as many journalists have, as one of those players whose extreme natural ability coincided with – or even depended on – his colourful off-table lifestyle. But as we'll see in this chapter, the story of O'Sullivan isn't that simple. Two things are certain – first, he deserves his own pedestal, free from White and Higgins, as a player who has offered so much to the game while always being forced to publicly share his ongoing bouts of psychological highs and lows; second, of course, is that there's so much of the story still to come.

Although famous for his Essex roots, O'Sullivan was born on 5 December 1975 in Birmingham, where his parents, Ronnie senior and Maria, moved shortly after marrying. The couple put their names down for a council flat in London soon after Ronnie's birth and when one became available in Dalston, they headed south. Maria got work as a waitress, while Ronnie senior started working in sex shops. It wasn't long before he opened his first shop in Berwick Street and he never looked back, setting up a string of stores, some of which were for his brothers to run, since he liked to involve the family. The young O'Sullivan was often given the job of cleaning his dad's car.

Ronnie's fascination with snooker started when he began playing on his uncle's 6x3-foot table when he was about seven. He was then given a table of his own as a Christmas present and it wasn't long before his practice became an addiction. When O'Sullivan was eight, his dad took him to the Ambassador's Club in the West End, where the youngster played on a ten-footer before eventually moving up to a full-size table.

By this stage, the family were living in Ilford and O'Sullivan joined a local club at Green Lanes, where he annoyed some of the other members with his lippy attitude and habit of throwing food around while eating his dinner. 'When I was little, I could be a pest,' he later admitted. 'Eventually, I learned that I had to keep my mouth shut – but it took me some time.'[1]

But he got into more serious scrapes than that. At a Pontin's holiday camp tournament in Brean Sands, O'Sullivan, being chased by a fellow player who was older than him, smashed a glass across the floor in an attempt to stop his assailant. Another guest complained and tournament referee John Williams ordered O'Sullivan from the site and banned him from all Pontin's events for a year (later reduced to six months). The story even made *The Sun* and O'Sullivan, at the age of ten, had taken his first step up the bad-boy ladder.

However, it was at that same age when he also took a significant leap on the way to snooker brilliance, becoming the youngest player to compile a century break, even keeping his cool to clear the table for a 117 at a club in Barking. He was also working hard to improve his attitude around the table. 'Nothing used to wind me up like snooker,' he admitted. 'I'd be f-ing and blinding whenever I missed a shot.'[2]

The word 'temperament' has gone hand in hand with O'Sullivan ever since he first appeared on our television screens. He certainly doesn't have the best one in the world, but it's hardly the worst either. Unfortunately, many analysts over the years have been tempted to use the lazy stereotype that, because of his 'poor temperament', he is either brilliant or terrible, with no in-between.

As his career has progressed, O'Sullivan has often dug in to get over the finishing line if playing below par. He may not have the 'B' game of players like Mark Williams, but O'Sullivan has proved time and time again that he is prepared to battle and focus. Even in his younger days, there are plenty of examples of him beating less-skilled opponents in the early rounds of tournaments by more than simply out-potting them.

Many pundits have also glossed over the consistency of his excellent safety play, claiming that, like many young, quick break-builders, O'Sullivan had no patience to learn and develop a safety game. Again, utter nonsense. O'Sullivan's deft touch, which he uses for position when building big breaks, is also used to perfection many times when playing a long safety. He has shown frustration at the table, once injuring his foot when kicking a plant pot, but that anger rarely, if ever, comes from being bogged down in a safety exchange – more often than not he is annoyed with himself for missing a pot he expects to make.

Building on that first century break, O'Sullivan went on to win the £450 first prize in an Under-16s tournament when he was 11. His dad, with the sex-shop empire thriving, then built him his own snooker room at the bottom of their garden, complete with its own toilet, settee and television.

At 14, O'Sullivan made a major breakthrough by winning a big pro-am tournament in Stevenage, beating Marcel Gavreau, the world No. 34 at the time, and Anthony Hamilton on the way. O'Sullivan was by now making serious waves, but attracted some criticism on the snooker circuit. A few of his rivals claimed his dad's money and the advantages that came with it (i.e. his own snooker room) were the reasons why he was doing so well and beating a stack of older players. O'Sullivan reacted to this envy in the best way possible – by shrugging it off, keeping up the meticulous day-to-day practice and playing as many matches as he had time for. 'As I grew up, I became increasingly passionate about snooker, about winning,' he said. 'You can't be a champion without having that hunger.'[3]

This desire came to the fore when O'Sullivan, at 15 years old, became the youngest player to compile a recognised maximum 147 break.[4] That same year, he was in Thailand competing in the World Amateur Championship when suddenly his world turned upside down. His mum rang him from home to tell him his dad had been arrested. There had been a fight in a Chelsea nightclub and someone had been killed. Ronnie senior was charged with murder.

When he was released on bail a few months later, he travelled to Blackpool to watch his son try and qualify for his first World Championship. It was the boost O'Sullivan needed and he won his early-round matches before beating Mark Johnston-Allen in the final qualifying round in September 1992. But when his dad returned to London for the trial, he was found guilty of murder and sentenced to life. The judge recommended Ronnie senior should serve eighteen years, six more than average, amid claims the crime was racially motivated – something the O'Sullivan family have always vehemently denied.

Young Ronnie was in bits, not just at the disappointment of losing his father, but also because he felt the length of the sentence was an injustice. 'He shouldn't be serving any more than the normal tariff,' he said years later. 'Sometimes I think he received such a harsh sentence because he was my dad and I was well known, and also because his business was sex shops.'[5]

The loss of his father is something that has had a huge effect on O'Sullivan's life, and still hangs over him. The suspicion of being persecuted because of his fame has never quite left him and has led him into altercations with authority figures over the years. 'His biggest problem is his dad, to whom he is deeply attached,' wrote Mordecai Richler. 'Ronnie junior believes his father was shafted, [that] the cops had it in for him because he was a porn dealer.'[6]

That sense of loss and injustice at such a crucial time in both his professional and personal life would have hit anyone hard, but O'Sullivan seems to have been affected particularly badly. 'It quickly turned him from a cheerful young lad with a vast talent and not a care in the world into a young man who soon became so engulfed in problems that he sank into despair,' wrote *Snooker Scene* editor Clive Everton.[7]

Because he is in the public eye, O'Sullivan is regularly urged to discuss his personal ordeals in the media. He deals with it in a variety of ways – sometimes putting on a brave face, saying he's just got to get on with it as that's what his dad's doing, while at other times he admits to being cut up and thinking of giving up the game. After knocking in five centuries on his way to beating Alan McManus in the UK Championship in November 2003, he revealed he was struggling to deal with unresolved emotional issues, saying, 'I sat in the bath during the interval crying my eyes out for 20 minutes because there is stuff I can't deal with. I've not fallen out with snooker, but there are things I can't handle and it's crippling me.'[8]

In coping with personal anguish in regular doses over a long period of time while also trying to perform in public, O'Sullivan has been put in a situation few sports stars have experienced, but somehow he has still managed to mix this vulnerability with a fair degree of consistency. He has been in the world's top four every year since 1998, while in his first professional season, 1992–93, he won his first 38 matches and went on to win a staggering 74 out of 76 – a record, of course, and further proof that his 'inconsistent' tag can be some way off the mark. This moved him up to No. 57 in the world after just one year on the circuit.

In November 1993, O'Sullivan reached new heights by becoming the youngest player, a week shy of his 18th birthday, to win a world-ranking event, the UK Championship in Preston. In front of a live television audience, the man snooker MC Alan Hughes had just dubbed 'The Rocket' produced a supremely accomplished performance to beat world No. 1 Hendry 10–6 in the final, picking up £70,000 for his trouble.

O'Sullivan was being praised in all quarters for his bravery and fluency, and had moved into the world's top 16. He won the British

Open the following April and was by then regular back-page material and one of the most popular players around. But with the extra attention came more questions about his private life. O'Sullivan decided to be open about things, announcing that his dad would be running his fan club and that all post should be sent to him at D-wing, Wormwood Scrubs. 'Journalists seemed surprised that I was so upfront about Dad. I don't know if they expected me to deny that he was inside,' he said. 'I did sound so confident . . . but most of it was front. Inside I was doing the opposite. I was crying like a baby, and I was beginning to crack up.'[9]

Things got worse in 1994 when his mum, looking after her husband's business, was arrested for tax evasion, increasing O'Sullivan's fears that there was a police vendetta against the family. She was later sentenced to a year in prison and served seven months, leaving O'Sullivan to take care of his little sister, Danielle. He was 19 and she just 12, and it was a struggle. A family friend later helped out, looking after Danielle, but the burden was still weighing heavily on O'Sullivan's shoulders. He occasionally turned to dope, went on drinking and food binges, and his form fluctuated. He discovered he could be addicted to anything if the mood took him and, at one stage, when hooked on takeaway food, he regularly rang up taxi firms and got them to pick up a giant order from McDonald's and drive it round to him.

His weight went up to nearly 16 stone in 1996, but he still managed to reach the furthest he ever had at the World Championship, edging past John Higgins 13–12 in an exhilarating quarter-final before losing out to Peter Ebdon in the last four. It was also at this tournament that O'Sullivan's feud with authority reached boiling point. He was with his then coach and mentor, Del Hill, in the players' lounge when press officer Mike Ganley told Hill to leave because he was wearing jeans. A frustrated O'Sullivan head-butted Ganley, who reported the incident immediately. The Rocket was fined £30,000 and received a suspended two-year ban.

Shortly after the Higgins quarter-final, a former girlfriend of O'Sullivan's claimed he was the father of her baby daughter, Taylor. O'Sullivan denied it at first, but started paying for her maintenance after a blood test proved positive. With all these off-table troubles, he still managed to perform magic amongst the balls on a fairly regular basis. Just as he could gain weight, O'Sullivan would lose it almost as quickly by putting himself through ruthless fitness regimes when the mood took him. He was either feeling very positive about himself and sticking to rigorous circuit training, or he was back on a food or drink binge and spending too much time in nightclubs.

As in his 1996 campaign, his assault on the 1997 world title was a story of ups and downs. In his first-round match against Mick Price, O'Sullivan created another piece of history which he himself believes will never be repeated – scoring a maximum 147 break in 5 minutes 20 seconds, the fastest ever by some distance. With a £147,000 reward, as well as £18,000 for the tournament's highest break, it worked out that he was earning £515 a second.

The images of him racing around the table, dropping his chalk when clearing the colours but refusing to pick it up as it would break his momentum, are repeated year after year on television and are firmly cast in Crucible folklore. Spectators were stunned by the sheer physical achievement of knocking in 36 pots with perfect position in such a short space of time. But the hysteria soon died down when he was knocked out 13–12 by a determined Darren Morgan in the second round. The army of fans waiting to see O'Sullivan lift the game's greatest prize would have to wait at least another year.

Before he headed back to the Crucible, there was another bout of controversy to wade through at the Irish Masters in March 1998. On a night out with friends during the tournament, O'Sullivan had tried a piece of 'puff cake' that was doing the rounds. 'It gave me the giggles and I was buzzing. It was a bad decision,' he later admitted.[10] He went on to beat Ken Doherty in the final, but tested positive for cannabis in his post-match drugs test. A disciplinary board later stripped him of the title and handed the winner's cheque to Doherty. O'Sullivan actually found out he had failed the test while in Sheffield that year at the quarter-final stage. He managed to get through to the semis, but was well beaten by a free-flowing John Higgins, who was unstoppable in his pursuit of the title.

O'Sullivan, at heart an open and perhaps easily led young man, often feels the pressure of what others expect of him. He has always been eager to please, like taking a bite of puff cake and going with the flow rather than be the only one in his group of friends to reject it.

In 1998, desperate to find a cure for his regular bouts of depression, he sought professional help. He was referred to sports psychotherapist Mike Brearley, the former England cricket captain, but O'Sullivan soon stopped the sessions, feeling he wasn't gaining any quick results. There was more drink and dope, not to mention anguish at upsetting his parents, who were constantly encouraging him to pick himself up from the floor and get himself together. His lows were getting lower and he wasn't sure if snooker was the source of the problem or the cure. After a heavy drink-and-dope bender in Ireland, O'Sullivan pulled out of the UK Championship, a title he was defending, citing exhaustion.

However, his form picked up for the 1999 World Championship, where he reached the semi-finals against Hendry. More than just playing his part in a fabulous match full of high-quality action, O'Sullivan only missed out on another 147 on the pink before Hendry eventually ground him down in the final session on his way to a seventh world crown.

By 2000, O'Sullivan decided it was time to step up his efforts on his road to salvation. Following the disappointing results of his time spent with Brearley, he went into The Priory in Roehampton for a month to take on the Twelve Steps Programme in a bid to ditch his addiction to smoking joints. He was in two minds at first and even left for home on his third day in frustration, but returned within four hours to see it through. By speaking to other patients and trained therapists on a daily basis, he learned a lot more about himself, about being an addict, and about how to accept it and how best to deal with it.

In the first tournament of his return, the Champions Cup, he came from 4–1 down in the final against Mark Williams to take the trophy 7–5 and celebrated with a cup of tea. After leaving The Priory, he enjoyed eight months of total abstinence before lapsing, but it seems from this point on the lapses came at less regular intervals. He was dealing with them better, knowing how important it was to keep the number of binges under control, but not beating himself up about it too much when he did slip up. He accepted it was a constant battle, kept going to local Narcotics Anonymous meetings and recognised the groundwork that needed to be put in. By this time in his mid-20s, a more reflective and laid-back O'Sullivan was starting to act more maturely both on and off the table.

The following year, O'Sullivan achieved what many fans, with Jimmy White in mind, feared he never would – triumph at the World Championship – and he did it the hard way. Going into the tournament, he wasn't drinking or smoking, but was feeling depressed, suffering from anxiety and panic attacks, and couldn't figure out why. Del took him to a doctor, to whom O'Sullivan admitted he had contemplated suicide several times. The doctor recommended Prozac tablets and convinced O'Sullivan to give them a proper go.

He hadn't taken any of the tablets by the opening Saturday of the championship, when he phoned the Samaritans for help. After that, he revealed in a radio interview that he wasn't feeling up to playing in the tournament and would be relieved when it was over.

But he had now developed a dogged style of snooker which enabled him to win matches without his 'A' game when necessary. After an easy win over Andy Hicks in round one, he eventually gave the Prozac a try, despite warnings that it could affect his game by making him dizzy, sick or high. Unlike his previous experiments with marijuana, Prozac was perfectly legal, and it seemed to work in his second-round match against Dave Harold, which he won 13–6, again without playing particularly well, but the style of victory didn't bother him – a win was a win.

O'Sullivan was feeling more comfortable, both with his play and the effects of the Prozac, by the time he faced Peter Ebdon in the quarter-finals and cruised through 13–6. 'Prozac gave me the confidence to think about my game in the same way any other player might,' he later revealed. 'I was thinking objectively for the first time in four or five years.'[11] After the match, Ebdon conceded he had been well beaten and added, 'Ronnie was just superb. I think he's snooker's equivalent to Mozart.'[12]

He beat Joe Swail 17–11 in the semi-finals before taking on Higgins in the final. O'Sullivan, fully prepared in mind and body, took it a session at a time, 6–2 up, then 10–6. By now, he was completely at ease with the Prozac and was full of energy. He ended the third session 14–10 up and the pressure of emulating White as the best player never to win the sport's biggest prize was now a long way off.

They shared the next six frames to go 17–13 before O'Sullivan wasted a great chance to wrap it all up in the next frame when he missed a simple red, allowing Higgins in to reduce his arrears to 17–14. In the next frame it was Higgins's turn to miss a straightforward red and O'Sullivan nipped in to clinch an 18–14 win and the world title at the age of 25. His hero, White, was backstage to join in the celebrations which lasted well into the next morning. Ronnie O'Sullivan, the man who couldn't face the world two weeks previously, was now on top of it. 'It buried so many demons,' he revealed. 'If I'd finished my career and never won it, there would have always been a little cloud over me.'[13]

There was more success the following season when he won the UK Championship, pulverising Ken Doherty 10–1 in the final, proving once again what a force he was when ahead. O'Sullivan's ability to kill off matches also dispels another common myth about him – that, because of his struggle to deal with his off-table problems, he lacks mental toughness.

Of course, O'Sullivan has lost matches that have turned into psychological battles over the years, as have all players, but to suggest he lacks strength upstairs is ludicrous. His record of winning matches when in front is way above average. Many a time players freeze when in sight of the finishing line, but O'Sullivan just speeds up. His potting and break-building skills are well documented, but he should be recognised as one of the most commanding front-runners snooker has ever seen.

To show that kind of confidence in your own ability when you're winning and therefore expected to wrap up the match is hardly the sign of a fragile mind. It is also another example of how O'Sullivan, a proven performer on the big stage, refuses to fit the traditional 'wayward genius' stereotype of 'big on talent, small on bottle'.

He continued to show marvellous consistency in his game following the thrashing of Doherty, but, in terms of world titles, 2002 wasn't to be his year. Attempting to become the first player to successfully defend the World Championship at the first time of asking at the Crucible, he fell just short.

He was looking good until the semi-finals, where he lost to a resilient Hendry. The Scot's own motivation to win was, in all probability, boosted by some ill-judged and unwarranted comments O'Sullivan made before the match. He said he wanted to 'beat Hendry up' and send him back to his 'sad little life' in Scotland. O'Sullivan had spent the hours before those interviews in the gym with a friend, the boxer Prince Naseem Hamed, and by his own admission had got carried away. The whole episode upset Hendry and the two have hardly spoken since, despite O'Sullivan showing regret over his actions in later interviews.

There had been a fair bit of needle between the pair even before that incident, stemming from their aforementioned world semi-final in 1999. O'Sullivan was left fuming after Hendry made him play a shot again following a snooker, suggesting, O'Sullivan felt, that he had missed the ball deliberately.

O'Sullivan's Crucible experience of 2003 was back to the days of immediate highs and lows. He didn't get the chance to build a run after falling at the first hurdle to Hong Kong's Marco Fu, but he still managed to create history, knocking in another 147 break – although not as fast as his momentous effort in 1997 – to become the first player to compile two maximums at the World Championship. The fact that there have only been five in total since the tournament began in 1927, and O'Sullivan is responsible for two of them, shows just how far he has taken the game and the high standards that future players will be up against.

The 2003–04 season got off to a surreal start when newspapers reported that O'Sullivan had converted to Islam over the summer. He later explained that he hadn't, at least not intentionally, and the reports were a misunderstanding of a ceremony in which he had taken part. He went along with some Muslim friends to a London mosque and was asked to repeat some words after them, which he did. 'I thought it was just a social thing, their way of welcoming a stranger,' he was quoted as saying in *Snooker Scene*. 'I'm the kind of person who doesn't want to offend and I just thought I'd keep everyone happy, then politely leave.'[14]

Confusion reigned off the table, but not on it. O'Sullivan won the Welsh Open and reached the final of the British Open and the Masters, playing some diligent and steady snooker. During that Masters tournament, he revealed he had gone seven months without alcohol or cigarettes (an impressive spell of abstinence instigated after a six-week drinking bender the previous summer following his Crucible defeat to Fu) and that he was taking his running more seriously than ever before, now doing about 35 miles a week.

Later in 2004 he even talked about using his left-handed shots in a more deceptive fashion. Many journalists had claimed O'Sullivan had been disrespectful towards his opponents by playing sporadic spells of matches left-handed. However, it was more a signal of him being annoyed with his own game than anything else. Now O'Sullivan was contemplating using his left hand even when playing well, in an effort to shake things up and make it harder for opponents to figure out his state of mind. It was a further sign of his increasing aptitude and desire to seize the psychological stranglehold on a match.

This tactic was highlighted a few months later at the Crucible, where he changed between his left and right hand so seamlessly it was often difficult to tell the difference. During his first two matches, though, O'Sullivan caused controversy once again, this time for his table manners. He raised his middle finger at a pocket after missing a shot in his opening match against Stephen Maguire and in the next round made an obscene hand gesture (aimed at either himself or the table again) after running out of position on a 39 break. This unacceptable behaviour led to the BBC receiving a number of complaints, while new WPBSA chairman, Sir Rodney Walker, voiced his disapproval. However, despite these ructions, O'Sullivan was playing outstandingly well. He had proved his consistency that season by winning the inaugural £50,000 LG Electronics Order of Merit[15] and was playing with stubborn authority and excellence. A 10–6 victory over European Open champion Maguire was an impressive result, as was his 13–11 second-round win over an inspired Andy Hicks, who was playing some of the best snooker of his career.[16]

It was in his next match, a quarter-final against Anthony Hamilton, that O'Sullivan ditched the occasional rude conduct and produced sublime play throughout. The 2001 champion triumphed 13–3 with a session to spare, outplaying Hamilton in every department. But the best was yet to come. O'Sullivan's semi-final against Hendry was billed as a clash of the titans, but it ended up being a walkover. The Essex man, playing some delightful snooker with a supreme effectiveness that even Hendry in his prime would have struggled with, powered home 17–4. If that wasn't enough, winning that semi-final ensured O'Sullivan snatched back the world No. 1 spot.

Against surprise finalist Graeme Dott, O'Sullivan, despite his break-building not being as impressive as it was against Hendry, maintained his focus to win 18–8, having been 5–0 down. Dott simply couldn't cope with his overwhelming long-safety game. It may not have been as tense as his final victory over Higgins three years previously, but this one had been won by setting even higher standards. There was no doubt O'Sullivan had been the player of the tournament and no one since Hendry in the mid-1990s had made winning the Crucible crown look such a certainty.

On the eve of the tournament, O'Sullivan, now 28, enlisted Ray Reardon as a coach and the six-time world champion seemed to have had a positive effect. After letting out his frustrations in those first two matches, O'Sullivan had seemed to get stronger as the tournament went on, displaying patience, fluency and determination in equal measure. As clear favourite throughout the final week of the event, he appeared to relish the expectancy laid upon him. And all of this came just a few weeks after making yet another threat to quit during the Irish Masters, when he said he was fed up with being at tournaments and was wondering whether snooker was what he really wanted to do. The mood swings were clearly not going to go away, but his domination at the Crucible proved he was still maturing, something he admitted himself in Dublin: 'I'm a true professional. I apply myself instead of bashing the balls about, so I suppose it's not all bad.'[17]

A self-labelled perfectionist, O'Sullivan wanted so much from the game, and has taken so much from it, but still doesn't know whether to laugh or cry. A troubled soul, tortured inside since his dad was sent to prison, life has dished him some incredible highs and devastating lows, and all he has tried to do is stay on the tracks, remain true to himself and be surrounded by the people he wants to be with. No other player in this book has been blessed with the same strengths, hampered by the same weaknesses nor dealt such a rough hand of fate.

Triumphs have been achieved, mistakes have been made, but there is no doubt he has come out the other side stronger and wiser. His mood swings may still be erratic, but he constantly speaks of taking it one day at a time in an attempt to keep on the straight and narrow. The story of Ronnie O'Sullivan is an elaborate maze – but at its core lies a somewhat complex young man, forever seeking happiness but not knowing where to find it, always wanting to impress and win people over, and a unique snooker player who will be remembered for a very long time.

TWENTY

PETER EBDON

Thinking of Newton's Cradle

Journalists and fans alike have always found it difficult to pigeon-hole Peter Ebdon. Never what you would call a typical snooker player, he has consistently separated himself from the rest of the pros, never quite fitting into any media-suited niche, always possessing a unique look and attitude about him. Passionate, committed and talented are certainly all accurate tags that have been attached to him over the years, while his intense mental approach to the game has earned him the nickname 'Psycho'.

Bursting onto the world scene in 1992 sporting a glitzy waistcoat and a long ponytail, fans welcomed his youthful, explosive energy. As the years went by, Ebdon's image gradually turned into one of ardent concentration as the pace of his game slowed down (brought on partly by problems with his cue action) and he became one of the most gritty players on the circuit.

His immense inner application only bubbled to the surface occasionally, but when it did, it came with tumultuous results. The image of him erupting with joy after rolling in a crucial long black during a World Championship match against Stephen Lee in 2001 is what many remember when thinking of Ebdon. Fists pumping, veins looking set to burst out of his shining forehead and several earsplitting shouts of 'Come on!' were met with a mixture of shock and bemusement. No other player had ever shown such emotion at the table and the outburst only added to Ebdon's peculiar demeanour.

He stood out from the start. Born in London, he grew up in Islington and stubbornly supported Tottenham despite going to a school half a mile away from Arsenal's home ground, Highbury. He was also a fan of classical music and decided to take up the oboe ('It wasn't the normal instrument that everybody played and I was drawn to that'[1]). There was no history of snooker in the family – his father was an accomplished cricketer who worked for Surrey's ground staff, while he also played darts semi-pro. It wasn't until Ebdon's parents bought him a snooker cue for his 14th birthday that he first took up the game.

He refused to blend in even then. While most players showed up for pro-am tournaments in jeans and a T-shirt, Ebdon strode in complete with wing-collar shirt, cufflinks, immaculately ironed trousers, bow tie and waistcoat. He looked different, but he didn't care. What concerned him was playing well and if that meant dressing like a professional, that's what he did. He was one of the best juniors around in the late 1980s, winning the £1,500 first prize in a national handicap tournament when he was 16 during the 1986–87 season. After that, he became a regular winner of events and soon built up a reputation as one of the most feared amateurs in the country. He enjoyed a particularly successful season in 1988–89, winning the Rothmans Amateur Championship and the Pontin's Open, beating Ken Doherty in the final. It was around this time that Ebdon and his wife Deborah moved out of London to a more central base in Northamptonshire, settling down in Wellingborough, where his manager Keith Warren now also lives.

Success continued apace in 1989–90, when Ebdon lifted the World Under-21 Championship and he eventually turned professional in 1991. During his debut season, he qualified for every ranking event bar two. His furthest run was to the last 16 at the Grand Prix until he made a major name for himself at the Crucible. In the opening round, he was drawn against Steve Davis, still a formidable performer and ranked No. 2 in the world. Ebdon took the first frame with a 92 break before the six-time champion recovered to lead 4–3. But Ebdon, delighting the crowd with an array of flash pots as well as proficient shot selection, racked up seven successive frames to take the match 10–4 as a stunned Davis could do nothing to halt the tide. The youngster managed to produce another impressive surge in his second-round match against Martin Clark. Tied at 4–4, Ebdon won nine frames in a row to go through 13–4. In his quarter-final against Terry Griffiths, Ebdon compiled three centuries but eventually bowed out to the veteran 13–7.

However, Ebdon's impressive first season saw him rise to No. 47 in the world rankings and named WPBSA Young Player of the Year. He enjoyed another fruitful campaign in 1992–93, reaching the last sixteen in four tournaments. In the opening half of the following season, he clinched his first ranking title, beating his old amateur rival Doherty 9–6 in the final of the Grand Prix. That performance, and a run to the last four in the Regal Welsh, saw him break into the top 16. His rise up the game's ladder seemed relentless.

In 1994–95, he beat Stephen Hendry to lift the Irish Masters crown, while during the next season he progressed further than ever before at the Crucible. After beating Dene O'Kane 10–1, Ebdon needed a 123 break in the deciding frame of his second-round match to sneak past Jimmy White 13–12. A quarter-final victory over Davis was followed by an enduring 16–14 win over Ronnie O'Sullivan in the last four, which put him in his first world final. His opponent was Hendry, who had beaten Ebdon 10–3 in the UK Championship final earlier that season and was fishing for his sixth world crown. Ebdon was always behind and didn't have the reserves of energy or the experience to catch the Scot, who won 18–12. Although he was no slouch, Ebdon admitted years later that a lack of physical stamina had played its part. 'My fitness deficiency was one reason I look back on the final and think I wasn't quite ready to win it. I promised myself next time I got there I'd do whatever it takes to win,' he said.[2]

He would have to wait some time for that chance again, but in 1996–97 he made do with the Thailand Open crown, his second ranking title, and victory at the invitational Scottish Masters. However, four opening-round defeats that season signified the beginning of a tough period in Ebdon's career. He began to get bogged down with his cue action, a process which in itself often expands the problem, and slipped down the rankings. One semi-final and two quarter-final appearances were all he could manage in 1997–98 and snooker aficionados were beginning to suspect this once-bright prospect was all washed up. A year later, he fell to No. 13 in the world, a drop of ten places in three years.

He stopped the rot by reaching the final of the 1999 British Open, where he lost to Hendry again, but this was the catalyst for a resounding return to form in 2000–01. He started the campaign by battling through to his second straight British Open final, in which he beat White, while the following spring he took the Scottish Open title. He impressed in his first two matches at the Crucible, before being knocked out by eventual champion O'Sullivan in the last eight.

It was O'Sullivan who, in terms of endearment rather than disdain, had labelled Ebdon 'Psycho', and it was during this tournament that he lived up to his nickname. During the aforementioned second-round match against Stephen Lee, Ebdon unleashed his infamous ferocious celebration after making a difficult long pot. Lee, sitting in his chair reflecting on the loss of a vital frame, looked on as Ebdon paced around the table with his fists in the air shouting in ecstasy. Luckily, play on the other table had already finished for the night. Ebdon clearly puts a lot into the sport and is understandably overjoyed when this hard work results in success, but he recognised his celebration had gone too far and apologised afterwards. He has refused, though, to lighten up around the table, recognising that his deadpan approach is necessary for him to do his job. His 'Psycho' tag has also helped intimidate his opponents over the years, and cleverly he has appreciated the advantages of this. He was once asked about his reputation amongst the other players and replied, 'They might be right that I'm a psycho. Who knows? Let's hope they don't have to find out.'[3]

Ebdon was by this stage up to No. 7 in the world and enjoyed another successful season in 2001–02. Two final appearances and two semi-finals set him in good stead before his return to Sheffield. He kicked off with fairly comfortable wins over Michael Judge (10–4), Joe Perry (13–7) and Anthony Hamilton (13–6), but the wheels were expected to come off in the semi-finals against Matthew Stevens. The Welshman had enjoyed a string of fine results at the Crucible over the previous years, most notably coming within a whisker of lifting the trophy in 2000. Ebdon pushed him all the way, though, and looked like going down bravely when trailing 16–14, but a quick toilet break at that point suddenly changed the course of the match.

'I was under extreme pressure, and it just came to me in a flash of inspiration,' he revealed later. 'I came back from the toilet and actually saw myself shaking hands with Matthew having just beaten him. I saw it and then it happened the way I saw it. It was incredible.'[4] In the frame after that break, Stevens, needing just one more for victory, was leading by 33 points with 35 left, but Ebdon, knowing it was now or never, bravely took on a difficult pink and potted it. The Wellingborough player, in a trance of utter self-belief, cleared the table and then knocked in a 138 break in the next to pull level. He held his nerve in the decider to take the match 17–16 and seal a thrilling and unexpected comeback from the brink of defeat.

Like in 1996, Ebdon had to pick himself up from an exhausting semi-final and unfortunately for him he was up against the same opponent in the final – Hendry. Ebdon showed fighting spirit, and no little skill, in sticking with his opponent all the way. The first session ended 4–4 and, although Ebdon led 10–6 after the second, the seven-time world champion had pulled it back to 12–12 by the end of the third. The Scot moved 14–12 ahead in the final session, but then seemed to lose his touch in the safety department, allowing Ebdon to level at 14–14. The underdog sneaked 17–16 ahead and looked to have victory in the bag in the 34th frame, but missed a straight black off its spot when 52–27 ahead. Ebdon jumped up as soon as he had hit the cue ball, knowing he had miscued it. The crowd and most of the millions watching on television thought he'd bottled it, and witnessed Hendry clearing up to take the match to a final frame.[5] Both players made nervous mistakes until Ebdon produced a measured 59 break. The pressure was on Hendry, who had won a final-frame finish in 1994, of course, but he was unfortunate to go in-off when attempting a safety and Ebdon – a 33–1 shot before the tournament – punished him by clinching victory at his next visit to the table.

His win, although a shock, was nothing on the scale of the likes of Joe Johnson. Ebdon, at 31, was seeded seventh and stated publicly during the tournament that he had improved vastly since his final appearance in 1996. But few believed him, largely because his frenzied mental approach to the game was seen as just too severe. Ebdon went into great depth about how he had put himself on a ruthless fitness regime in order to get himself in tip-top shape for the longer matches. The daily half-mile swims had now turned into mile swims, he had forced himself into a strict diet, relentlessly cutting down on carbohydrates and sugars, while he was constantly re-reading Napoleon Hill's classic 1930 self-improvement book *Think and Grow Rich*. He took a copy (of which he owns several) with him wherever he went. None of the other players felt the need to go this far, so onlookers automatically assumed this was the wrong way to prepare.

Ebdon was clearly regarded by the punters, bookies and experts within the game as an outsider. How could anyone who worked himself up so much actually win the game's biggest prize? Not for the first time, those who thought they knew best were proved wrong. Ebdon, the loner who prepared for his matches by locking himself in his dressing-room and listening to self-help tapes or reading psychology books rather than sitting in a bar relaxing with his mates, had in fact planned it all out perfectly. When he needed to keep his head cool and his cue arm relaxed, he had been ready.

As with many first-time winners, the following year flew by for Ebdon, his schedule packed with promotional appearances. It was hard to find enough time for his ideal preparation for matches, but he did reach two ranking-event semi-finals. He made a brave stab at retaining his world title, beating Tony Drago in a second-round match in which tempers threatened to boil over. In the second session, with the run of the balls going against him, the Maltese player was getting increasingly frustrated with Ebdon's frequent toilet breaks between frames and slow deliberation over his shots. On one occasion when Ebdon returned following a fairly lengthy recess, Drago sarcastically applauded his opponent before breaking off. Ebdon, applying the cunning matchplay approach he has picked up over the years, kept his cool in a heated atmosphere to take a commanding 11–5 lead. By the time the players returned the following morning for the final session, the situation had calmed down significantly and Drago looked a lot more relaxed. But he had already blown his chance – Ebdon was too far ahead and needed just 22 minutes to complete a 13–5 win.

The champion's run ended at the next hurdle, though, an in-form Paul Hunter knocking him out 13–12 in a vigorous encounter during which Ebdon had fought back from 12–10 down to 12–12. Despite his best efforts and his unmatchable will-power, his below-par form throughout the season had made it all the more difficult to win five gruelling matches in a row at the Crucible. Obviously, no player wants to peak before the season's-end trip to Sheffield, but very rarely has a defending champion gone into the event on the back of a string of poor results and walked off with the trophy, relying on inspiration rather than form to carry him through.

It had also been a heated season for Ebdon off the table. A staunch supporter of the game's governing body, the WPBSA, he was pleased to see a breakaway group led by Griffiths, Hendry and Davis fail in their attempt to remove the board (which had been forced to cut prize money due to increasing financial problems) in November 2002. In the spring of 2004, with the question of who should govern the sport still the subject of much debate, Ebdon was appointed to the WPBSA board as part of a fresh strategy outlined by the organisation's new chairman, Sir Rodney Walker. Sir Robin Miller (chairman of music retailer HMV), David Richards (chairman of the Football Association's Premier League) and Adrian Metcalfe (a Great Britain 4 x 400m

Olympic relay silver medallist in 1964 and former head of sport at Channel 4) were also named board members, while Jim McMahon and Tony Murphy were the only existing directors invited to stay on by Walker.

The new scheme had its supporters, but also its sceptical opponents. An editorial in *Snooker Scene* read:

> Varying degrees of disappointment have been expressed about Sir Rodney's decision to retain McMahon and Murphy, the lynchpins [*sic*] of the board which has allowed WPBSA to sink into such dire straits . . . To some, this is bound to look like a continuation of the old regime, albeit with a new king.

The article also reflected the surprise many felt at Ebdon's appointment as the board's players' representative, rather than a more 'middle-of-the-road figure in the sport's internal politics'. It went on, 'Some players were angry because they would never have voted for the constitutional changes giving Sir Rodney a free hand if they had realised that Ebdon was in his plans.'[6] Ebdon expressed his own backing for the regime, insisting, 'I think I speak for most players when I say that there is enormous encouragement and support for Sir Rodney being at the helm of the sport.'[7]

Ebdon's life away from the table isn't just about involving himself in snooker politics – in fact, it has been the subject of much curiosity over the years. Not one for a few rounds of golf in his spare time, when he is not at home with his wife and four children, he is on his laptop researching the line breeding of racehorses. He has a computer database with details of a million horses stored on it and designs his own pedigrees. This often involves going back seven or more generations. He is a member of an internet breeding syndicate that in 2003 bought an Entrepreneur filly named Perle D'Or for £38,000, which is in training with William Haggas in Newmarket. Ebdon also owns a couple of brood mares who have produced some promising foals.

A proud member of his Wellingborough community, Ebdon became the first president of the town's re-formed football club in May 2004. Wellingborough Town, the sixth-oldest club in England, had gone out of business two years previously but were being resurrected, with Ebdon taking a leading role in the venture – another example of him seeking an alternative and active challenge away from snooker.

Back on the table, Ebdon lifted his second Irish Masters crown in

2003–04, the sixth ranking-event title of his career, displaying solid matchplay skills to see off O'Sullivan and Quinten Hann before beating Mark King 10–7 in the final. 'I've been practising very hard recently and I've got what I deserved,' he said, again reiterating how important that work ethic was to him.[8] He also revealed that his game had sharpened up thanks to playing with practice partner Ding Jun Hui. The highly rated Chinese teenager had recently moved to England and settled in the Northamptonshire area, basing himself at Ebdon's Rushden Snooker Centre.

Ebdon went on another good run at the next tournament, the Players Championship in Glasgow, but in the semi-finals he lost a 5–3 lead against White, the Londoner battling hard to scrape through 6–5 in a classic match that earned them both a standing ovation at the finish. Ebdon's game was therefore in pretty good shape as he headed for Sheffield, but he was to suffer from the growing trend of players outside the top 16 proving their class as well as mettle. Stephen Maguire (No. 41) had won the European Open earlier that season, while Barry Pinches (36), Joe Swail (27) and Lee Walker (81) knocked out White, Doherty and Stephen Lee respectively in the opening round at the Crucible. Ebdon was another big name to fall to a qualifier, world No. 26 Ian McCulloch beating him 10–8.

Ebdon had often been portrayed as an overly focused sportsman with a quirky nature – until, that is, his World Championship victory made people who thought they knew the game think again. He was not an idiosyncratic character simply adding colour to the circuit's supporting cast, but a highly skilled performer, a champion in the making, waiting to take his chance. He had faith in himself because he knew that if he worked hard enough for his opportunity, he would be prepared for it when it came along.

His pursuit of snooker immortality acts as a lesson to us all, in life as well as sport. If you're not where you want to be, it's because you're not trying hard enough, so step it up a level. Ebdon has stood out from the rest in so many ways during his career, but it was through his extreme powers of self-motivation and discipline that he proved the greatest goals can be achieved. 'You only get out of it what you put in,' he says. 'That's the iron law. Reaping and sowing. It's like Newton's cradle, the amount of force you put in, you get an equal reaction . . . work hard, make the breaks, get the breaks.'[9]

TWENTY-ONE

JIMMY WHITE

Whirlwind Romance

The story of the World Snooker Championship would be incomplete without reference to the greatest player never to lift the crown, as well as one of the sport's true entertainers, and we therefore make no apologies for including a chapter on Jimmy 'The Whirlwind' White in a book otherwise solely devoted to world champions.

White's seemingly cursed quest to lift snooker's greatest prize has seen him acquire iconic status. Six defeats in the World Championship final, coupled with numerous other setbacks – testicular cancer chief among them – would have broken a lesser man, but the south Londoner has always retained an air of boundless optimism, while his flair and positive philosophies have never wavered. 'I am a purist,' he once declared. 'When I have to choose between a tactical shot or one from the heart I will usually go for the heart.'[1]

The narrative of White's extraordinary career took a romantic twist in 2004 when his refusal to bow to the conventional wisdom that he was finished as a top competitor received its just reward when he ended a 12-year ranking-title drought by lifting the Players Championship. It was a remarkable triumph for the power of hope over rationality, even if, Jimmy being Jimmy, he lost in the first round of the World Championship less than two weeks later – a demonstration of the maddening inconsistency that makes his triumphs all the sweeter.

James Warren White was born in a prefab in Balham on 2 May 1962 – a date that, in a perverse twist of fate, regularly coincides with the World Championship final. His family were south London to their core, father Tom hailing from Merton, while mother Lilian was from Tooting. 'South London is in my bones and I'm part of its fabric, which makes me feel good,' White once claimed. 'You have to be from south London to understand it.'[2] Tom and Lil never married, but were together fifty-three years, with Jimmy the youngest of five children.

White's childhood was the archetypal misspent youth. A persistent truant, he whiled away his days ripping off fruit machines and pretending he was an orphan to elicit free food from shopkeepers. One day, while escaping from a bout of fisticuffs, an 11-year-old White ducked into Zans Snooker Hall and his life changed forever. Entranced by the seductive click of the balls, he visited the club for nine months before picking up a cue, whereupon he practised for one hundred hours in just one week.

White received no formal tuition, but played fast with a silky left-handed action. A phenomenal potter blessed with considerable cue power, his control of the white ball was astounding and made his artistry appear effortless. At thirteen, he knocked in his first century, another fifty following within two years. His ability was amply illustrated by an incident in a snooker club in Neasden. He had recently broken his foot and stunned a watching Steve Davis by nonchalantly potting balls with his walking stick rather than a cue.

By then, White and another Zans regular, Tony Meo, were being managed by cab driver Bob Davis, who drove them across the country on money-match missions. While under Bob's auspices, White and Meo even met Joe Davis, although his reported assessment of the youngsters to their manager – 'I'd send them back to school, they're a pair of wankers'[3] – was not exactly the sort of first impression they had hoped to make. Of more importance to White's future was his first encounter with Alex Higgins during a charity exhibition. 'You get loads of promising kids,' the Northern Irishman told White's father. 'Some burn out. But one like Jimmy shines.'[4] Higgins took White under his wing, offering him work at several exhibitions, and the duo's soul-mate status would later be sealed during a heart-stopping World Championship semi-final in 1982.

White's housemaster at Ernest Bevin Comprehensive was soon concerned by how much lesson-time his pupil was spending at Zans and proposed a deal whereby he could leave school in the afternoons, if he turned up in the morning. It worked for only one day – White was too deeply in love with snooker to worry about formal education. By his mid-teens, he was leading a schizophrenic existence, flirting between the twilight world of late-night money matches while also dressing up in his Burton's suit to play on the amateur circuit.

In 1977, he lifted the national Under-16 title and took part in what he still sees as one of his three greatest matches ever – an 8–8 draw against Charlie Poole, an extravagant talent who never turned pro, for a fiver a frame in Earlsfield. 'There were balls going in everywhere, in the lampshades, off the cushions,' he said with pride.[5] His amateur progress continued apace when, a month before his 17th birthday, he became the then youngest winner of the English Amateur Championship.

A trip to Tasmania, Australia, for the 1980 World Amateur Championship reinforced White's reputation for brilliant snooker and fast living. He and fellow teenage tearaway Joe O'Boye gambled away their expenses almost immediately and were forced to cadge food for the duration of the tournament. Despite such chaos, White became the youngest winner of the title at 18 years and 191 days, thrashing Australian Ron Atkins. So confident was he of success that he held his victory party before the final, then won, despite a hangover. 'I could have done it just by potting because in those days I was so good,' he recalled.[6]

While the British press were hailing him as snooker's greatest discovery since Higgins, White headed to India, winning the country's national snooker title. The grandeur of official functions bored him and O'Boye, so instead they ducked out and spent time with local street children. On his return to England, White turned professional and qualified for the World Championship, losing 10–8 against eventual winner Davis in round one. The performance helped catapult him to No. 21 in the world rankings and a few months later he captured the Scottish Masters, becoming the then youngest winner of a professional event – albeit a non-ranking one. During the final against Cliff Thorburn, White played with an arrest warrant hanging over him for alleged looting during the Brixton riots, although he was later acquitted.

In the 1982 World Championship, White made a huge impact, disposing of world No. 1 Thorburn in the first round and then seeing off Perrie Mans and Kirk Stevens to set up a semi-final showdown with Higgins. At just 20, White was in with a chance of beating

Higgins's record as the youngest world champion. The match, described in depth in Chapter Eight, was a classic, but also a gut-wrenching 16–15 loss for White, who missed a regulation red on the verge of victory.

Although now tenth in the rankings, this defeat seemed to knock the stuffing out of White and the following season was a disappointment; although he reached two finals, he lost both to Ray Reardon and fell in the opening round of the World Championship to old pal Meo. Many people questioned whether White was as good as the hype surrounding him, and he answered his critics in a classic semi-final shoot-out against Stevens in the 1984 Wembley Masters. Stevens notched a 147, just the third ever televised, but White won the match 6–4, his Canadian opponent applauding him as he potted the final pink and black with crowd-pleasing flair. A 9–5 victory against Terry Griffiths in the final saw White pick up the biggest pay day of his career to date – £35,000 – as well as the sport's most prestigious invitational title.

He carried this form to Sheffield, defeating Stevens 16–14 in another illuminating semi to set up a showdown with the omnipotent Davis. Drained from his battle with Stevens, White's cause looked hopeless when he trailed 12–4 at the end of the first day; but on the Monday, courtesy of some virtuoso play, he reduced the deficit to 13–11, 16–15 and then 17–16, before a wild miss on the green in a tight next frame gave a relieved Davis the chance to close out the match 18–16. This absorbing contest reduced Higgins, in the crowd cheering on White, to tears, but the manner of White's display won him much acclaim. It seemed only a matter of time before he lifted the title himself.

A disappointing 1984–85 campaign ended with defeat against Tony Knowles in the World Championship quarter-finals, but the following season White finally captured his first ranking title, the Mercantile Credit Classic, with a 13–12 victory over Thorburn. Two ranking-event trophies were won in 1986–87, helping White scale a career high of second in the world rankings, although his path to World Championship glory remained blocked first by Davis, who knocked him out in 1986 and 1987, and then by Griffiths and Parrott.

As the 1990s began, White was at the peak of his powers. His rest play was established as the best in the world, his safety was tidier than ever and his raw talent now well complemented by a surer grasp of the demands of tournament play. From 1990, he reached the World Championship final a remarkable five times in a row – only to lose on each occasion. In 1990, Stephen Hendry, spurred by a sense of destiny, out-potted him to win his first title 18–12, while the following year a flawless Parrott was an 18–11 victor. 'I don't think he even missed a safety shot, let alone a pot,' White quipped.[7]

The 1992 championship saw White enjoy his greatest moment – and also suffer one of his most demoralising defeats. The highlight of his smooth progression to the final came in the first round against Tony Drago, as he became only the second man after Thorburn to make a 147 in the World Championship. The route to the magical maximum was opened when Drago missed a long red and left the balls invitingly spread. White's ensuing clearance was not perfect, but whenever he ran out of position he rescued the situation with assured potting and some wonderful cuts. After finishing too straight on the blue, he potted a long pink in ice-cool fashion before dispatching the black to earn a £114,000 bonus. 'Tony, bless his heart, was so moved he wept,' White reflected. 'I was so moved I soon gambled it away.'[8]

When it came to the final against Hendry, White raced 14–8 ahead, but the Scotsman somehow roused himself to win ten consecutive frames and secure an 18–14 victory. Despite such a shattering defeat, White showed great heart to lift the UK Championship in November, his biggest title to date, and fight back to the World Championship final again in 1993, whereupon a rampant Hendry thrashed him 18–5.

The 1994 World Championship final, the third in a row between White and Hendry, was the most heartbreaking of all for Whirlwind fans. After falling 5–1 behind, a repeat of the previous year's massacre looked likely, but White responded with gusto and led 9–7 overnight. The final day's play was one of the most memorable in the tournament's history, with the momentum ebbing and flowing from one player to the other. Hendry moved 15–13 ahead, but White responded with a 116 to halve the deficit; Hendry again edged two frames ahead at 16–14, before White stole two tight frames with brilliant clearances. Yet again, the Scotsman responded, a 47 putting him 17–16 ahead.

Displaying the coolest nerves of his career, a 75 break took White to 17–17 and a final-frame shoot-out. When he moved 37–24 ahead in the 35th frame and was among the balls, he must have thought the title was his. However, in a moment that still sends a chill down the spine of his fans, White missed a black off its spot. Hendry didn't flinch in constructing a match-winning 58 and White's best chance of lifting the title was gone. Characteristically, he was honest and charming in defeat. 'That black was a disaster,' he said. 'A rush of blood on my part.' Turning his attention to Hendry, he added, with perfect comic timing, 'He's beginning to annoy me.'[9]

Between 1995 and 1998 White hit rock bottom. His brother Martin was diagnosed with cancer and soon after White himself discovered he had testicular cancer. Although he survived the disease, Martin did not and just over a year later he also lost his mother. White was also convicted of drink-driving, suffered a terrible reaction to a baldness cure and saw his marriage to long-suffering Maureen enter its most turbulent phase yet. His dog Splinter was even kidnapped – although a £300 ransom eventually secured his return. Unsurprisingly, White's snooker disintegrated. A miserable sequence of losses in 1996–97 culminated in a first-round exit at the World Championship against Anthony Hamilton, which sent The Whirlwind spiralling out of the top 16.

Gradually, White began to fight back. In 1998, no one gave him a prayer when he drew Hendry in the first round of the World Championship – a few weeks previously, White had lost to world No. 150 Mark Gray and he hadn't beaten the Scotsman since 1991. Yet he rolled back the years with a real demolition job on the six-time champion, transforming a 7–1 first-session lead into a 10–4 victory which raised the roof of the Crucible. White went on to reach the quarter-finals, but it was not enough to regain his top-16 place. He did squeeze back into the elite bracket a year later, but dropped out yet again after just a season.

In 2000–01, a notable upturn in form led to an appearance in the British Open final. Although White lost to Peter Ebdon, the result helped him regain his top-16 place for the second time – an unprecedented feat. The only disappointment of a successful campaign was that he failed to reach the televised stages of the World Championship for the first time after a qualifying-round loss against Irishman Michael Judge.

By maintaining a less hectic lifestyle than in years gone by and slowing the pace of his game, White has held on to his top-16 place ever since. In 2003, he even enjoyed one of his greatest victories – on the poker rather than the snooker table – shocking the card-playing establishment by beating Joe 'The Elegance' Beevers to win the £80,000 first prize in the Ladbrokes Poker Million, Britain's most famous poker tournament. 'I've been gambling since the age of 12,' he shrugged afterwards. 'Horses, dogs, dice, roulette, you name it.'[10]

In the 2003–04 season, his snooker renaissance also began to scale new heights as semi-final appearances at the UK Championship and Wembley Masters prefigured an appearance in the final of the European Open. However, with a first ranking title in 12 years within his sights, and his legion of fans holding their breath expectantly, White stumbled to defeat against outsider Stephen Maguire.

Remarkably, he dusted himself down and went all the way in the penultimate ranking event of the season, the Players Championship, beating Paul Hunter 9–7 in a scrappy but compelling final, confounding the critics who felt there was no chance of him lifting a significant title again. At the conclusion of the match, White embraced his 84-year-old father, Tom, his most loyal supporter. 'It was very tough out there, but I was thinking of [boxer] Roberto Duran,' White said after the match. 'He used to say, "Keep on punching, just keep on punching." I had to keep believing that I had it in my heart to win. There have been some tough times for me in the last 12 years.'[11]

The victory made White, at 41, the oldest winner of a major title since Doug Mountjoy lifted the 1989 Mercantile Credit Classic and only the second player, after Hendry, to win ranking events in three separate decades. It also moved him onto a career total of ten ranking-tournament wins – a tally surpassed only by Hendry, Davis, Mark Williams, John Higgins and Ronnie O'Sullivan. This display raised hopes of a significant showing by White at the World Championship. It was not to be, though, as the rigours of an emotional campaign caught up with him and he fell to a first-round defeat against Barry Pinches. The season also ended with a police caution for possession of cocaine and an emergency appendix operation – the world of Jimmy White is certainly never dull – but with his ranking bolstered to No. 11 for the 2004–05 season, all the signs are that he has plenty more snooker in him yet.

With typical eccentricity, White has rated Charlie Poole, Patsy Houlihan and Alex Higgins as the three greatest snooker players he has ever seen, reasoning that they were 'potters and entertainers. Safety shots were too boring for them'.[12] His own place in snooker history, unless he miraculously wins that world title, seems destined to remain the subject of fierce debate. The resilience he has recently demonstrated has certainly bolstered his legacy, but many still argue that his career is predominantly defined by two missed pots – namely, 'that' red against Higgins in 1982 and 'that' black against Hendry in 1994. His failure to win the world title, it has been argued, disqualifies him from being considered among the game's greatest performers.

Such a theory is based on the assumption that White has primarily been the architect of his disappointments. However, this is true only to a certain extent, for it must also be said that White has not been overburdened with good luck. Along with O'Sullivan and Higgins, he is arguably the most naturally talented player to ever pick up a cue, but he was unfortunate that his peak coincided with the almost total dominance of Davis and Hendry, the two greatest competitors of the modern era. Furthermore, in his 1994 World Championship-final loss to Hendry, White was unlucky that one error in the final frame was so ruthlessly exploited by his opponent – contrast that with the good fortune of Dennis Taylor and Ebdon, who spurned several match-winning chances before finally crossing the finishing line in their final-frame world-title triumphs.

Whenever White has appeared in a World Championship final, he has run into opponents at the peak of their form. In 1991, Parrott played faultlessly to race 7–0 ahead and the match was virtually over after one session. Davis has called White 'one of the greatest matchplayers of all time'[13] and his Crucible performances over more than two decades bear this out – six final appearances, four semi-finals and five quarter-finals in twenty-four tournament entries is a sterling record.

Besides, whatever he has lost in trophies, White has more than compensated for in public adulation. His appeal transcends all boundaries of age and class largely because, for all his rough-around-the-edges behaviour away from the table, on it he is a gentleman who always calls his own fouls and never makes excuses in defeat. Furthermore, White is that rarity – a superstar who still seems like an ordinary bloke and remains resolutely untouched by fame. Attempts to make him more corporate-friendly by successive management teams have all ended in failure, which only adds to his appeal. 'If Jimmy endorses anything, no one, least of all him, remembers it,' noted journalist Will Buckley. 'If Jimmy makes any money, you can rest certain that he will blow it on the horses or at a party, or both.'[14] This unique mixture of qualities has made White equally popular with grandmothers and teenagers. The violin player Yehudi Menuhin was also a huge admirer of White's talents, while the American comedian Bill Hicks constructed a routine based around him.[15]

Like motor-racing driver Stirling Moss, White has never won his sport's World Championship, but remains a hugely significant figure. Snooker, with its miniscule margins for error, is not necessarily a discipline which rewards flair as much as caution; but it needs the artistry of players such as White to maintain its hold on the public's imagination. 'It doesn't really matter what people like Hurricane Higgins and Jimmy do; it's how they express it,' argued Jonathan Rendall, who included a cameo from White in his novel *Twelve Grand*. 'They have "it", whatever "it" is, in the way that great painters, writers, poets and violinists have it.'[16]

White may not be a great winner, but he is inarguably a great player. He captures fans' hearts because his failings reflect their own fears, while his flair offers them the eternal hope that maybe, just maybe, he might finally win that elusive world title. If the brilliant and neurotic Higgins is snooker's Hamlet, then White is its Romeo – a romantic hero who reminds us how liberating it feels to play from the heart and live in the present. 'The past belongs to the pundits and the statistics boys,' is White's philosophy. 'There is only "tomorrow" to deal with, which is as it should be. Look to the next shot.'[17]

TWENTY-TWO

WHO IS THE GREATEST?

In an effort to evaluate more precisely what the aforementioned players achieved on the snooker table and the levels of their lasting effects on the game, we have decided to round off this book by compiling our ten greatest players of all time. This list is based on achievements already proven (up to the time of writing), not potential, which is why several modern-day players who have won one or two world titles but promise more may be missing or ranked lower than expected.

We would also like to stress that this chapter, like all 'best of' lists of a similar ilk, is subjective by its very nature. We rated the players in each of six categories which we believe are crucial at the highest level of the game – break-building, potting, safety play, temperament, bravery and impact – with each category worth twenty points, and added up the totals. These categories are all pretty self-explanatory, but it should be noted that in assessing players' 'impact' we not only take into account the effects they have had on snooker itself in terms of developments in technique and tactics, but also to what extent they popularised the game as a whole or brought it to a wider audience. These ratings, and consequently the order of our top ten, are based on our opinion only, while taking into account the thoughts of several commentators, analysts and fans of the game.

10. CLIFF THORBURN

There are many one-time World Championship winners, but Thorburn is the only one who sneaks into our top ten. Horace Lindrum's disputed 1952 victory aside, Thorburn was the first overseas player to win the big one and this achievement must not be understated.

Adapting to the game in another country, with vastly different playing conditions and traditions to his home in Canada, was by no means easy but Thorburn, a natural at working hard against the odds, gritted his teeth and made a huge success of himself. Unlike many other one-time winners, he also reached three world finals and, of course, created one of the most golden moments in Crucible history, becoming the first player to compile a 147 maximum break in the biggest pressure-cooker atmosphere of all.

Break-building	18
Potting	16
Safety	16
Temperament	17
Bravery	17
Impact	16
Total	100

9. FRED DAVIS

The only player to beat his older brother on level terms, Fred was a legend who dominated his era despite adopting a more laid-back attitude to the game compared with Joe.

Fred won eight world titles, the second-highest total ever, and deserves utmost respect for competing at the top for longer than anyone else (he was still in the world's top 16 at the age of 67). But, like his older brother, the scope of Fred's achievements is diminished slightly due to the time in which he lived. Through no fault of his own, the competition in the late 1940s and '50s was nowhere near as fierce as it is now, which is why he only makes it this high on the list.

Break-building	16
Potting	16
Safety	17
Temperament	19
Bravery	18
Impact	16
Total	102

8. MARK WILLIAMS

Williams deserved much credit for winning his first world title in 2000, but what stands out more is the fact that he managed to win it again three years later when many of his great rivals – O'Sullivan, Higgins, Ebdon, Doherty – were still stuck on one world crown.

Many commentators have labelled Williams the most ruthless single-ball potter in the game, but his ability to stay cool under pressure was another major factor in his string of successes at the start of the twenty-first century. In October 2003, he held the world title, UK Championship, Masters crown and LG Cup all at the same time. Dominating any generation is tough enough, but standing tallest in that ultra-competitive era merits ample respect.

Break-building	18
Potting	19
Safety	17
Temperament	17
Bravery	17
Impact	15
Total	103

7. JOHN SPENCER

Three-time champion Spencer took the standard of snooker up a notch with his revolutionary deep screw shots that delighted the crowd and baffled his opponents. He won the World Championship the first year he entered it in 1969 and lifted his third and final crown eight years later using a different cue.

His timing at turning pro in 1968–69 couldn't have been better. Snooker needed new blood at this stage and Spencer, a thrilling talent with exquisite cue technique and steely matchplay temperament, fitted the bill perfectly.

A comfortable member of the top ten, he doesn't make it into the top five because he was unable to maintain his peak form for as many years as others, but there's no doubt he was one of the classiest players ever.

Break-building	17
Potting	18
Safety	17
Temperament	17
Bravery	18
Impact	17
Total	104

6. RAY REARDON

Reardon's record in World Championship finals – losing just one of seven – was exceptional. The Welshman, an uncompromising character who, like Joe Davis, maximised the potential of his intimidating personality, was also the first player to regain the world No. 1 spot. However, Reardon's game entered a fairly steep decline after his final world title in 1978 and his trophy haul outside of the World Championship – he never won the UK Championship and lifted just one Masters crown – wasn't nearly as impressive as that of others.

Reardon's pragmatic style of play also meant he scored lower in areas like bravery and impact than the likes of trailblazer Higgins, who dared to be aggressive at a time when caution was often rewarded more than attacking prowess. But it's not Reardon's fault that his opponents failed to match him, and he still faced more competition than the likes of John Pulman and the Davis brothers. It's tempting to slip Reardon higher up the list based on the theory that he was good enough to win stacks of world titles in any era, but then we're getting into conjecture.

Break-building	18
Potting	18
Safety	19
Temperament	19
Bravery	16
Impact	17
Total	107

5. RONNIE O'SULLIVAN

In an age when many punters bemoan the lack of characters in the game, we have in fact been fortunate to witness O'Sullivan, a truly unique player and human being, strutting his stuff.

Some of the facts backing O'Sullivan's case are astonishing – 74 wins out of 76 matches in the 1992–93 season after turning pro, he has compiled more centuries than any other player in history with the sole exception of Hendry, and, in terms of natural ability, he is referred to by many as the No. 1.

But it's clear there are weaknesses that go alongside his exquisite strengths, namely the mood swings that have plagued him over the years. His frustration at not playing his best has often affected his game in the negative and has, up to now, prevented the two-time world champion matching the achievements of others.

Break-building	20
Potting	19
Safety	18
Temperament	14
Bravery	19
Impact	18
Total	108

4. ALEX HIGGINS

Many would argue that Higgins's inappropriate behaviour over the years, as well as his inconsistent playing record, does not warrant such a high place. Of course, a string of frailties plagued Higgins for years, but in the case of his strengths, he was often way above the rest. His frantic style may have resulted in mixed results, but there's no denying that, in his 1982 World Championship semi-final against Jimmy White, he pulled off one of the most exceptional breaks under pressure in the sport's history.

Performing under maximum levels of tension is what snooker is all about and Higgins's haphazard 69 break that night when one frame away from going home was as astonishing as it was brave. Despite it being brief, it deserves to go down as one of the most significant achievements in the game. Another key reason why Higgins breaks into the top five is impact – only he and Joe Davis score the maximum points in this section. If it wasn't for Higgins, snooker's renaissance in the early 1970s would have been nowhere near as vigorous or successful. So many future professionals picked up a cue because of the Northern Irishman.

Finally, whatever his critics may hold against him, you can't argue with the facts: Higgins won the big one twice, his world titles separated by a full decade, suggesting he was no fly-by-night wannabe just chasing fame. He loved the game, and he loved it for years.

Break-building	20
Potting	20
Safety	16
Temperament	13
Bravery	20
Impact	20
Total	109

3. STEVE DAVIS

King of the 1980s, Davis was a snooker genius whose dedication to the sport made him a great role model as well as a ruthless champion. He is still immensely popular, but doesn't break into the top two here, mainly because – despite his magnificent skills and enthusiasm – he did lose three big matches during his peak.

Sport is, after all, about winning and losing, and it's easy to forget that Davis's record in major finals wasn't perfect. He lost the 1983 UK Championship final 16–15 to Alex Higgins after being 7–0 up, the 1985 world final to Dennis Taylor 18–17 after leading 8–0, and the 1986 final to rank outsider Joe Johnson. He received much criticism for over-cutting the black in the penultimate shot of that unforgettable 1985 final, but, to be fair to Davis, the nature of snooker often means missed shots like that are highlighted more than they are in other sports – if a striker receives five good chances in a cup final and scores two of them, he is forever remembered as a hero, while his three misses are quickly forgotten.

But Davis was also at the heart of perhaps the most astounding collapse of a defending Crucible champion in the shape of his 10–1 defeat to Tony Knowles in 1982. Although known as 'The Romford Robot' due to his superb bouts of consistency, there were these odd glitches which means he falls just behind the top two.

Break-building	19
Potting	19
Safety	19
Temperament	20
Bravery	17
Impact	19
Total	113

2. JOE DAVIS

Davis didn't have a weakness. His technique and desire were faultless, while his matchplaying skills were second to none. Only Fred ever beat him on level terms and, of course, Joe never lost a World Championship match. A monumental talent as well as a gutsy fighter, Davis was undoubtedly the finest player of his day, while some still regard him as the greatest ever.

Unlike any other player, Joe also had the disadvantage of having to teach himself the practicalities of winning snooker matches. There was no one to watch on television, no heroes to influence him or senior players to show him different shots and methods (a young Steve Davis, of course, read Joe's books when learning the game). The equipment was also harder to play with back then – the balls were heavier, while the cloths were not as smooth, making positional shots more tricky and today's 'cue-power' shots impossible.

But not all of Davis's fifteen world-title triumphs came from tournament play – some of them were arranged on a challenge basis, meaning he only had to beat one player to defend his title. This was first the case in 1928, when Fred Lawrence won the right to take on Davis, the challenger going down 16–13. In 1929, the World Championship reverted back to a knockout tournament, but there were only five entrants, while in 1931 there were a mere two – Davis and Tom Dennis. In 1932 and 1934, the championships attracted only three and two entrants respectively. In all, Davis beat just one player to win four of his fifteen world titles, and another four of those tournament victories came after beating only two opponents. It wasn't until 1936 that Davis had to negotiate four matches, while from 1937–40 and in 1946 he had to win three.

Davis dominated his generation as much as it was possible to, but

231

the player we have positioned as No. 1, who ruled his own era with just as much skill and savagery, had to overcome more competition and public pressures to earn his glories.

Break-building	20
Potting	20
Safety	18
Temperament	19
Bravery	17
Impact	20
Total	114

1. STEPHEN HENDRY

Considering the vast array of skills Hendry developed to dominate snooker's most competitive era of all, it's entirely plausible to believe that the Scot would have ruled the roost to an even greater extent had he been around in Joe Davis's day. However, measuring these two giant names up against each other is not as easy as that.

While both of them did so much for the game, it's almost impossible to compare the two in terms of raw ability – the mechanics of snooker have evolved over time and both players used all the skill and tactical knowledge available to them to rule their respective generations. It's no surprise, then, that Hendry cultivated a deeper array of technical craft in certain areas of the game that developed in later years (most notably long potting) than Davis did. But there are more substantial reasons why the Scot tops this list.

In Davis's day, there were few excellent players to conquer (Fred Davis and Horace Lindrum were arguably the only ones capable of posing a real threat) and little outside pressure from the media to deal with, a situation which is very different on both counts today.

As well as having fewer opponents to beat, the significant length of the matches back then also favoured the stronger player, allowing for fewer upsets. During the first half of the twentieth century, most World Championship matches were played over several days or even weeks, while in the modern-day championship, the eventual winner has to overcome a variety of short and long matches to lift the crown. Many big names have fallen in the first round, played over the best of 19 frames, a format deliberately designed to test the top players against hungry young qualifiers looking to take a scalp, while the best-of-35 final is a test of stamina as well as class.

Snooker crowds are also more hostile towards players nowadays.

There are always exceptions, of course, but in the early days of snooker the majority of punters turned up to marvel at the skills on display and would applaud exceptional play whoever was at the table. Today, many spectators go to watch with the strict intention of supporting one player and opposing the other. On many occasions, Hendry has fallen into the latter of these categories and has had to put up with examples of inappropriate behaviour from sections of the crowd.

Some critics have claimed that Hendry had less natural ability than others. If so, it's certainly not by much (Hendry is the only player to score a 147 at the Crucible beyond the second round – his occurred during a semi-final, where the stakes were higher). But what immense talent the Scot did have, he put to better use than anybody. A major component of his overall ability was playing to his maximum potential under the highest amounts of pressure – something that didn't come to other players as naturally, which is why he is our choice as the greatest player ever.

Break-building	20
Potting	20
Safety	17
Temperament	20
Bravery	20
Impact	19
Total	116

WORLD SNOOKER CHAMPIONSHIP FINALS

1927	Joe Davis (Eng)	bt	Tom Dennis (Eng)	20–11
1928	Joe Davis (Eng)	bt	Fred Lawrence (Eng)	16–13
1929	Joe Davis (Eng)	bt	Tom Dennis (Eng)	19–14
1930	Joe Davis (Eng)	bt	Tom Dennis (Eng)	25–12
1931	Joe Davis (Eng)	bt	Tom Dennis (Eng)	25–21
1932	Joe Davis (Eng)	bt	Clark McConachy (NZ)	30–19
1933	Joe Davis (Eng)	bt	Willie Smith (Eng)	25–18
1934	Joe Davis (Eng)	bt	Tom Newman (Eng)	25–23
1935	Joe Davis (Eng)	bt	Willie Smith (Eng)	25–20
1936	Joe Davis (Eng)	bt	Horace Lindrum (Aus)	34–27
1937	Joe Davis (Eng)	bt	Horace Lindrum (Aus)	32–29
1938	Joe Davis (Eng)	bt	Sidney Smith (Eng)	37–24
1939	Joe Davis (Eng)	bt	Sidney Smith (Eng)	43–30
1940	Joe Davis (Eng)	bt	Fred Davis (Eng)	37–36
1941–45	No tournament held			
1946	Joe Davis (Eng)	bt	Horace Lindrum (Aus)	78–67
1947	Walter Donaldson (Sco)	bt	Fred Davis (Eng)	82–63
1948	Fred Davis (Eng)	bt	Walter Donaldson (Sco)	84–61
1949	Fred Davis (Eng)	bt	Walter Donaldson (Sco)	80–65
1950	Walter Donaldson (Sco)	bt	Fred Davis (Eng)	51–46
1951	Fred Davis (Eng)	bt	Walter Donaldson (Sco)	58–39

BA&CC Championship:

1952	Horace Lindrum (Aus)	bt	Clark McConachy (NZ)	94–49*

World Professional Matchplay Championship:

1952	Fred Davis (Eng)	bt	Walter Donaldson (Sco)	38–35
1953	Fred Davis (Eng)	bt	Walter Donaldson (Sco)	37–34
1954	Fred Davis (Eng)	bt	Walter Donaldson (Sco)	39–21
1955	Fred Davis (Eng)	bt	John Pulman (Eng)	37–34
1956	Fred Davis (Eng)	bt	John Pulman (Eng)	38–35
1957	John Pulman (Eng)	bt	John Rea (NI)	39–34
1958–63	No tournament held			

Challenge matches:

1964	John Pulman (Eng)	bt	Fred Davis (Eng)	19–16
1964	John Pulman (Eng)	bt	Rex Williams (Eng)	40–33
1965	John Pulman (Eng)	bt	Fred Davis (Eng)	37–36
1965	John Pulman (Eng)	bt	Rex Williams (Eng)	25–22
1965	John Pulman (Eng)	bt	Fred van Rensberg (RSA)	39–12
1966	John Pulman (Eng)	bt	Fred Davis (Eng)	5–2
1967	No tournament held			
1968	John Pulman (Eng)	bt	Eddie Charlton (Aus)	39–34

Knockout format:

1969	John Spencer (Eng)	bt	Gary Owen (Wal)	37–24
1970	Ray Reardon (Wal)	bt	John Pulman (Eng)	37–33
1971	John Spencer (Eng)	bt	Warren Simpson (Aus)	37–29**
1972	Alex Higgins (NI)	bt	John Spencer (Eng)	37–32
1973	Ray Reardon (Wal)	bt	Eddie Charlton (Aus)	38–32
1974	Ray Reardon (Wal)	bt	Graham Miles (Eng)	22–12
1975	Ray Reardon (Wal)	bt	Eddie Charlton (Aus)	31–30
1976	Ray Reardon (Wal)	bt	Alex Higgins (NI)	27–16

Played at the Crucible:

1977	John Spencer (Eng)	bt	Cliff Thorburn (Can)	25–21
1978	Ray Reardon (Wal)	bt	Perrie Mans (RSA)	25–18
1979	Terry Griffiths (Wal)	bt	Dennis Taylor (NI)	24–16
1980	Cliff Thorburn (Can)	bt	Alex Higgins (NI)	18–16
1981	Steve Davis (Eng)	bt	Doug Mountjoy (Wal)	18–12
1982	Alex Higgins (NI)	bt	Ray Reardon (Wal)	18–15
1983	Steve Davis (Eng)	bt	Cliff Thorburn (Can)	18–6
1984	Steve Davis (Eng)	bt	Jimmy White (Eng)	18–16
1985	Dennis Taylor (NI)	bt	Steve Davis (Eng)	18–17
1986	Joe Johnson (Eng)	bt	Steve Davis (Eng)	18–12
1987	Steve Davis (Eng)	bt	Joe Johnson (Eng)	18–14

1988	Steve Davis (Eng)	bt	Terry Griffiths (Wal)	18–11
1989	Steve Davis (Eng)	bt	John Parrott (Eng)	18–3
1990	Stephen Hendry (Sco)	bt	Jimmy White (Eng)	18–12
1991	John Parrott (Eng)	bt	Jimmy White (Eng)	18–11
1992	Stephen Hendry (Sco)	bt	Jimmy White (Eng)	18–14
1993	Stephen Hendry (Sco)	bt	Jimmy White (Eng)	18–5
1994	Stephen Hendry (Sco)	bt	Jimmy White (Eng)	18–17
1995	Stephen Hendry (Sco)	bt	Nigel Bond (Eng)	18–9
1996	Stephen Hendry (Sco)	bt	Peter Ebdon (Eng)	18–12
1997	Ken Doherty (Ire)	bt	Stephen Hendry (Sco)	18–12
1998	John Higgins (Sco)	bt	Ken Doherty (Ire)	18–12
1999	Stephen Hendry (Sco)	bt	Mark Williams (Wal)	18–11
2000	Mark Williams (Wal)	bt	Matthew Stevens (Wal)	18–16
2001	Ronnie O'Sullivan (Eng)	bt	John Higgins (Sco)	18–14
2002	Peter Ebdon (Eng)	bt	Stephen Hendry (Sco)	18–17
2003	Mark Williams (Wal)	bt	Ken Doherty (Ire)	18–16
2004	Ronnie O'Sullivan (Eng)	bt	Graeme Dott (Sco)	18–8

*The BA&CC held this event despite there being only two entrants. Following a row with the BA&CC, all the other players boycotted the tournament to form the World Professional Matchplay Championship, deemed the true World Championship by the public until 1958.

**Although generally regarded as the 1971 championship, this tournament was actually played in November 1970.

NOTES

INTRODUCTION – FROM JUBBULPORE WITH LOVE

1. Thankfully for the world's elephants, ivory balls were eventually eschewed after the development of Celluloid, Bakelite and then Crystalate.
2. There are some doubts about Chamberlain's claim to inventing the game. The Garrick Club Snooker Room, for example, contains a poster which outlines the rules of 'Savile and Garrick Snooker', which pre-dates Chamberlain by six years. It is a letter from Sir Compton Mackenzie to *The Billiard Player* (published in April 1939), however, backing up Chamberlain's claim, which is generally accepted as the definitive account of snooker's origins.

   Although Chamberlain did not design the game entirely, he certainly shaped its rules sufficiently to ensure it caught on and, as such, he has the best claim to be the game's 'inventor'.
3. Later renamed the Billiards Association and Control Council.
4. In November 2004, World Snooker annouced there was a chance the event could be moved from the Crucible from 2006, with six cities – including Sheffield – bidding for the right to host it.
5. *The Observer Sport Monthly* magazine's '100 Most Memorable Sporting Moments' rated the Steve Davis–Dennis Taylor black-ball finish ninth, with Alex Higgins's 1982 World Championship victory eighty-eighth. Channel 4's '100 Greatest Sporting Moments' also placed the Davis–Taylor final ninth.
6. The two products of the snooker-movie boom – one of the British film industry's more surreal interludes – are now almost entirely forgotten: Les Reid's *Number One* (1984) features Bob Geldof as Harry 'Flash' Gordon, an Alex Higgins-style maverick who comes from nowhere to win the world title. Mel Smith, Alison Steadman, Ray Winstone and legendary lost snooker talent Patsy Houlihan all pop up in a film that plays like a poor episode of *Minder*. Meanwhile, Alan Clark's *Billy the Kid and the Green Baize Vampire* (1985) is a Brechtian musical which pits Alun Armstong's Dracula (based on Ray Reardon) in a grudge match against Phil Daniels's Billy the Kid (a Jimmy White clone).

   Television also joined in the snooker craze. BBC's *Give Us A Break* was a snooker-themed comedy-drama starring Robert Lindsay and Paul McGann, while many snooker players popped up in cameo roles in other series, including Joe Johnson in *Supergran*.

1 JOE DAVIS – IT BEGAN WITH A LEGEND

1. Joe Davis, *The Breaks Came My Way* (W.H. Allen, 1976; now Virgin Books), Chapter 10.
2. Ibid. Chapter 3.
3. Joe Davis, 'World's Snooker Champion Deplores Popularity of Game' (*The Sporting Globe*, 22 August 1934).
4. Clive Everton, 'Joe Davis: The Master of the Green Baize' in Chris Nawrat, Steve Hutchings and Greg Struthers, *The Sunday Times Illustrated History of Twentieth Century Sport* (Hamlyn, 1996), pp.70–1.
5. *The Billiards and Snooker Archive* Volume 3 (video series compiled by Roger Lee).
6. *The Breaks Came My Way*, Chapter 15.
7. Ibid.
8 Ibid.
9 Ibid. Chapter 16.
10. 'The Greatest Player' (embassysnooker.com, 2003).
11. 'Joe Davis: The Master of the Green Baize'.
12. Ibid.
13. *The Breaks Came My Way*, Chapter 16.
14. Ibid. Chapter 20.
15. 'Joe Davis: The Master of the Green Baize'.
16. *The Breaks Came My Way*, Chapter 1.
17. John Parrott, *Right on Cue* (Robson Books, 1991), p.126.
18. Ibid. p.19.
19. 'The Greatest Player'.

2 WALTER DONALDSON – THE GREAT IMPERTURBABLE

1. Clive Everton, *The Embassy Book of World Snooker* (Bloomsbury Publishing, 1993), p.19.
2. 'World Snooker Champion Donaldson' (*The Billiard Player*, November 1947).
3. Our London Correspondent, 'Nursery Cannons' (*Manchester Guardian*, 17 June 1922).
4. Joe Davis, *The Breaks Came My Way* (W.H. Allen, 1976; now Virgin Books), Chapter 20.
5. 'World Snooker Champion Donaldson'.

3 FRED DAVIS – THE AMBASSADOR SUPREME

1. Dennis Taylor, *Frame by Frame* (Futura Publications, Macdonald & Co., 1986), p.69.

4 HORACE LINDRUM – PROPHET WITHOUT HONOUR

1. Horace Lindrum, *Billiards and Snooker for Amateurs* (Sir Isaac Pitman & Sons, 1962 edition), p.xi.
2. For the definitive account of Walter Lindrum's career, see *Walter Lindrum Billiards Phenomenon* by Andrew Ricketts (Brian Clouston, 1982). A

substantially expanded and revised edition is planned for publication in late 2006.

3. Horace Lindrum, *Horace Lindrum's Snooker, Billiards and Pool* (Paul Hamlyn, 1974), p.73.

4. Ibid. p.74.

5. Joe Davis, *The Breaks Came My Way* (W.H. Allen, 1976; now Virgin Books), Chapter 15.

6. *Horace Lindrum's Snooker, Billiards and Pool*, p.76.

7. Bizarrely, O'Donnell did not turn up for the final session of this match and, according to Lindrum, was never heard of on the snooker scene again.

8. 'Snooker Pool: World's Professional Championship' (*The Times*, 27 April 1936).

9. *Horace Lindrum's Snooker, Billiards and Pool*, p.77.

10. *The Billiards and Snooker Archive* Volume 2 (video series compiled by Roger Lee).

11. *Billiards and Snooker for Amateurs*, p.ix.

12. *Horace Lindrum's Snooker, Billiards and Pool*, p.74.

13. Ibid. p.79.

14. Ibid. p.85.

15. In 'Crowe ties the knot' (*Sydney Morning Herald*, 8 April 2003), Richard Jinman reported, 'One of the guests at the wedding, Arthur Downes, gave Crowe a snooker cue signed by world champion Horace Lindrum and won in an exhibition match in London in 1953.'

16. *Horace Lindrum's Snooker, Billiards and Pool*, p.89.

5 JOHN PULMAN – FOR THE LOVE OF THE GAME

1. Alex Higgins with Tony Francis, *Alex Through the Looking Glass* (Pelham Books, 1986), p.12.

2. John Pulman, *Tackle Snooker* (revised edition, Stanley Paul, 1974), p.10.

3. Ibid. p.10.

4. Ibid. p.144.

5. Ibid. p.11.

6. Ibid. p.129.

7. Ibid. p.124.

8. Ibid. p.11.

6 JOHN SPENCER – THE MAN WITH THE PREMIER STREAK

1. Joe Davis, *The Breaks Came My Way* (W.H. Allen, 1976; now Virgin Books), Chapter 22.

2. John Spencer, *Spencer on Snooker* (Cassell & Co., 1978), p.4.

3. Ibid. p.5.

4. Ibid. p.7.

5. Ibid. p.7.

6. Ibid. p.10.

7. Clive Everton, *The Embassy Book of World Snooker* (Bloomsbury Publishing, 1993), p.36.

8. *Spencer on Snooker*, p.11.

9. Ibid. p.21.

7 RAY REARDON – THE AURA OF GREATNESS

1. Ray Reardon with Peter Buxton, *Ray Reardon* (David & Charles, 1982), p.26.
2. 'Reardon for the snooker championship' (*The Billiard Player*, February 1957).
3. *Ray Reardon*, p.65.
4. Ibid. p.70.
5. Ibid. p.80.
6. Ibid. p.81.
7. *Like a Hurricane: The Alex Higgins Story* (Sunset + Vine North documentary, BBC2, 17 April 2001).
8. *Ray Reardon*, p.93.
9. Ibid. p.93.
10. Post-match interview, 25 April 1974.
11. *Ray Reardon*, p.121.
12. Alex Higgins with Angela Patmore, *'Hurricane' Higgins' Snooker Scrapbook* (Souvenir Press Ltd, 1981), p.65.
13. Post-match interview, 24 April 1977.
14. Post-match interview, 16 May 1982.
15. Interview with BBC *Breakfast* television, 23 October 1983.
16. *Ray Reardon*, p.34.
17. Bill Borrows, *The Hurricane: The Turbulent Life & Times of Alex Higgins* (Atlantic Books, 2002), p.89.
18. Interview with *Sky Sports News*, 4 May 2004.

8 ALEX HIGGINS – THE PEOPLE'S CHAMPION

1. In 2004, Carlton Television announced they were to make a two-hour television drama based on Bill Borrows's book, *The Hurricane: The Turbulent Life & Times of Alex Higgins* (Atlantic Books, 2002). 'My hope for this project is that a fully three-dimensional portrait of Alex "Hurricane" Higgins re-emerges,' Borrows commented. 'People might be shocked by what they see but this country has got to get away from embracing a willing suspension of disbelief.'
2. Alex Higgins with Tony Francis, *Alex Through the Looking Glass* (Pelham Books, 1986), p.7.
3. Ibid. p.26.
4. Ibid. p.30.
5. Ibid. p.33.
6. Ibid. p.37.
7. *Hurricane Higgins* (Thames TV, 4 September 1972).
8. Alex Higgins with Angela Patmore, *'Hurricane' Higgins' Snooker Scrapbook* (Souvenir Press Ltd, 1981), p.26.
9. Clive Everton (ed.), *World Snooker* magazine (February 1972), p.10.
10. *'Hurricane' Higgins' Snooker Scrapbook*, p.33.
11. *Like a Hurricane: The Alex Higgins Story* (Sunset + Vine North documentary, BBC2, 17 April 2001).
12. *Alex Through the Looking Glass*, p.54.
13. See Chris Dunkley, 'Hurricane Higgins: Thames' (*The Times*, 5 September

1972). A quintessential pool movie, *The Hustler*, directed by Robert Rossen, was released in 1961.

14. *The Hurricane: The Turbulent Life & Times of Alex Higgins*, p.100.
15. *The People's Champion* (BBC Worldwide Ltd, 1992).
16. *Like a Hurricane: The Alex Higgins Story*.
17. Ibid.
18. Ibid.
19. Ibid. Davis is referring here to Ken Russell's 1975 film of The Who's 'rock opera' *Tommy*. The eponymous hero is a blind, deaf and dumb boy who nevertheless possesses supernatural abilities on pinball machines, which bring him fame and fortune.
20. John Hennessey, *Eye of the Hurricane: The Alex Higgins Story* (Mainstream Publishing, 2000), p.25.
21. *'Hurricane' Higgins' Snooker Scrapbook*, p.73.
22. *Like a Hurricane: The Alex Higgins Story*.
23. *'Hurricane' Higgins' Snooker Scrapbook*, p.71.
24. *I Love 1982* (BBC2, 2001).
25. *The Hurricane: The Turbulent Life & Times of Alex Higgins*, p.1.
26. *Tobacco Wars* (BBC1, 27 July 1999).

9 TERRY GRIFFITHS – FINDING THE RIGHT BALANCE

1. Terry Griffiths with Julian Worthington, *Griff: The Autobiography of Terry Griffiths* (Pelham Books/Stephen Greene Press, 1989), p.1.
2. Ibid. pp.14–15.
3. Ibid. p.24.
4. Ibid. p.28.
5. Post-match press conference, 2 May 1988.

10 CLIFF THORBURN – GRINDING TO GLORY

1. Cliff Thorburn, *Playing for Keeps* (Partridge Press, 1987), p.28.
2. Ibid. p.28.
3. Ibid. p.31.
4. Ibid. p.39.
5. Ibid. p.43.
6. Ibid. pp.96–7.
7. Thorburn was also dubbed 'The Rhett Butler of the Green Baize' – a less well-known nickname referring to his elegant style and hairbrush moustache, which resembled Clark Gable's appearance in *Gone With the Wind*. Thorburn himself wanted to be called 'Champagne Cliff', but that would never have caught on, for obvious reasons.
8. *Playing for Keeps*, p.97.
9. Ibid. p.99.
10. Thorburn's name has since been added to Canada's Sports Hall of Fame.
11. Mordecai Richler, *On Snooker* (Yellow Jersey Press, 2002), p.103.

11 STEVE DAVIS – SNOOKER SUPERSTAR

1. Simon Hattenstone, 'Davis returns to snooker's top table' (*The Guardian*, 3 February 2004).

2. Steve Davis (as told to Brian Radford), *Steve Davis: Snooker Champion* (Arthur Barker, 1981), p.19.

3. Ibid. p.19.

4. Ibid. p.61.

5. Ibid. p.47.

6. Ibid. p.11.

7. Ibid. p.102.

8. Sydney Friskin, 'The world could soon be in his pocket' (*The Times*, 4 December 1980).

9. *Steve Davis: Snooker Champion*, p.143.

10. Ibid. p.143.

11. Post-match press conference, 20 April 1981.

12. Post-match press conference, 11 January 1982.

13. Post-match press conference, 2 May 1983.

14. Post-match press conference, 4 December 1983.

15. Gordon Burn, *Pocket Money* (Heinemann, 1986), p.65.

16. Peter Batt, 'A champion at all costs' (*The Times*, 9 November 1982).

17. 'Davis returns to snooker's top table'.

18. 'A champion at all costs'.

19. Andrew Longmore, 'Mr Interesting sticks to work ethic in quest for greatest feat' (*The Times*, 23 April 1994).

20. Post-match press conference, 25 January 2004.

21. Steve Davis, 'Welsh Open is just the start' (BBC Sport Online, 26 January 2004).

12 DENNIS TAYLOR – SEIZING THE MOMENT

1. Dennis Taylor, *Frame by Frame* (Futura Publications, Macdonald & Co., 1986), p.19.

2. Ibid. p.38.

3. Ibid. p.63.

4. Ibid. p.68.

5. Ibid. p.86.

6. Ibid. p.132.

7. Ibid. p.137.

8. Ibid. p.139.

9. Ibid. p.7.

10. John Parrott, *Right on Cue* (Robson Books, 1991), pp.146–7.

11. *Like a Hurricane: The Alex Higgins Story* (Sunset + Vine North documentary, BBC2, 17 April 2001).

12. Ibid.

13. Ibid.

13 JOE JOHNSON – ORDINARY JOE

1. Peter Sanderson, 'Snooker's forgotten man' (BBC Sport Online, 30 April 2001).

2. Gordon Burn, *Pocket Money* (Heinemann, 1986), p.204.

3. Post-match press conference, 5 May 1986.

4. Press conference, 2 May 1986.

5. Ibid.
6. *Pocket Money*, p.205.
7. Post-match press conference, 5 May 1986.
8. Ibid.
9. Ibid.
10. *Pocket Money*, p.211.
11. Ibid. p.214.
12. Post-match press conference, 5 May 1986.
13. 'Snooker's forgotten man'.
14. Ibid.
15. *Pocket Money*, p.205.
16. Post-match press conference, 5 May 1986.

14 STEPHEN HENDRY – WINNING THE BRAVE WAY
1. John Parrott, *Right on Cue* (Robson Books, 1991), p.140.
2. It wasn't the first time Hendry conquered severe pain during a tournament. He damaged his heels when jumping off a bed prior to the New Zealand Masters in 1988 and played in carpet slippers on the way to winning the title.
3. Post-match press conference, 3 May 1999.
4. Mordecai Richler, *On Snooker* (Yellow Jersey Press, 2002), p.75.
5. Ibid. p.155.
6. Clive Everton (ed.), 'Hendry forced to change cues' (*Snooker Scene*, October 2003), p.9.
7. Jim White, 'The Stephen Hendry Interview' (*The Guardian*, 15 October 2001).
8. *On Snooker*, p.69.
9. Ronnie O'Sullivan with Simon Hattenstone, *Ronnie: The Autobiography of Ronnie O'Sullivan* (Orion Publishing Group, 2003), p.172.

15 JOHN PARROTT – STANDING TALL AMONG GIANTS
1. John Parrott, *Right on Cue* (Robson Books, 1991), p.57.
2. Ibid. p.105.
3. Post-match press conference, 22 April 2004.

16 KEN DOHERTY – THE DARLING OF DUBLIN
1. Post-match press conference, 3 May 2003.

17 JOHN HIGGINS – FOLLOWING IN THE MASTER'S FOOTSTEPS
1. By the end of 2003–04, Higgins had made 298 first-class career centuries, with Steve Davis fourth on the list at 297. Stephen Hendry was top on 639, with Ronnie O'Sullivan on 368.
2. Ronnie O'Sullivan was tied with Higgins on 16 ranking-event titles at the end of 2004.
3. This record was broken by Hendry, who made 16 centuries in the 2002 championship.
4. Post-match press conference, 26 April 2004.
5. Those back-to-back maximums made it a career total of four for Higgins

in tournament play. The previous two both occurred in 2000, at the Nations Cup and Irish Masters. (He later laid claim to his fifth 147 break at the Grand Prix in October 2004.)

18 MARK WILLIAMS – CASTING CONVENTION ASIDE

1. Nick Townsend, 'I'd rather be in the bingo hall than in the players' lounge' (*The Independent*, 1 February 2004).
2. Ibid.
3. 'Marvellous Mark going for the treble' (Embassy World Snooker Championship programme, 2004), p.13.
4. Post-match press conference, 9 April 2000.
5. Post-match press conference, 29 April 2000.
6. Post-match press conference, 1 May 2000.
7. Ibid.
8. Press conference, 30 April 2000.
9. Post-match press conference, 22 November 2003.
10. Post-match press conference, 5 May 2003.
11. 'Marvellous Mark going for the treble', p.13.
12. Post-match press conference, 28 April 2001.
13. 'I'd rather be in the bingo hall than in the players' lounge'.
14. Post-match press conference, 15 December 2002.
15. BBC television interview, 5 May 2003.
16. Post-match press conference, 5 May 2003.
17. 'Griffiths: Williams to rule roost' (BBC Sport Online, 6 May 2003).
18. 'Marvellous Mark going for the treble', p.13.

19 RONNIE O'SULLIVAN – A MYSTERY WRAPPED IN AN ENIGMA . . .

1. Ronnie O'Sullivan with Simon Hattenstone, *Ronnie: The Autobiography of Ronnie O'Sullivan* (Orion Publishing Group, 2003), p.8.
2. Ibid. p.14.
3. Ibid. p.41.
4. This record was broken by 14-year-old Judd Trump in March 2004.
5. *Ronnie: The Autobiography*, p.60.
6. Mordecai Richler, *On Snooker* (Yellow Jersey Press, 2002), p.125.
7. Clive Everton, 'The highs and lows of Ronnie O'Sullivan' (*Snooker Scene*, May 2003), p.24.
8. Post-match press conference, 25 November 2003.
9. *Ronnie: The Autobiography*, pp.64–5.
10. Ibid. p.100.
11. Ibid. pp.182–3
12. Post-match press conference, 2 May 2001.
13. *Ronnie: The Autobiography*, p.193.
14. Clive Everton, 'O'Sullivan misunderstands ceremony in mosque' (*Snooker Scene*, November 2003), p.7.
15. This was effectively a league table where points were awarded depending on how far a player had progressed during the previous seven ranking tournaments in 2003–04.
16. During this win, O'Sullivan equalled the record of five century breaks

during a best-of-twenty-five-frame match at the Crucible.
17. Clive Everton (ed.), 'Dublin Notebook: I'm a snooker player . . . get me out of here' (*Snooker Scene*, May 2004), p.13.

20 PETER EBDON – THINKING OF NEWTON'S CRADLE

1. Jonathan Rendall, 'A breed apart' (*The Observer*, 6 April 2003).
2. Jim White, 'The Peter Ebdon Interview' (*The Guardian*, 14 April 2003).
3. 'A breed apart'.
4. Ibid.
5. The peak viewing figure of nearly eight million for that match was a higher audience than that year's FA Cup final.
6. Clive Everton (ed.), 'New WPBSA board appointed' (*Snooker Scene*, May 2004) pp.3–5.
7. 'Sir Rodney Walker "delighted" as Miller, Richards, Metcalfe and Ebdon agree' (*World Snooker* press release, 1 April 2004).
8. Post-match press conference, 28 March 2004.
9. 'The Peter Ebdon Interview'.

21 JIMMY WHITE – WHIRLWIND ROMANCE

1. Jimmy White with Rosemary Kingsland, *Behind the White Ball* (Hutchinson, 1998), p.45.
2. Ibid. pp.10–11.
3. Ibid. p.46.
4. Ibid. p.47.
5. Ibid. p.49.
6. Ibid. p.80.
7. *Jimmy White: Close to the Wind* (Vision Video Ltd, 1994).
8. *Behind the White Ball*, p.152.
9. Post-match interview (BBC television, 2 May 1994).
10. Interview (Sky Sports, 16 March 2003).
11. Post-match press conference, 11 April 2004.
12. *Behind the White Ball*, p.49.
13. *Jimmy White: Close to the Wind*.
14. Will Buckley, 'Why gentlemen prefer Jimmy' (*The Observer*, 18 April 2004).
15. Hicks, the dark poet of stand-up comedy, became intrigued by White's seemingly constant presence on British television during frequent transatlantic visits. His musings on the subject can be found on the CD *Bill Hicks: Live at the Oxford Playhouse 11.11.92* (Invasion Group, 2003). In common with White and Alex Higgins, Hicks was a flamboyant talent who developed cancer. The disease killed him in 1994 aged just 32.
16. Jonathan Rendall, 'Join the cue' (*Independent on Sunday*, 24 January 1999).
17. *Behind the White Ball*, p.265.

BIBLIOGRAPHY

BOOKS

Borrows, Bill *The Hurricane: The Turbulent Life & Times of Alex Higgins* (Atlantic Books, 2002)

Burn, Gordon *Pocket Money* (Heinemann, 1986)

Davis, Fred *Talking Snooker* (A & C Black Ltd, 1979)

Davis, Joe *The Breaks Came My Way* (W.H. Allen, 1976; now Virgin Books)

Davis, Steve (as told to Brian Radford), *Steve Davis: Snooker Champion* (Arthur Barker, 1981)

Docherty, John *Remember My Name: The Authorised Biography of Stephen Hendry* (Pelham Books, 1990)

Everton, Clive *The History of Billiards and Snooker* (Cassell & Co., 1979)

Everton, Clive *The Embassy Book of World Snooker* (Bloomsbury Publishing, 1993)

Everton, Clive 'Joe Davis: The Master of the Green Baize' in Chris Nawrat, Steve Hutchings and Greg Struthers *The Sunday Times Illustrated History of Twentieth Century Sport* (Hamlyn, 1996)

Griffiths, Terry with Julian Worthington *Griff: The Autobiography of Terry Griffiths* (Pelham Books/Stephen Greene Press, 1989)

Hennessey, John *Eye of the Hurricane: The Alex Higgins Story* (Mainstream Publishing, 2000)

Higgins, Alex with Angela Patmore *'Hurricane' Higgins' Snooker Scrapbook* (Souvenir Press Ltd, 1981)

Higgins, Alex with Tony Francis *Alex Through the Looking Glass* (Pelham Books, 1986)

Lindrum, Horace *Billiards and Snooker for Amateurs* (Sir Isaac Pitman & Sons, 1962 edition)

Lindrum, Horace *Horace Lindrum's Snooker, Billiards and Pool* (Paul Hamlyn, 1974)

Morrison, Ian (ed.) *The Hamlyn Encyclopedia of Snooker* (Hamlyn Publishing, 1985)

O'Sullivan, Ronnie with Simon Hattenstone *Ronnie: The Autobiography of Ronnie O'Sullivan* (Orion Publishing Group, 2003; paperback edition, 2004)

247

Parrott, John *Right on Cue* (Robson Books, 1991)

Pulman, John *Tackle Snooker* (Stanley Paul, 1974)

Reardon, Ray with Peter Buxton *Ray Reardon* (David & Charles, 1982)

Richler, Mordecai *On Snooker* (Yellow Jersey Press, 2002)

Ricketts, Andrew *Walter Lindrum Billiards Phenomenon* (Brian Coulston, Australia, 1982)

Spencer, John *Spencer on Snooker* (Cassell & Co., 1978)

Taylor, Dennis *Frame by Frame: My Own Story* (Futura Publications, Macdonald & Co., 1986)

Thorburn, Cliff *Playing for Keeps* (Partridge Press, 1987)

White, Jimmy with Rosemary Kingsland *Behind the White Ball: My Autobiography* (Hutchinson, 1998)

ARTICLES

Batt, Peter 'A champion at all costs' (*The Times*, 9 November 1982)

Buckley, Will 'Why gentlemen prefer Jimmy' (*The Observer*, 18 April 2004)

Davis, Joe 'World's snooker champion deplores popularity of game' (*The Sporting Globe*, 22 August 1934)

Davis, Steve 'Welsh Open is just the start' (BBC Sport Online, 26 January 2004)

Dunkley, Chris 'Hurricane Higgins: Thames' (*The Times*, 5 September 1972)

Everton, Clive 'Higgins splits from manager' (*The Guardian*, 11 October 1994)

Everton, Clive 'The highs and lows of Ronnie O'Sullivan' (*Snooker Scene*, May 2003)

Everton, Clive (ed.) 'Hendry forced to change cues' (*Snooker Scene*, October 2003)

Everton, Clive 'O'Sullivan misunderstands ceremony in mosque' (*Snooker Scene*, November 2003)

Everton, Clive (ed.) 'New WPBSA board appointed' (*Snooker Scene*, May 2004)

Everton, Clive (ed.) 'Dublin Notebook: I'm a snooker player . . . get me out of here' (*Snooker Scene*, May 2004)

Friskin, Sydney 'The world could soon be in his pocket' (*The Times*, 4 December 1980)

'The Greatest Player' (embassysnooker.com, 2003)

'Griffiths: Williams to rule roost' (BBC Sport Online, 6 May 2003)

Hattenstone, Simon 'Davis returns to snooker's top table' (*The Guardian*, 3 February 2004)

Hudson, David and Caroline Malone 'My two dads' (*Daily Star*, 7 May 1986)

Jinman, Richard 'Crowe ties the knot' (*Sydney Morning Herald*, 8 April 2003)

Longmore, Andrew 'Mr Interesting sticks to work ethic in quest for greatest feat' (*The Times*, 23 April 1994)

'Marvellous Mark going for the treble' (Embassy World Snooker Championship programme, 2004)

May, Harold 'Talking sport' (*Sunday Empire News*, 9 March 1952)

Our London Correspondent, 'Nursery cannons' (*Manchester Guardian*, 17 June 1922)

'Reardon for the snooker championship' (*The Billiard Player*, February 1957)

Rendall, Jonathan 'Join the cue' (*Independent on Sunday*, 24 January 1999)

Rendall, Jonathan 'A breed apart' (*The Observer*, 6 April 2003)

Sanderson, Peter 'Snooker's forgotten man' (BBC Sport Online, 30 April 2001)

'Sir Rodney Walker "delighted" as Miller, Richards, Metcalfe and Ebdon agree' (World Snooker press release, 1 April 2004)

'Snooker Pool: World's professional championship' (*The Times*, 27 April 1936)

Townsend, Nick 'I'd rather be in the bingo hall than in the players' lounge' (*The Independent*, 1 February 2004)

White, Jim 'The Stephen Hendry Interview' (*The Guardian*, 15 October 2001)

White, Jim 'The Peter Ebdon Interview' (*The Guardian*, 14 April 2003)

'World Snooker Champion Donaldson' (*The Billiard Player*, November 1947)

World Snooker magazine (February 1972)

TELEVISION PROGRAMMES AND VIDEOS

The Billiards and Snooker Archive (Volumes 1–4, compiled by Roger Lee)

Hurricane Higgins (Thames TV, 4 September 1972)

I Love 1982 (BBC2, 2001)

Jimmy White: Close to the Wind (Vision Video Ltd, 1994)

Like a Hurricane: The Alex Higgins Story (Sunset + Vine North, BBC2, 17 April 2001)

The People's Champion (BBC Worldwide Ltd, 1992)

Tobacco Wars (BBC1, 27 July 1999)

WEBSITES

BBC Sport (www.bbc.co.uk/sport)

Global Snooker Centre (www.globalsnookercentre.co.uk)

Chris Turner's Snooker Archive (www.cajt.pwp.blueyonder.co.uk)

World Snooker official site (www.worldsnooker.com)

110sport official site (www.110sport.com/snooker)

INDEX